SOUNDINGS

Books by Peter S. Prescott:

A World of Our Own:
Notes on Life and Learning in a Boys' Preparatory School

Soundings:
Encounters with Contemporary Books

PETER S. PRESCOTT

SOUNDINGS

• • • • • • • • • • • • • •

ENCOUNTERS WITH
CONTEMPORARY
BOOKS

COWARD, McCANN & GEOGHEGAN, INC.

New York

for
ANNE,
*many hours, months
taken from her own work*

Acknowledgments

I am grateful to the editors of *Newsweek, Look, Women's Wear Daily,* and the Chicago *Daily News* for permission to reprint these pieces. Nearly all were first published in their pages, occasionally in somewhat different form. I thank those editors who encouraged me to write them, especially Charles Boland, John Fairchild, Martin Goldman, and Jack Kroll. I also wish to thank my father, Orville Prescott, for setting an example of integrity and style, and for his encouragement, even when (as must have often happened) he disagreed both with my approaches and evaluations. My debt to my wife, Anne Lake Prescott, surpasses analysis: She has improved each of these pieces by her insights, chiding, and persuasion.

P. S. P.

Contents

SIX

SEVEN

Preface

The first book reviews I wrote were of a rather private sort, done when I was an editor at a book publishing firm. I was expected to make several judgments daily on the ebb and tide of manuscripts that sloshed across my desk. Most of these submissions were dreadful, requiring only a few succinct lines of dismissal, but some were dreadful in an impressive way: They came to me with recommendations from editors who outranked me. We were never supposed to know what another editor thought of a book, but editors have a way of lounging against your doorframe while saying, "I do want to know what you really think of this because it seems to me his best and most commercial book to date." These manuscripts had to be dealt with carefully, sometimes to the length of five pages, single-spaced. There were, occasionally, some recommendations and endorsements to write; it is always harder to praise than to condemn, but then there are always more books to condemn than to praise. Eventually, all the books anyone cared for came before our editorial conference. Then the president of the firm would look at me and say, "Well, Peter, Jack and Jill here, who have had a lot of experience with this kind of thing, like (don't like) the book. How can you be sure you're right?" Jack and Jill would glare patiently at me.

In those days I was less inclined to doubt my judgments than my future as an editor. I liked writing about books. A clear case of arrested development: The only boy in the fourth grade who actually *likes* writing book reports finds, in adult life, that writing book reports is still what he wants to do. My fourth-grade ambition, however, was not to write about books but simply to get all the good ones free, and that has come about, but the price is that all the bad books come free, too.

In time, by processes not worth describing, I stopped writing about books for editorial conferences and file drawers and began writing about them for magazines and newspapers that had never published any critical writing about books before. I did not make the shift suddenly. For one thing, book reviewing is not a task that many people feel obliged to pay for. As a profession, it ranks—even in the eyes of many who practice it—somewhere between cleaning chimneys and calling people up to ask what television program they are watching. We can live without it, is the general consensus, and anyway, nobody much cares. "A dusty business," said an editor I knew at the *Times Book Review* as he carefully protected me from my error of attempting to start at the top. So much for my early image of myself as Cerberus guarding the gate of Civilization, six rows of fangs bared against the barbarian invaders.

My problem from the start was, quite literally, how to lure readers away from trade news about hosiery and metal climax conventions and toward a column devoted to books. "Be original," I was told at the time, "we don't want the same old stuff." Since few people were likely to read me at all, I was given some time to fumble around. It became clear to me, after I outgrew the idea that I was inevitably going to present the infallible truth about books, that all a reviewer could offer a reader was a certain perspective, a certain tone of discourse that the reader would in time come to recognize and evaluate, taking it into account when making up his own mind about what I said of the books I had read. It is really the only advantage that the regular reviewer has over his free-lance colleagues: Whereas the specialist can, or should, provide a greater expertise, the generalist can, or should, provide a continuity of criticism. Continuity is the key, not consistency: The books themselves must elicit from us our response, whether in gravity or jest. The point is to have the reader, after a time, be able to say: Well, yes, there's Prescott again, for good or ill, and by now I know which is which.

To this end, one develops his own eccentricities. One of mine was to build, as other writers have done, an elaborate persona, with a past history for which I drew upon my family and friends for anecdotes. Another was a dissatisfaction with the amount of space carved from a review by synopses of plots and long quotations. Surely no one wants to read such stuff? Surely this is what people mean when they insist that book reviews are parasitic? So I cut such roughage back as far as conscience allowed, to save precious space for precarious digressions or excursions into what struck me as worth remarking about a book, an author, a way of writing, or even the times that produced the combination.

Finally, I decided that the only kind of review I wanted to write, was perhaps fit to write, was the kind that, like most other pieces of writing that begin here and go to there, did not depend entirely upon the subject. Exceptions must be made, I suppose, for reports of governmental commissions and the kind of pieces one finds in magazines like *College English,* which cannot be read without a prior addiction either to the subject or to the pathology of prose. The point, though, that an essay should exist for itself, holds for book reviews. There are those who disagree. One famous publisher, bellowing down the length of a luncheon table, suggested that my only function was "to announce the existence of the book and persuade people to buy it. The rest is shit!" Well yes, but the dreary truth revealed to all book reviewers is that many of the books we have to review are not worth reading, whereas our editors assure us that our business is to write, if we can, something that *is*; a couple of times a week we must run through a few compulsory figures and a pleasant free-form improvisation—just to keep the reader's attention.

The reviews and occasional pieces in this collection are drawn from the comments I have made on more than eight hundred books in the past ten years. They are, with whatever limitations the word implies, encounters with books that attracted or demanded my attention at the time, quick plunges in and out, taken (I like to think) at some risk because I am always writing not only against an inflexible limitation of space, but against a deadline, beginning in the cheery hours of late afternoon and too often ending in the dread minutes of early morning, and therefore publicly exposing hasty judgments, two and sometimes three of them, each week. Before pressing such pieces between hard covers, there is a temptation to congeal the parts into something that looks more like an organized and sustained work of criticism. It is a temptation to be put down, presuming as it does that the concealed virtues of what one has written may be better revealed by a face-lifting. Not so. These pieces were written in a certain time and under certain pressures, and I have to believe that such virtues as they may have are inextricably entwined with their faults. Of course, if I were writing about these books today, I would write differently. Norman Mailer's *Armies of the Night,* for instance, has become, among sophisticated readers, accepted as something of a contemporary classic, but it was not thought such at the time of its publication, when many intelligent readers were appalled by what they thought to be little more than gratuitous vulgarity and exhibitionism. At that time, the book required an explanation and a defense that I presume is no longer necessary.

In any event, one edits by what one leaves out. I notice, in looking over this selection, that I have left out most of the reviews I have written about important nonfiction—all those biographies of Tolstoy and Thomas à Becket, for instance, the Kennedy books and the polemics about ecology and foreign policy—because writing about such books requires more summary, more leaden exposition than I can bear to reread.

If any reviews are worth looking at again, they may be those that deal with books which show us something about how we live now. And those books are often written by fine people of whom one has heard little, perhaps nothing. They may be books of very limited scope. And, perhaps more important, they may be very bad books indeed, self-help books by psychiatrists and society matrons. Bad books often give a reviewer more to chew on than good ones do, and the only point of a collection like this is to see the reviewer chewing.

P. S. P.

One

. . . . Shall Saul
Reign over Us?

Saul Bellow is something more than a writer; he is a cultural frame of reference. This is a critical condition, known to lead to arteriosclerosis of the artistic capabilities, and yet, it may prove unavoidable. Like the editors of film fan magazines, the editors of literary journals nominate their superstars and pit celebrities against each other in senseless and vulgar conflicts: *What Does Liz Really Think of Jackie? Is Saul a Better Novelist Than Norman?* Superstar authors, unable to keep their mouths shut, squabble among themselves. Norman Mailer creates a marketable personality by insisting that he is winning the footrace or the boxing match or whatever it is he thinks novelists do, and Bellow flails his colleagues for their lack of intelligence in their approach to fiction.

The trick—if one wants to become a cultural frame of reference—is to combine the talking and the writing so that both peak out together. Mailer has difficulties with this—he tends to talk best when he writes worst—but Bellow pulled it off in 1964 with *Herzog,* a very good and demanding novel that, against all odds, zoomed up the best-seller lists. Philip Rahv and other members of America's literary *Cosa Nostra* applauded and declared Bellow the winner in the battle for the job of Top Novelist. On any subway in New York you could see pretty young girls clutching a strap in one hand and a closed copy of *Herzog* in the other. You could see, too, a bookmark sticking out of *Herzog* somewhere among the first fifty pages, about the place where the same girls had stuck bookmarks in *Ship of Fools* and *Doctor Zhivago* just a few years earlier.

Bellow had made it, but he must have had some doubts. He was often praised for his intelligence and erudition but not so often praised for the compassion that pervades his books, for the warmhearted sweetness that sometimes gums up his endings, for the sensuality that must make him sympathize with pretty young girls who buy his books but never reach page 50. Bellow had scrambled over the corpses of the colleagues he had criticized, and here he was, *numero uno,* but was he not still a rather shy and gentle man? Were the partisan infighting, the sneers and rivalry, worth it? And what could he do now? Even his admirers agreed that *Herzog* marked a climax; there was nothing more that Bellow could profitably do with his particular breed of hero, the intellectual victim, the sensitive, self-conscious man aware of his superiority but a bit scornful of it, a man out of place in American society, inclined to remain aloof and yet inevitably drawn into the messiness of living as he sought for a meaning in life itself.

And so, nearly six years later, we have Bellow's new novel, *Mr. Sammler's Planet,* a story about just such a man. Artur Sammler is over seventy. He is a Jew, a Pole who had lived in England and had been a friend of H. G. Wells. Early in the war, the Germans nearly killed Sammler. He literally crawled from his own grave, and now, a Lazarus of the after-Auschwitz generation, he is half-blind, "a refugee in Manhattan," dependent on the kindness of relatives. An intellectual who has heard all the explanations men have given for life, Mr. Sammler is paring his own to the core of the spirit. He has given up reading Marx and Spengler and peers now with his one good eye at the Bible and the Latin devotions of Meister Eckhart. He is at odds with the overstuffed variety of life in America today, with dirty, ignorant students, with young people's clamorous demands for instant gratification. Toward his family and the noisy bustle of the world, Mr. Sammler responds with an amiable contempt, an affectionate inattention.

But, of course, the world will not let him alone. Relatives force their confessions on him, importune him to intervene in their affairs. Crime seems to erupt everywhere. What is he to make of his benefactor, dying of an aneurysm in the brain, who seems to have taken money from the Mafia? What of the Negro pickpocket who follows him home and exposes himself? And what of his own daughter, a deranged girl who steals an Indian scholar's manuscript that speculates on the unguessed possibilities of life upon the moon? Taking off from earth, heading out toward the universe—a release from the pressure of our lives—appeals to Sammler, who has been through death and has thought too long on finalities and withdrawals. Sammler, at his age, must remember what he has always known about the business of living.

Mr. Sammler's Planet is, in several ways, a beautiful book, so neatly joined, with every part bearing in upon every other, that one could wish for roughness. Bellow has never been one of our most graceful stylists in prose, but he yields to few in the sharpness of his observations, in his precise choice of words. Here, as elsewhere, he displays erudition, sensuality, and a wry humor washing over all. Here, as elsewhere, he has worked hard to define our human agitation, our despair, the reasons for our greed, our lusts, and our prevarications. Bellow has also constructed a mirror image of all those tedious novels about soulful youth rebelling against a square society: Sammler is old, square, and a dropout from the ignorance and smelly self-indulgence of the young.

And yet the book is not quite satisfactory. It is unreasonable for us to ask our best writers to exceed with each book their past performances, and Bellow has not done that here. Still, writers as talented as Bellow should at least develop, if not improve; they should change and astonish us with something other than a theme-and-variations approach to fiction. Sammler tells us early on that he has heard all the arguments, all the explanations—and so have we, but Bellow gives them to us again. For a moment I felt like Sammler: Who needs this? Why won't Bellow, like Mailer, run the risk of major failure?

Nor does this novel remove my suspicion that Bellow might secretly prefer to be remembered for his ideas and for his sensitivity rather than for his skill as a novelist. At one point, Sammler and the Indian scholar sink into a philosophical debate. The novel can't bear it; the reader barely can. The poet, wrote Sir Philip Sidney three hundred and seventy-five years ago, "yeeldeth to the powers of the minde an image of that whereof the Philosopher bestoweth but a wordish description." Bellow's fiction falters when he interrupts his images for wordish descriptions of ideas circulating inside Sammler's skull. Intelligence, as Bellow reminds us, is an excellent thing in fiction, but, like grease in a pan, it tends to congeal when the heat is turned off beneath it. It was not by accident that Dostoyevsky wrote about murder and Camus about a plague: Novels about ideas work best when they are about something else, something that arouses not only our intellect but our feelings and imagination. Bellow seems only half convinced. He writes about men who dream of disengagement but who are determined, now, to talk—and that is why, good as Bellow's novels are, parts of them read like college lectures.

1970

. . . . ". . . And You Don't Know What It Is, Do You, Mr. Jones?"

Why do revolutions fail? Because the leaders, who are supposed to draft proclamations and hurl stones from the barricades, are worrying about their sex lives, that's why. The point of the Broadway musical *1776* is that Thomas Jefferson's horniness nearly prevented him from writing the Declaration of Independence. A damn close call it was, and a mystery to me how our historians could have overlooked it.

It's the same thing with *The Merry Month of May,* a novel that James Jones has set against the 1968 student uprisings in Paris. You might think that there was turmoil enough for any novelist in that, but no: When the arts come to revolution, Freud, not Marx, provides the determining imperative. "Do not forget," says one of Jones' characters to a group of revolting students, "that the audiences of this world don't give a damn about the truth, unless it is presented to them in a way in which they can personally associate." A cynical argument, but Jones agrees: For him, the May uprising is no more than a diorama, a spectacle of *son et lumière* such as cautious tourists might observe. His real story, as tedious as any this side of Jacqueline Susann, involves some dropouts from that revolution and the sexual bowline that ensnares them.

Jack Hartley, a failed poet, failed novelist, and failed husband, tells the story of his attraction to the Harry Gallagher family. Hartley and Gallagher are both Americans living on the Ile St. Louis in Paris. Hartley fusses over shaving, confesses he is undersexed, and waits for his mistress to call him. Gallagher, a Marxist screenwriter, is rich and expansive on the twin themes of his philosophy—the bar as the modern equivalent of the church and the American male's obsession with that part of the female that is found between her navel and her knees. Gallagher dreams of taking two women to bed at once. Samantha, a nineteen-year-old black American, obliges: After she sleeps with Gallagher's son and tries to seduce Gallagher's wife, she runs off with Gallagher and another girl.

Meanwhile, James Jones guides the reader through a walking tour of the revolution—up one street and down another—and you can probably make sense of it all if you unroll a map of Paris. I didn't get around to that because I kept waiting for Jones to explain the *real* geography of the revolution—the conditions and motives that led to it—but he didn't get around to *that.* In fact, Gallagher and his son, who fall out over the proper way to make a film of the revolution, never get around to making the film at all because—well, the sex takes so much time and thought.

I don't mean to imply that there is a lot of sex in the book—there isn't. Some lively pornography, some lively anything, might have lent redeeming social value to the story, but in keeping with Jones' present concern with breakdown and exhaustion, most of the sex is kept offstage. People *talk* about sex instead. Reading about sexual acrobatics is one thing; reading about people talking about sexual acrobatics is another. A kind of voyeurism for the ear, I suppose; we shall have to call it *écouteurism* if it catches on with our novelists. I hope it doesn't.

So, too, is the revolutionary action kept well out of sight. Hartley strolls around to watch the barricades go up, to inspect the damage after, to listen in at meetings of a revolutionary cinema committee. His friends show him their wounds. Hartley drinks a great deal, listens to the radio for news of the riots, sniffs at the tear gas lingering on the warm spring air. He distracts the reader with great indigestible gobs of irrelevant information. Hartley is a charmless prig, one of life's tourists rebuffed by a spasm of history. In fact, an air of impotence and anticipation hangs over all these expatriate Americans; I can almost believe they know they are occupying Hemingway turf some forty years too late. They rut with each other, snarl at each other, and drink beer at the Brasserie Lipp, but it's not the same, even if each one of them seems lifted from *The Sun Also Rises*. There's no style in the way they live, none of that peculiar intensity and anguish, that sense of impermanence that informed the lives of Hemingway's originals.

Nor has the novel any of the virtues of Jones' best work. The author of *From Here to Eternity* and *The Thin Red Line* is capable of handling a Parisian street revolution, but he has chosen not to. This is a more determinedly literary book, as if Jones wanted to convince us that he has grown up, is out of the Army now and hanging out with intellectuals. His book is the poorer for it. The brutality, the pessimism, the ability to see that the problem is not war, but the men who make war—Jones used these to effect before, but they are missing here, and there is nothing to replace them.

What he gives us is a flaccid, ill-disciplined novel that only the Book-of-the-Month Club could love. *The Merry Month of May* is possibly the worst-written novel ever published by an American with a claim to a major literary reputation. Jones is, of course, writing in the voice of his narrator, Jack Hartley, but Hartley is also a writer; he is even the improbable author of a book called *The Rhythms of Early English Prose*. Even so, Hartley can say that the French "don't understand concrete like we do," and "this thing of a film-job thing is a complicated matter." "The fame of being famous," he writes later on, and "By the time the war came at the end of 1941, at the age of 23, Harry had written," and so on. Hartley breaks rules, tends to favor officialese: "I do not choose to comment on what will be history's verdict" and (of his marriage): "Fortunately, we were without issue."

Only a writer who has long since ceased to make demands upon himself can write like that. Reading the book is like looking at a painting by an artist who can't tell burnt umber from canary yellow, or hearing a sonata played by a pianist who is not quite sure of the difference between B and B flat.

1971

. . . . The Last
Gentle Novel

Walker Percy has published only three novels, yet each is better than its predecessor, and, as far as fiction is concerned, we must now recognize Dr. Percy—who is indeed a medical doctor and an occasional practitioner of psychiatry—as the chief diagnostician of our American anomie. He writes about neurosis and existential terror, about malaise and the general breakdown of function in machines, in institutions, and in people. The protagonist of *The Moviegoer* suffered from apathy and an identity crisis. The central character in *The Last Gentleman* was a victim of amnesia and *accidie*. Dr. Thomas More, the narrator of *Love in the Ruins,* is afflicted by simultaneous exultation and depression, but alone among Percy's damaged heroes he may be a genius; he may be able to save the world.

The scene is Louisiana in the 1980's. Polarization has broken up the country. Conservative Christians, complaining of rages and large-bowel disorders, are aligned against liberal atheists, who complain of impotence and "morning terror." The Auto Age is over because no one is interested in repairing cars. Lichen and mimosa spread over interstate highways; "vines sprout in sections of New York where not even Negroes will live. Wolves have been seen in downtown Cleveland. . . . Some Southern states have established diplomatic ties with Rhodesia." For fifteen years the United States has interfered in a civil war in Ecuador and, in the swamps at home, live "ferocious black Bantus" who raid the shopping centers, white derelicts who smoke Choctaw ·cannabis, and "deserters from the Swedish Army." "The center did not hold," Tom More observes. "However, the gross national product continues to rise."

More, a collateral descendant of the English saint, proposes to save America with a gadget he has invented: the Qualitative Quantitative Ontological Lapsometer, which, as its name implies, measures man's falling off. More precisely, it charts the electrical activity of exact areas of the human brain: Its readings are then "correlated with the manifold woes of the Western world," thereby producing a diagnosis of man's mental imbalance. "A stethoscope of the spirit," More calls his gadget. He hopes it will cure the sickness of his time, that sense men have that their self is slipping away from them. But there are problems. More, an alcoholic, a bad Catholic and unsuccessful psychiatrist, has escaped from an asylum. Consequently, only lunatics and lovers believe in his invention—the doctors don't. More has three women competing for him and a sniper trying to kill him, all as the world is about to end. Even the devil appears to show More how an attachment to his gadget will cure people of the ills it diagnoses.

Percy is an amiable prophet, an even-handed satirist, and a charming writer. There is in his work an elegant wit, a delicate refusal of solemnity, and a disciplined guilelessness that inhibit him from winding issues to the sticking point. He lacks the ferocity to create a dystopia like *1984*, with all its organized claustrophobia, preferring instead to make playful fun of Catholicism, euthanasia, sex clinics, and half a hundred other aberrations of our culture.

Tom More may raise dire metaphysical questions—why are so many living people actually dead? why do a few men find life in the presence of death?—but Percy deflects them. Lacking pretentious answers, he returns to simpler questions—"Why did God make women so beautiful and man with such a loving heart?"—to which there are no answers either. He rejoices in the flesh and (because he is a clever doctor) wittily celebrates sensuality in medical textbook terms. Such answers as occur to More are humble, even banal, yet charming still: "What does a man live for," Tom muses, "but to have a girl, use his mind, practice his trade, drink a drink, read a book, and watch the martins wing it for the Amazon and three-fingered sassafras turn red in October?" Even Percy's devil, a seedy character, a cross between a traveling salesman and an FBI agent, provides good advice (as the devil in literature often does): "Work! Love! Music!" he shouts. "That's what makes a man happy."

Have I said how much I like this book? *Love in the Ruins* is Percy's best novel, his least elusive and least mannered novel, his gentlest, his funniest novel. Charming: There is no other word for it.

1971

. . . . The Fire
Last Time

Of the making of bad books there is no end, but there is, at least, variety. Sometimes an important author writes so staggeringly bad a book that the reader recoils, stumbles to his bookshelf, and, fumbling among the pages of the author's earlier work, seeks for whatever it was that once he had admired. We all know such novels—John Updike's *Couples*, Norman Mailer's *An American Dream*, William Styron's *Set This House on Fire*—novels so awful they seem to discharge laser beams or lethal gases that damage the reader's sensibilities. They are, to coin a phrase, positive in their negativism.

I wish I could say as much for James Baldwin's new novel, *Tell Me How Long the Train's Been Gone*. It did send me back to Baldwin's earlier books to see if I had been wrong in my assessment of them, but it does not itself attain the monstrous malignancy that one can respect in authors of importance. It is simply a nullity, banal in conception, construction, and content. Fortunately, it wasted more of Baldwin's time writing it than it did mine reading it; I hope you will not bother.

Baldwin today is an anomaly among writers. For a while, with Richard Wright dead and Ralph Ellison silent for so many years, Baldwin was *the* radical Negro writer, defining, better than anyone had done, what being both black and bright meant to a man in America. No longer. There is in the writing of Eldridge Cleaver, a paroled convict whose book *Soul on Ice* appeared earlier this year, a hard-edged calmness and austerity of anger lacking in Baldwin's recent work. Cleaver, not Baldwin, is now the man to watch.

Black men like Cleaver have denounced Baldwin for selling out to Whitey. In fact, Baldwin was adopted, perhaps against his will, by the white Establishment. He has become Whitey's token Negro writer. His essays appear in every freshman-English anthology, and any writer you can assign to freshmen can't be very dangerous. Baldwin is *safe*. He spoke, but nothing happened. He predicted the fire next time, but Stokely Carmichael may have made it happen. You won't find Carmichael in the anthologies.

This absorption of James Baldwin is the matter of his new novel. *Train*'s narrator is Leo Proudhammer, most successful of all Negro actors. Leo has a heart attack and remembers his past: his struggles in Harlem; his love for his brother; his affairs with various black men and white women (no one, it seems, can resist Leo's loving); and his entirely implausible rise to fame as an actor. Leo's problem, Baldwin implies, is that he has never learned to hate Whitey sufficiently. He began his acting career because he worshiped white film stars. His first heterosexual passion was for a white actress, but this dissolved when a male black militant captured Leo's affections. The novel ends equivocally: Has success spoiled Leo as a black man? Are guns the only answer? Baldwin hasn't the guts to come out for or against guns, but obviously he is smarting from charges that he (thinly disguised as Leo) could not be so successful had he not sold out to Whitey.

Train clatters over many obstacles along its lengthy track. Chief among these is that the reader cannot believe the engineer is black. No one can insist that black writers write black novels, but *Train* offers no more than a white man's truth about the Negro. The stale news about Broadway movie palaces, subway routes, and theater life seems real enough, but only because we have read it all before. The characters are incredible; their problems, secondhand. Baldwin has made it now and perhaps has no more to say, but this does not mean that he didn't write well once: *The Fire Next Time,* even on reexamination, remains one hell of a book.

Reynolds Price's third novel, *Love & Work,* is another bad book. Everything about it makes the reader root for it—come on, Reynolds, make it work!—but it doesn't work. There is, nevertheless, much to admire in it: It is a compact, chilly little story, much too carefully constructed; writers will gasp in appreciation as readers yawn in boredom. A clue to the debacle can be found on page 52: "glaborous," Price writes, describing a couple making love. The word he wants is "glabrous," but even if he hadn't misspelled it, it is the wrong word for the occasion, and anyway, virtually no one knows what it means.

Love & Work concerns a writer, Thomas Eborn, who believes that only one's work gives meaning to life because everything else one has can be taken away. Eborn does not seem to know what love—and the dependence love requires—means. He has a wife, a woman possessed of more than reasonable patience, but Eborn is really wed to his parents. After their death, he seeks to make them live in a book; the crisis he precipitates estranges him not only from his wife but from life itself.

The book is all lean meat and gristle. Professionals will admire it because Price has set himself obstacles known to be almost insurmountable. His material is the stuff that amateurs grasp at because they think familiarity makes writing fiction easy: the hospital scene, the car accident, the discourses on work, love, and responsibility, and—most dreaded of all—the novel within a novel. Nobody can cope with so much corn; Price knows this, and he is showing off. He brings new life to all the old clichés, but in doing so, he drains the guts out of his book. His novel is, in fact, a triumph of manner over matter: The abounding symbols bound into each other with dullish clanks. From time to time Price stops the action to point out neat connections the reader might have missed. The end is dark and difficult. It is a pity such skill was not applied to a less self-conscious exercise in fiction.

1968

. . . . My Mind to Me
a Kingdom Is

Last summer, on a tiny island south of St. Vincent, a flabby Britisher and I drank rum and fruit juices. The Britisher's son by an American wife engaged a native in a Caribbean version of Chinese checkers. I was explaining baseball.

"It's the statistics that count," I babbled. "If a man hits .400, that means he gets four hundred hits for every thousand times at bat in one season, but nobody bats a thousand times in one season."

More rum, more fruit juices. The Britisher's son was winning his game: Pop-pop-pop, and all the brightly colored marbles fell to Anglo-American imperialism. The native ground his finely pointed teeth.

"Only Ty Cobb turned that trick twice," I said, always at ease with sportswriters' jargon. "In 1912, he hit .420. Nobody's topped that."

With a machine-gun staccato of pops, the Britisher's boy raked in all the marbles. The native reached for his knife. "Wrong," said the boy. "Cobb hit .420 in 1911. Rogers Hornsby beat him with .424 in 1924. They both hit over .400 three times. George Sisler hit over .400 twice."

"How do you know *that*?" I asked.

"I've memorized the record book," the boy replied, setting out the marbles for another game.

The moral of this story is that there are people for whom baseball assumes an unwieldy significance; indeed, there are people who think of baseball less as a game than as a mythical translation—into terms ordinary guys can understand—of the ultimate laws of existence. Such a man is the hero of Robert Coover's *The Universal Baseball Association, Inc., J. Henry Waugh, Prop.*

Henry is introduced in one of the most expertly conceived and executed opening chapters in modern American fiction. He is, apparently, at a baseball stadium watching a rookie pitcher complete a perfect game. But no, Henry goes out to a delicatessen; he must have been at home, watching the game on television. But wait: It is night when Henry goes out, yet the game is being played in the afternoon. Then the truth comes through: The game is in Henry's mind.

Henry, we learn, is a cipher—a fifty-six-year-old accountant and a miserable bachelor who talks to himself. Henry is also an insane genius: In baseball, with its nearly perfect balance of offense and defense and its obsession with statistics, Henry finds the insignificant accountant's dream of trivia on a heroic scale. He has created an eight-team league as, with a few exceptions, it might have existed a hundred years ago. He knows every player—his quirks and ulcers—on every club as intimately as any manager would; and he has recorded, in many volumes, the fifty-six-year history of the league, its legends, player interviews, and obituaries. In the winter, Henry trades players, haggles over salaries, and fires managers, but in the season, he plays the game: *every* game of every team, rolling dice and consulting charts to determine every play. "Ball stadiums and not European churches were the real American holy places," Henry remarks. "Sometimes I wished I could do something heroic, something tremendous and legendary, a testing of the very limits of the record system."

The testing comes, of course, as the crisis of the novel. Henry may be the god of his game, but he is a god subject to the roll of the dice. What happens when circumstances seem to justify fixing the roll? Will this work toward a more perfect order or toward a destruction of Henry's world? Henry tends to identify with his ballplayers, and, inevitably, the time comes when they take over, Henry vanishes, and the game assumes the character of a Passion play, or perhaps a Dionysian sacrifice.

Coover's novel is a brilliant and original tour de force, a very funny book, and a triumph of modern mythmaking. It has its faults: It is a little too long; the reader will not be able to sort out the baseball players as easily as Henry can; and a familiarity with baseball may be necessary to ease the reader through the complexities of the story. Even so, Coover has captured the magic of the game—from its numerological concern with three's and nine's to its hagiography—and in doing so, he has also caught something of the ambitions and frustrations of the Universal Human Association.

The narrator of Brian Moore's new novel, *I Am Mary Dunne,* is in almost as bad shape as Henry Waugh. Mary also lives too much in her mind; she, too, totters on the edge of mental breakdown. The novels have no other resemblance. They are, in fact, so different that few readers will enjoy both. Coover's is a tale for men, imperfectly stamped with genius; Moore's is a woman's story, imprinted with his impeccable competence. Coover is a fantasist; Moore, a traditionalist—a realist so skillful that he switches sexes in his narration to write a narrative about sex as seen from the opposite perspective. This is, of course, the gimmick of the pornographer, who writes from what he would have us believe is the woman's point of view on sex. Actually, the pornographer tells us only how most men would like to think women respond to sex—which explains why most women take a dim view of pornography. Moore's approach is different: It is honest and, for all I can tell, the way it probably is.

At fifteen, Mary Dunne told her teacher, "We are what we remember." The teacher was amused. Now, at thirty-two, Mary has been married three times; she spends the day the novel describes remembering her marriages. Her feelings, complicated by premenstrual tension, subject her to what she calls "the dooms"—gloomy thoughts in which she loses both her husband and her sanity. Mary is a Canadian living in New York. During this fateful day, various strangers remind her of her vulnerability, but she is most disturbed by visits from two Canadian friends of yesteryear: a vulgar woman who, Mary now realizes, once betrayed her, and an intolerable oaf of a man who has diddled away his life in loving Mary.

Mary is in trouble. "You have sex on the brain," her vulgar friend tells her, and this judgment is close to the truth. She has changed husbands and allegiances too often; even in her own self, a "mad twin" is likely to break out, scattering all coherence before it. Mary has been called by so many names that she begins this day by forgetting her name. "I am a changeling," she says, "who has changed too often, and then there are moments when I cannot find my way back, moments when whoever is the current me goes away and leaves me here, a me who is no me, a person with no identity." By the end of the story, she can only insist on her identity, echoing the words of Webster's famous heroine: "I am Duchesse of Malfy still."

Like all realistic novelists, Moore spends much time passing on stale news: news of *Marat/Sade,* the Turner exhibition, the chatter of cabdrivers, the tassels on sherry bottles. Moore wants us to believe this is indeed a woman talking: "There was a cold spring wind as I got off the bus," Mary says, "cold on my thighs between my stocking tops and girdle." Okay, I'm convinced. Scores of thousands of readers look for this kind of verisimilitude in fiction, the satirical portraits sharply etched, the flashbacks and flashbacks-within-flashbacks effortlessly handled. Why should anyone complain? I don't. *I Am Mary Dunne* is an easy read, and Moore copes with this kind of thing, for whatever it is worth, better than anyone now writing in the genre.

1968

. . . . The Worst of
Bruce Jay Friedman

Let me write out all the bad words at once and then we can cry, for a paragraph or two, over Bruce Jay Friedman's talent, which he cannot be accused of hiding in the earth, but which has nonetheless gone to seed.

The bad words I have been collecting about *The Dick,* Friedman's third novel, are: heavy-handed, self-indulgent, clumsy, sentimental, repetitious, smart-aleck-nasty in a prepubescent way. It is also embarrassingly old-fashioned. Reading it is like stumbling over a 1950 Packard: a classy number in its time, no doubt, but that time was mothlike brief, so why is it still crouching in the streets, its wheels gone and its paint flaking, its bumpers twisting out to catch us on our shins?

Stern, Friedman's first novel and one of the best American novels of the past decade, appeared in 1962. All the good words apply to *Stern*— taut, selective, funny, and sad, it touched off tremors of apprehension in its readers. In fact, only after I reread the opening pages of *Stern* did I realize how disappointing *The Dick* is. Friedman's second novel should have warned us what to expect: *A Mother's Kisses* was an overblown farce, a pre-Portnoy assault on Jewish motherhood that left readers with a kind of *ne plus ultra* enervation—but there is always an *ultra.* Some writers, Friedman among them, seem determined to exceed their own excesses, and that is why Friedman's star, firmly in the ascendant only a short while ago, now seems about to complete its parabolic curve: from potency to decadence in only three novels and eight years.

Much of the agitation—I can hardly call it narrative—in *The Dick* concerns the natural violence of policemen attached to a homicide division, which (in case the thought did not occur to you) is sometimes called "the homicidal world." These detectives like to shoot people up and whittle people down; they hang pistols in their crotches and cover them with cellophane so they can wear them in the shower. Friedman's intention (in case the thought did not occur to you) is humorous, and this combination of sadistic cops and lots of yuks might have been funny, even useful, once, before Chicago, or even further back when we dozed in the benign complacency of Eisenhower's Silver Age.

It doesn't seem funny or useful now—in fact, it seems downright retarded. Friedman's humor is grounded in jokes about mutilation, sex, and race. He talks about " 'Oven faces,' girls from a nearby home who had all at one time been involved in various types of explosions." He giggles over a teen-age girl who has porno photos taken of herself to give to her father, and titters over a white child sent to an all-black school: a "heavily spaded atmosphere," Friedman writes; the child is "educated in almost total darkness." Ho, ho. I haven't laughed like that since I was a kid. But that's the point: Friedman's humor is kids' humor. Not the Pooh Bear and Mr. Toad kind of humor that delicate adults think children like, but the real thing, the jokes about your sister's anatomy that the crazy-eyed kid down the block told you while his big friend held your arm behind your back. At puberty, they tell me, our bodies change and empathy develops. Perhaps, but the weight of Friedman's jokes, which he delivers two or three to a page in the manner of a stand-up comic who has to get a certain number of laughs, snickers, and guffaws from his audience every minute, is affectless, even brutalizing.

There is a plot of sorts, though it is barely discernible. Ken LePeters, né Sussman, public relations detective for "a large, violent but somehow conscience-stricken homicide bureau," is not opposed to violence and bigotry, but he lacks the "bond of authentic homicidal fury" that would have made him brother to his fellow dicks. Predictably (in this book we tend to hope Friedman does not mean his metaphors), LePeters' badge is only half size. He has trouble with his wife but loves his daughter and is dismayed when, through a zoning fluke, she must attend the town's "spade school." LePeters gets a hernia, then a mistress. His wife takes a lover. LePeters' Jewish background is leaked to his colleagues (much merriment there, I assure you). LePeters takes more mistresses, then restores order to his domestic affairs with an act of violence. There is a lesson for us here, I am sure, but ask me about it some other time.

The Dick is not all bad. If my response is chilly, it is because the novel reads like a first draft. With six more weeks of rigorous conditioning, Friedman might have reduced this three-hundred-and-ten-page lump of a book to a one-hundred-and-eighty-page story in fighting trim. I grieve, too, because Friedman, a talented writer who helped create the literary mood of the sixties, seems to grow more strident, but not more imaginative, with each novel. Other writers, bent on social satire, have progressed to more apposite forms of fiction. Still, there is good stuff in his novel, whole pages that are funny, perceptive, warmly sentimental. Sorting them out, however, is like picking through the laundry hamper when your clean socks have been mixed in with the dirty. I'm old-fashioned enough to think that the sorting-out process is what we pay laundries and novelists for.

1970

. . . . Three Concerti for
Symbols and Allegory
(*Ma non troppo*)

That is no country for dumb men. The lame
  Of intellect, the sluggards of dull wit
—Readers who moistly move their lips—complain
  That what an author means does not quite fit
With what he seems to say. "Come now, explain!
  I almost understand. With just a bit
Of help," the reader says, "some charity,
  I'll cash your symbols in at parity."

And then like you, O William Gass, I'll come
  Serenely sailing to Byzantium.
  —Fragments of a manuscript found in a bottle in the
  washroom of the Public Library

Since William H. Gass begins the title story in his collection *In the Heart of the Heart of the Country* with a mangled quotation from Yeats' famous poem ("So I have sailed the seas to come . . . to B . . ."), I thought it only proper to return the favor here. Symbols are an integral part of Gass' fiction; they work, as symbols should, to change the perspective of the stories, to ease the reader's progress from the realm of realistic detail to a moral and metaphysical plane on which those same details will be repeated, now metamorphosed into something rich and strange.

Such signs and portents pose no problems; on the contrary, they strengthen Gass' fiction. What may perplex a casual reader is the high-compression ratio that drives these tales. Much is condensed into little, and every syllable is nudged firmly into its significant place. The plots that begin so simply dissolve into a fog, mere action yielding to a vision of the rot festering in the mind and heart of man: the triumph of the invisible worm of spiritual decay.

Take, for instance, "The Pedersen Kid," the longest and most impressive of the five stories, and one which, more fully than the others, develops themes that are common to them all. On one level, Jorge, the narrator—a callous boy indeterminately advanced in adolescence—tells how a neighbor's boy stumbled through a blizzard to his father's barn. Half-frozen, the boy babbles about a mysterious gunman who is holding his parents prisoner in their cellar. Jorge, his father, and the hired man, armed with guns, go to the Pedersen farm. Shots ring out; the hired man flees, the father dies, and Jorge exults in delirious joy. On another level, the story concerns Jorge's murder of his hated father—an act Jorge had anticipated for years, but which, like everything else in the story, may take place only in Jorge's fevéred imagination. Does the gunman actually exist? Did the Pedersen kid really survive the blizzard to tell a lurid story suspiciously like every Western thriller ever written?

The reader must decide for himself. Gass' concern lies elsewhere: with Jorge's rapidly deteriorating mind. Moving inexorably through progressive states of physical, spiritual, and mental alienation, Jorge finally arrives at madness—a madness in which everything in the world is revealed as a sign pointing to something within *him*, and every person in the world behaves as he must to conform with Jorge's mad melodrama. Even the blizzard, with its connotations of numbness and death, is absorbed by Jorge: "The cold storm in my belly," he says, likening it to ". . . a white blank glittering waste like the waste outside."

A similar psychological imperialism prevails in all of Gass' stories. Each concerns a falling off from humanness: "I have succeeded to the idleness of God," says one narrator; "I am in retirement from love," another muses. Still another believes that property is in possession of *him*; and another, that insects are superior to women. Those narrators who do not succumb to madness combine obsession with despair, a peculiarly disabling combination. Each is capable, as his story opens, of observing the evil in others; each, as his story progresses, is revealed to be as corrupt as those whom he labors to despise; each, as his story ends, has been swallowed by the world from which he had set himself apart.

A grim picture, but a sternly moral one, more moral, perhaps, and certainly more exciting, than anything we have had in the field of short fiction since the death of Flannery O'Connor.

Snow is also the principal symbol in Hans Erich Nossack's *The Impossible Proof,* but for Nossack, snow is rather like what you get from a defective television set: a blur that impedes communication. For all the communication accomplished in its pages, the novel itself might have sunk into the snow. It took a dozen years to import this trifle of metaphysical masochism from Germany, but the wonder is that it was imported at all.

The novel, which runs without an intermission, involves a nameless defendant elaborating upon the banality of his behavior before a nameless judge. The defendant's wife has disappeared, and the court assumes the defendant is criminally involved. The defendant is friendless, dependable, vacuous; his life has been "irreproachable to the point of tedium." He sells insurance for any of the possessions that encumber our existence, but he cannot, he confesses, insure against life itself. "Aha!" I exclaimed, like the horse that smelleth battle, and sure enough, after endless yards of boring chatter, it turns out that his wife has escaped—not from life but to it. The defendant wishes the court to find him guilty because he lost courage and, like Lot's wife, cast a glance behind him.

Any reader of Kafka knows you don't need evidence of a crime to put a man on trial for his life, and as long as you have him on trial, you may as well consider his entire life a crime. It may, however, require a Kafka to make rewarding reading from such juridical irregularity. Nossack cannot do it. He has not the talent. He lacks Kafka's anger and anguish; he cannot muster Kafka's horror or wit. His characters admit to "giving importance to statements apparently devoid of it." They *are* devoid of it. Nossack's inquiry is tedious; his point, banal. He cannot, as Kafka could, persuade us that either has anything to do with us. There may be more to his story than I have indicated, but there is not much more. Michael Lebeck's ponderous translation does nothing to lighten the situation.

Lane Kauffmann's *Another Helen* is such frothy fare it hardly belongs in this formidable company. Nevertheless, both Kauffmann and his characters belabor an unnecessary and unconvincing parallel between Helen, who after the Trojan defeat returned to live peaceably with Menelaus, and Eleanor Davenport, a stunning beauty who left her husband, son, and soft suburban home only to return six years later when her lover, a French aristocrat, died racing his car in the Grand Prix de Monaco.

How can you keep them down on the farm after they've seen Paris? Eleanor is only forty when she returns, a firm Francophile (which disturbs her husband) and a confirmed skeptic about American women (which disturbs her son of college age). Eleanor's return predictably creates a scandal, but only when she imports a genuine French girl to distract her son from his American fiancée does the plot get under way. Eleanor's ruse backfires. As the curtain falls, everyone is happily joined in new respect for everyone else, with the superfluous characters who briefly entertained us now brusquely cast aside.

Another Helen is a book women will love because the men in it are well-meaning and stupid, and the women (including the maid and the teen-age girl) are brilliantly witty. It seems such an obvious formula for success, I wonder no one has thought of it before. Still, it would have made a better play than a novel. Had Kauffmann had a director at his elbow, the novel's dross might have been eliminated; as a well-paced, brittle comedy in which well-groomed characters play conversational Ping-Pong amid the well-groomed furniture, it might have been believable. But as a novel, it collapses. The plot is clumsy, cracking with corn. Only Eleanor redeems it: Eleanor is not only witty, she means exactly what she says, which must, I am sure, make her unique among women anywhere. When she is on stage, the novel sparkles; when she is off, the reader wishes he were reading another book.

1968

................The Case of the Calcified Novelist

If, as we are told, a hundred monkeys banging at typewriters can eventually write a play like *King Lear,* then surely a computer could, in one great creative spasm, cough up a facsimile of a novel by Henry James. You may not have given much thought to that possibility, nor, to tell the truth, had I until I read James Gould Cozzens' ninth novel, *Morning Noon and Night.* At first glance, it appears to be simply a very bad novel; at second glance, it looks unreadable. By the third or fourth page, however, the reader, remembering novels by Cozzens that he admired, grows suspicious.

Is this where Cozzens has been heading? Or—and the thought creeps slyly in—is it a hoax, wrought upon an unsuspecting public by a publisher whose accounting department sent him a memorandum to the effect that (a) it had some time available on its computer, and (b) it was tired of waiting eleven years for a novel as successful as *By Love Possessed*? Isn't this novel, in fact, a parody, skillfully composed by an electronic gizmo programmed for all the obsolete, inkhorn words that good writers have abandoned—if they ever knew them? Isn't it a travesty of a novel deliberately designed to play to Cozzens' weaknesses and avoid his strengths?

In earlier and better novels, Cozzens displayed an astonishing familiarity with the military and medical professions, with the church and the law. Management consulting, by contrast, may seem a cool crucible in which to forge a soul, but the soul of Henry Worthington, attenuated WASP and narrator of this new novel, has no metal in it; like a fallen soufflé, its exterior Puritan crust has collapsed because there is nothing but soggy pulp inside. Henry is a man of staggering triviality. He mumbles over his life: the shabby pretension of his career, his exceptional luck, his faulty memory, and his penchant for delivering "ethical wise saws." One wife divorced him, another committed suicide. He might have taught, but he didn't; he wanted to write, but he couldn't;

and, like many WASP's, he talks interminably about his ancestors. He bumbled through college and fumbled through sex; he grumbles over writers who are committed to the world—in particular those who argued for Sacco and Vanzetti—and he had a comfortable war.

Ho, hum. Yes, indeed, Henry is devoted, as he says of his ruminations, to "a laboring of the obvious," and so, unfortunately, is his author who should know by now that "the just representation of life and people" he holds so dear involves more than dull, gray literalism. If you can imagine Mr. Collins narrating *Pride and Prejudice,* you will have some idea of what Henry's narration does to this novel. And yet Cozzens seems to *like* Henry—almost as if many of Henry's fusty meanderings through climes of conservative opinion paralleled his own. Certainly, much of what Henry says about writing and its critics seems to come straight from some part of a horse's anatomy. "What a bore are today's books that harp on sex," Henry piously intones, but the first dialogue in the novel—and none appears until page 71—introduces his daughter's sexual autobiography, from her first experiments with herself through fulfillment and three husbands. Of such material are best sellers made. Henry may groan, but Cozzens knows what he is doing.

Henry, however, is the least of Cozzens' sins. The prose in this novel is so mannered, so opaque, that many sentences will not yield coherent meaning even after several readings. A wise author, I suppose, knows that such words as "innominate," "butyric," and "inconceptible" exist, but if Cozzens were wise, he would not use them. Nor would he describe a woman sleeping with a man as "featly accommodating him in conjoinment." Only a leaden ear would not wince from such a line as "satisfied with the courses of instruction he gave given as he gave them." And can you believe a person could *say*: "Feeling sees bad done to you through—so, by—them"?

More serious is the novel's apparent lack of design. No part of the novel seems necessary; at no point do we want or need to know anything more about Henry than we have already learned. Instead, the novel lumbers through endless epicycles, with never an indication of purposeful progress from one event or perception to another.

This in itself might suggest that Cozzens is not, or is no longer, the intellectual titan of the art of fiction that many critics once thought him to be. For too long too many readers have accepted his chilly disdain for man and his endeavors as if such sanitary pessimism were evidence of wisdom. It may be amusing to imagine Cozzens carefully washing his hands after going to the typewriter, but *Morning Noon and Night* shows just how shabby his glacial cynicism is, and how priggish his relish of man's barbarity to man—particularly if the form of that barbarism is sanctioned by tradition. Humor might have saved it, because the blackest view of man becomes bearable when lightened by wit or irony.

Drama or compassion might have alleviated the dullness. But there is none of these in Cozzens' novel, a book that is bad beyond believing.

1968

. . . . .Going Downward,
Toward the Dark

Now that I have finished Joyce Carol Oates' new novel, *them,* I'll be in a foul mood for weeks. I'll snarl at my wife and slap at my children. And why not? My daughter may be illiterate, but she is not excused; soon she must learn what literature says about life.

Well, you may say, there's variety in that. Poet A says this and Playwright B says that, and since there's no agreement, why bother with any of it? Not so. We forget that writers have always basically agreed. The variety is not in what they say about life but in how they say it, how they repeat, in endless artistic variations, a few homely, pessimistic truths. Life is lousy, they say, perfectly dreadful. The pain of life is a constant source of wonder and humor, as is the ability of a few poor cripples to keep shuffling along. Writers disagree about details, of course: Has life a meaning? Shall we laugh at suffering, like Chaucer and Joyce Cary? Or shall we weep, like Euripides and Dostoyevsky? Can man find an exultation in suffering that makes it all worthwhile? But even if half our writers think man can cope with his vicissitudes and the other half do not, they do not disagree about the facts. The phenomena of pain, of loss, and of betrayal remain the same.

Once upon a time, before Hawthorne showed us our neuroses, Melville showed us Armageddon, and Mark Twain laughed through the hole at the bottom of the world, most writers were affirmative, if not optimistic, fellows. Humanity can amount to something, they said, though it probably won't. Maybe here and there, a man will muddle through: Tom Jones marries Sophia Western at the end of Henry Fielding's novel, but nobody is fooled. Happy endings, as all writers know, are no more than personal enclaves pitched in the midst of general disorder.

Fielding knew that most men spend most of their time being nasty to one another, but nevertheless, life made *sense,* and his novels show what that sense was. Few writers of Joyce Oates' generation believe it. Miss Oates is more brilliant and more savage than most of her colleagues, but, like them, she finds a pattern in life where others found sense and cause for affirmation. The pattern repeats itself: Man's life is short and swinish; man's enthusiasms expire early and his aspirations vanish shortly after; man's spirit disintegrates as violence and boredom overcome him, as he succumbs to ugliness and desperation. Like all serious novels, Miss Oates' stories are a criticism of life. Unlike the greatest stories, Miss Oates' novels convey no sense of exultation, no sense of a struggle worth the pain and losing. Her books are too clever, too shallow, too acid for that. Instead, she offers something else: art as reparation for life. It is not a new thing; artists of all kinds, in times of deepest pessimism, have offered it before.

Miss Oates seems to say: For your pain, I give you a form. Not an explanation, and certainly not hope, but a pattern. It may help; it is all any of us has to offer. "I lived my life but there is no form to it," says one of the major characters in *them*. "No shape. All the people who lie alone at night squirm with hatred they can't get straight, into a shape, all the women who give themselves to men without knowing who those men are, all of us walk fast with hate like pain in our bowels, terrified, and what do you know about it? You write books. What do you know? . . . We are . . . waiting for something to come to us and give a shape to so much pain."

Them begins in 1937, with Loretta, a sixteen-year-old girl, looking in the mirror, feeling her youth and sensuality, still able to resist the ugliness of her family and the dull Midwestern city where she lives. Loretta is waiting for something important to happen to her. All her life she will wait, though she will grow beery and blowsy, though she will mate and breed and bitch about her life. Her son Jules takes up Loretta's search for freedom. Robbed of his childhood, he turns to petty, violent crimes and dreams of crushing his father's skull. Jules believes in himself, though everyone tells him he will be dead at twenty, preferably in an electric chair. But it is love that nearly kills Jules, love that Miss Oates calls "a delirium and a pathological condition." Only in violence can Jules find rest. Maureen, Loretta's daughter, fares worse. Men use her; her stepfather almost kills her; her spark of childish kindness is extinguished, and Maureen sinks into a stupor, a woman disguised as a child, "sleeping in her body, knowing she is safe." Maureen asks: How can people live in so much noise and cruelty and craziness, always afraid? Loretta forgets her questions: Her search for a self she never finds deteriorates into quarrelsome self-promotion.

How much we aggravate each other, Miss Oates exclaims, how much we wish each other ill! Men are brutish; women, unbalanced because of their need for men. Our lives are out of our control. If our emotions do not kill us, our lethargy will suffocate us. Stupidity is yoked to ambition. The good in us dies young, but the bad endures so that, as we grow old, our insides leak and our spirits turn to alum.

Brrr. *Them* is a long, depressing book that in less talented hands would prove unbearable. But Miss Oates is an artist, determined to surprise. She has read Stendhal and Flaubert. She tells her distinctly American story in the French romantic tradition of a century ago. She combines irony with intensity, obsession with frustration, and pessimism with melodrama. Pistols explode into the heads and chests of lovers, and lugubrious satire intrudes into a nightmare world. It is somehow frightening, if not quite real, like those unworldly photographs of a setting sun, squatting large and leprous in the smog above a city skyline.

1969

This is an off-year for Joyce Carol Oates: no novel ready, but—to keep her hand in—a collection of short stories, *The Wheel of Love,* which is twice as long as such collections usually are. Miss Oates is prolific; she is also one of the best living American writers. Remarkably, she has made her reputation with only minimal (and rather academic) experiments with style.

Her success, I think, is easily explained. First, she is peculiarly attuned to the numbness, madness, and chaos of our times. Second, she doesn't mess around. Miss Oates' stories threaten to explode in the reader's hands—perhaps from the melodramatic violence of their plots, perhaps from the bottled desperation of her characters. A teen-age girl on drugs threatens to murder a baby; a young man in love cuts his throat before his girl, spurting blood upon her coat; a child fears returning home from school because her mother, quite mad, crouches behind the furnace. Madness, I almost forgot to say, is the warp and woof of Miss Oates' fiction; it overtakes mothers and children who, stumbling dully through a world that has no meaning for them, awake to insanity. The characters in her stories do not affect each other much; they use their relation to other people to destroy themselves. Most of them are very much alone and prone to melancholy. They are fragile, vulnerable people who break down and nurse secret, shapeless fears, who open up and shut down within themselves. "There is a force inside me that wants to be let out," says one, speaking for all, "but I don't know what it is."

Most of the stories are set in Detroit, but it doesn't matter: Miss Oates' landscapes are interior. Most of the characters are moved by love, a few are even saved by it, and that does matter. Half a dozen of these twenty stories will haunt me for years. I urgently recommend that you read them.

1970

Some of us, in these degenerate times, find that our fantasy lives have been overtaken by headlines. I drive home alone from the station, improving the idle minutes by wondering whether, this evening, my driveway will be full of police cars, rotating lights, short men with bulky cameras. Joyce Oates whispers in my ear: "Yes, yes; that's the way it is!" Neighbors, standing on my lawn by the overturned tricycle, nudge each other and stare at me. The state trooper advances cautiously: "Mr. Prescott?"

"Gothicism," Joyce Oates wrote two years ago, "is not a literary tradition so much as a fairly realistic assessment of modern life." Gothic fiction, then, becomes realistic fiction, with grotesque people—monsters, really—devouring each other in a welter of everyday detail. We are used to it in newspaper reports and in our more fanciful nonfiction, but with novels one usually makes a choice: Gothic fiction (imperiled maidens in windy castles) over *here*; realistic fiction (junkies in slums) over *there*. Miss Oates' combination of the extravagant and the familiar comprises a perspective on fiction that is both personal and exciting.

A chart of one of her novels would look like an electrocardiogram gone berserk: a plateau or two and a few *longueurs* scattered among a dozen or more horrendous, superbly dramatic set pieces, self-contained episodes so securely crafted that they often appear elsewhere as short stories—which is perhaps not entirely salutary. *Wonderland* is as impressive, as admirable, as her other fiction, but perhaps those who will admire it most will be those who don't know her other work. For those of us who do, a certain sameness, certain patterns, are beginning to come clear. The connecting themes and images in *Wonderland*—of personality and the possession of one's self, of the devouring father and the parricide—recur throughout the novel without development. A suspicion grows: Perhaps the truth of Joyce Oates' novels is no more than the truth of journalism; perhaps the anguish behind the melodrama, for all the talk of fate and destiny, has not yet found a full articulation. Partly for this reason, *Wonderland*'s parts seem greater than the whole.

The story begins in 1939, in upstate New York, with Jesse, a fourteen-year-old boy, about to flee his father, who has just slaughtered his family, and who will try to get Jesse, too, before turning his gun upon himself. Jesse flees: He is a survivor, an Oates' hero, typically desperate, blood throbbing in his ears, fear banging in his brain, a scream rising in his lungs. Inside, Jesse is empty, his despair a hollowness like hunger. As an adult, Jesse would remember that he "did not have a personality. He did not want a personality. His heartbeat told him always: *here you are, here is Jesse, a survivor.*"

Other men, father figures to Jesse, try to fill his emptiness by making him grow into their own images. "He will become the complete form of the self I have imagined for him," says his adopted father. Jesse flees him, too. Another, a surgeon who takes Jesse on as a protégé, denounces personality as something monstrous: "We each have a hidden obsession,

I suppose, a kind of monster that has made our facial structures what they are . . . and we try to keep this monster secret. . . . This is the personality people defend." Not profound, perhaps—it is a bit like the lines they feed to Vincent Price in movies—but it is melodramatically effective, nonetheless. Again, Jesse presses for survival at the expense of personality. In time, his daughter will accuse him of seeking to devour her, will make her own break for survival, and the Kronos myth, always a highlight of Miss Oates' fiction, will be even further extended.

Miss Oates writes impeccably, as always, linking with metaphor her human and geographical landscapes: "this backyard of junk, the odor of smouldering rubber from a fire that is perpetually burning invisibly . . ." As always, she compresses much emotion in small space. In a brief paragraph, for example, she shows us fright, hurt, anger, love, impotence, and hostile weather, a tension between people that kills communication. She writes about the ordeal of interns and the hippie scene in Toronto: the kind of fictional journalism that she does so well, so much better than she does her characters with theories to expound (in this she shares a kinship with De Sade). She has a genius for the horrific detail: the medical student broiling and eating a woman's uterus, the girl at the vivisection lab brushing a piece of intestine from her hair.

Long sections are absolutely marvelous—stories, as I have said, that stand by themselves—but somehow, from a writer of Miss Oates' talent, it is not enough. We have had this, theme and variations, before. No one can ask a writer to write books other than those he knows how to write, but by establishing a pattern, a writer invites a closer scrutiny. Although I enjoyed *Wonderland* thoroughly, I am beginning to have doubts about the links Miss Oates establishes between melodrama and significance: They are not quite convincing.

1971

. . . . .Candide
Without Voltaire

There appear to be two Mary McCarthys. One is bright, tough, and witty, an acidulous author of satirical fiction and criticism who, in a squabble over the Vietnam War, eviscerated Diana Trilling in the pages of the *The New York Review of Books*. That was three years ago. Five years before that, Miss McCarthy's novel *The Group* was passed among horny hands on commuter trains, its spine broken at Chapter 2 in which a dull young virgin is serviced by a man who seems to have been trained by the people at Roto-Rooter. The first Mary McCarthy, then, is a writer whose books I know and love; the second, the false Mary McCarthy, is the author of *Birds of America,* the novel most likely to be left behind on Martha's Vineyard this summer.

Peter Levi is a college junior, about to take a year in France. He is a shy boy, fond of birds, an innocent who follows Kant's dictum that a man may not be used as a means: "The Other is always an End." Like Candide, Peter is an optimist, but he finds it difficult to do what he believes to be right—it is hard to be consistently good without offending others—so Peter, like many who attempt to apply a scheme to every action in their lives, is often foolish, often a prig.

Peter dearly loves his mother, who is thrice-married, bright, tough, and an artist—she plays the harpsichord on concert tours and is determined to cook only with real food, baking her own beans and complaining that unpackaged food is disappearing from the market. The mother, I suspect, must be a bit like Miss McCarthy herself: "She was too good to be true," Peter thinks; even her faults pleased him. "You confuse the ethical and the esthetic," Peter tells her, stirring my distrust of kids who analyze their parents' problems.

The early episodes are full of talk of food—"the cornbread and walnut stuffing, the green-tomato pickle, the mincemeat tarts with homemade vanilla ice cream," and so on—a weight watcher's erotic dream and Miss McCarthy's most saporific fiction yet. The later episodes, after Peter is in Paris and concerned with girls, bums, and architecture, are more politically inclined: "You may think I'm wandering from the theme of equality," he writes his mother. Throughout the book I kept thinking: How accurately sophomoric these conversations and interior monologues are; in real life they are just as protracted and as dull as they are shown to be here.

This is Miss McCarthy's problem: She tells the story from Peter's point of view. It limits her effectiveness because, although Peter is bright and good and his ideas are sweet, he is not interesting. The parallels between Peter and Candide do not help; although Miss McCarthy is well qualified to write an American *Candide,* her novel lacks altogether the irony, wit, and savagery for which she and Voltaire are famous, and her attempt at a sentimental *Candide,* emphasizing warmth, kindness, and realism, fails.

Nor can Miss McCarthy maintain a consistent tone. At times she condescends to Peter—"He had decided to be interested in art this year"; "Peter wished he knew where he stood about being an anachronism"—and in one unforgettable passage Peter takes five pages to tell his mother about his compulsion to clean out community toilets. The episode has a humorous point in that the filth of the toilets puts a block to Peter's Kantian ethics (all men cannot be equal if only some men clean up after themselves), but to write it Miss McCarthy abandoned the "niceness" of her narrative—and, by altering Peter's character (I cannot believe that this particular boy would write such an episode to his mother), she strains our belief in her story.

Irritating as *Birds of America* is to one who admires Miss McCarthy's other books, it is not a total loss. There comes a time in a man's life when he is too old to read the Freddy-the-Pig books and too young to read *Animal Farm*. Nice novels, written for adults, will teach him something of the real world. Teen-agers may learn from this book some elements of good taste in food, in people, in architecture, and in ethics. They will also learn some bad grammar ("somebody could trip on it and hurt themselves") and some banal thinking ("*Ars longa vita brevis* was a truth that could not be argued within the Eternal City"), but such stupidities are to be expected, I suppose, when a brilliant woman stoops to an adolescent's view of the world.

1971

. . . . How to Be a Loser: Three Novelists Reveal the Secret

Condon commercial. Take 17. Announcer (*smiles as patriotic music swells softly in background*): Friends, do your children snicker when you talk about Dick Tracy? (*Sympathetic grimace.*) Does your wife object to the Hardy Boy mysteries you leave about the house? (*He nods: We all know what wives are.*) Do your buddies giggle when you ask them in to watch Godzilla on *The Late Show*? (*Concerned expression.*) If you answered yes to these questions, you may be suffering from Tired Culture. (*Smile again.*) Modern medical discoveries prove that nine out of ten cases can be cured without surgery. (*Speaks with force and conviction.*) Come up come *all* the way up to Classy Culture simply by purchasing a copy of Richard Condon's novel *Mile High,* published by the people at Dial Press. (*Dissolve to book jacket.*) Your family and friends will be amazed because it looks and feels like a real book. (*Withdraw to show announcer looking at and feeling book.*) Only *you* will know that it's the same old stuff you've always liked: a comic strip without the pictures. (*Announcer winks. Fade out.*)

And that's what it is, folks. Condon appears to take it seriously, as if it were some kind of contribution to our American metaphysics, linking crime to democracy and violence to idealism, but comic books give us all that—Truth, Justice, and a Fist in the Snoot—without Condon's literary pretensions and, to be fair, without his formidable skills as an entertainer, either.

The protagonist of *Mile High* is Eddie West, the man who, for personal profit, brought us both Prohibition and the Crash of 1929. Like Charles Ives' Second Symphony, Eddie is less an original creation than an anthology of familiar American themes: He is part Jay Gatsby and part Daddy Warbucks, part H. L. Hunt and part Citizen Kane. He is also a paranoiac and a sexual maniac. His mother was a Sicilian lesbian; his father, an Irish immigrant who escaped the potato blight to crimp and pimp on the New York docks until, naturally, he owned not only a chain of brothels but the bars and gambling joints and Tammany Hall as well. "Ice in the veins," Paddy West would caution his son, "is money in the bank, and always take the long view." Eddie learned. When Paddy died at seventy-nine from a stroke brought on by punching a horse to its knees, Eddie took over his empire.

That was in 1911, the year Eddie decided that what the West fortunes needed was a dry America. Eddie knew how to collect liquor and distilleries, how to use the Mafia to his own advantage, how to force his bootleggers to finance their operations with short-term loans from Eddie's corporations. Because he grabbed one-sixth of the gross of every bootlegging operation, Eddie's income in the twenties averaged $13 billion a year. But there was time for fun, too: for breaking the bones of prostitutes, and sometimes killing them, all in memory of his mother. There is more—oh, much more!—which you may read for yourself.

The point, of course, is that Eddie's balloon must burst. Men who blow themselves up to comic-book proportions because they have whored after the American Dream—power! money! status!—all democratically, if shadily, arrived at, always fall hard. Too bad. But it makes a pretty story: Condon frequently pauses to illustrate it with fancy names, with menus and with descriptions of furniture, the interiors of private planes and railroad cars.

Mile High is one of those novels that make us feel good because its author is even more cynical than we are. Men, says Condon, are endlessly corrupt. Everybody can be bought or fooled: cardinals, cops, and senators take whatever they can get, and judges, actors, and athletes dance attendance on those outside the law. There is enough truth in this—look at Thomas Dodd and Joe Namath—to make us wince, but Condon carries it too far. Men like Eddie West, he says, will never be exposed because they are universally respected, even loved. Nonsense, of course. Such men are feared and usually exposed. Still, it is marvelously entertaining nonsense. Condon is one of the great slumlords of the current literary scene. Far from condemning what he builds, I enjoy it immensely: His are good books to visit if you don't have to live there.

The destruction of a man is also the theme of the late James Kennaway's last novel, *The Cost of Living Like This*. It is, I think, what is called an intelligent novel, meaning that it is a bit overly thought out, that the seams show wherever parts are joined, and that there is an endless quantity of talk about the nature of man.

Julian is young but dying of lung cancer. The pain feels like a crab clawing at his innards, but he fights it off with morphine and a final fling with an eighteen-year-old girl from his office. Julian's wife objects but blames herself. Through a series of coincidences too complicated to relate, she gets involved with a Scot named Mozart Anderson, to whom she offers an interminable confession in the form of rhetorical questions. Mozart replies with aphorisms on human nature.

It is all pretty stiff and artificial, which is a pity because Kennaway was a skillful writer and should have gone out with a novel that is easier to like than this one. Still, the characters are complex, and there is some interesting speculation on the organization that we give our lives, the games we play to deceive others and ourselves. Did Julian, dying, increase his pain by his affair? Or, by honing an edge for his remaining weeks, did he cease, for a while, to be a loser?

Better than either of these is Leonard Gardner's first novel, *Fat City*, a beautiful story of losers and their banal lives, of the futility that most men, sooner or later, feel creeping up on them, a spider crawling from some pocket in their minds that words and courage cannot reach.

Two men under thirty, Billy Tully and Ernie Munger, men of no talent whatsoever, try to make something of their lives by boxing in a California city. Tully is finished; he was never any good, and his attempt at a comeback is pitiful. Yet it is all he has to sustain him, to keep him from squatting and shuffling under the sun as a migrant worker—"Of all the hated work he had ever done, this was a torment beyond any"—breaking his back to pick fruit and vegetables before he boards the bus at the end of the long day and pulls his bottle from its paper bag. Ernie Munger is in his teens. He hopes that boxing will release him from pumping gas and from his wife: "A fear came over him that after marriage death was the next major event." But Ernie isn't any good either. His manager tries to work up a little professional enthusiasm for something that Ernie simply hasn't got. Ernie loses a few, wins one, but it doesn't seem to matter: Winning can be more like losing than losing, if you see what I mean. Ernie doesn't see. It would never occur to him. It just happens to

Ernie, and he's left there, at the end of the book, nowhere, not even wondering if anything has happened.

Fat City is a story about how men live, about the emptiness of life, about men's callousness, indifference, despair, and fear—the little gropings for oneself and the stubborn conviction that there must be something better. Men alone, Gardner seems to say, grow afraid; together, they grow coarse. We have lost what we had in the past. Perhaps what we had in the past wasn't as good as we remember it, but it was certainly better than what we have now. Why can't we get it back? Gardner writes about the anguish of living without love, about the exhaustion that comes over men who find nothing of importance left to feel. Some are inarticulate prisoners: "There was no hope except in eventual escape," he writes of one, "and of that he did not feel capable." Gardner writes as well of the mounting irritability that can overtake a man dissatisfied with "the meaningless expenditure of himself," of the fraud and incompetence that attend public careers, and of the pain that physical labor involves. Mostly, he writes about how hard it is for a man to find a safe and quiet place where he can learn something about himself.

Kennaway, in his novel, uses literary dialogue to put in formal exposition everything he has to say about the human condition. Gardner says nothing directly. He picks details, and a tone of voice, that give emotion and significance to the wasted and inconsequential. From weakness, he has drawn strength, and from dullness, beauty.

1969

. . . . The Most Offensive Novel of the Year

Already the gooey accolades are slopping in, but be of good cheer. You needn't read it. I didn't. I meant to. I spent two days on the damn thing and could scarcely engage my eyes and concentration in the oppressively solid type obliterating 1,200 outsize pieces of perfectly inoffensive paper. Two perfectly good days lost, too, but what of that when Marguerite Young has lost twenty years in writing it?

Think of it: three-quarters of a million words of intense and artistic prose, a quantity sufficient to fill eight or nine novels of ordinary length. Individual sentences run on for many hundred words. There is virtually no dialogue to break up the monolithic solidity of type on these huge pages. Nor is there a detectable plot to absorb the reader's interest. Litrachewer, that's what *Miss MacIntosh, My Darling* is; you can tell because it is aggressively sensitive. By the fourth page Miss Young, with all the delicacy of a bulldozer, is banging the reader about the ears with her insistence that This is Art: This Deals with the Biggest Themes. The nature of reality and illusion, too, of course. This is What Life is All About. A novel of ideas, conveyed by what passes, in our decadent age, for poetic language. There's symbolism, too, to prove Miss Young's case. The narrator's name is Vera Cartwheel (translation: She-who-rolls-on-in-search-of-truth) and she has an incapacitated mother, Catherine Cartwheel (you remember what happened to St. Catherine, broken on a wheel).

Well, the reader cannot help but be impressed. A novel that rivals *Remembrance of Things Past* in length *ought* to deal with ideas; still, *Miss MacIntosh* spews whatever ideas it has to offer all over the place so quickly—like Onan, before they can do any good—and so repetitively that there is no hope of an interesting development of themes that will keep the reader going to the end.

The reader sets his teeth, hunches down in his chair, and arms himself for battle. Pretty soon his eyes wander from the page. With a guilty feeling he realizes he has not even completed a sentence which began near the top of one page and showed no sign of finishing by the bottom of the next. Execrable prose it is, too, but it is his paid job to read the book (my editor offered me four times my regular fee to do it; he was so desperate—everyone else turned him down). He goes on; he knows the novel *has* to be good because he has already caught a sequence of images which will surely prove to be symbols: harbor cities, angels. Surely.

Given endless months, anyone—you, I, the bottle washer at the bar—could read *Miss MacIntosh* in its entirety. The problem is one of inducement, and here there is clearly no reason to do so. Such literary orgies never pass unnoticed, but they often pass unread. Miss Young is a published poet, but her novel will never be read if she cannot find a way to manufacture prose and her prose—well, it has a superficial resemblance to poetic diction (I think that is a phrase she would approve), but it invites irreverence; it is, in fact, *soupe anglaise*. We need not dwell upon such horrendous dialogue as: "Would I deflower the rose, I who am the last rose of the last summer on earth?" Take instead the following question: "What is a child that its heart shall be so superficial, so unthinking? What is a child?" The trouble with this is that it is garbage.

The psalmist David asked, "What is man, that thou art mindful of him?" Even Kipling asked, "What is a woman that you forsake her?" Similar questions, but both David and Kipling combine theirs with an attitude of wonder at an implied, unquestionable truth; Miss Young supports hers only with a questionable assumption. It is these assumptions that quell any attempt at taking the book seriously: No one embarked on it should be asked to read any part twice, but if one rereads these two questions about a child, a lot of time can be saved—simply because no intelligent reader who is not paid to do so will read further.

And yet Miss Young is capable of worse: "His tears were falling like the golden rain, like one who turned into his tears, his tears with their core of being, his tears enclosing suns, [etc.] . . . Ah, should he build a world from a tear?" John Donne said it so much better (and so much shorter) when he wrote:

> *So doth each teare,*
> *Which thee doth weare,*
> *A globe, yea world by that impression grow.*

After fifty pages or so, the haunting thought arises: It might be more fun to go back to David, Donne, and Kipling.

1965

. . . . Den of Irony

The original Daniel, you remember, was an uneasy man—a Jew who lived by his wits in the court of the Chaldean kings. These kings had no more use for Jews and intellectuals than have most governments in history, but (even as kings go) they were a stupid lot, sharing a baroque taste in dreams and executions while demanding instant obedience at the sound of the cornet, sackbut, and dulcimer. In such a political climate, what is Daniel's role? He works for himself, of course, and for his coreligionists. He may be, as the Dartmouth Bible suggests, "a Beacon of Faith in a Time of Persecution"; he may be something of a fanatic, too, a man angry at being trapped in a role fashioned for him by the state. Perhaps, seeing himself clothed in scarlet one day and tossed to the lions the next, Daniel has a certain sense of irony. We will never know. Irony is not the tone of the Old Testament.

The narrator of E. L. Doctorow's novel, *The Book of Daniel,* is the victim of certain stupidities and ironies of postwar America. This Daniel is the son of a Jewish couple who, in 1954, were electrocuted for stealing atomic secrets for the Russians. The Rosenberg case, of course: Doctorow uses it fully, with significant variations, but the genius of his story is that his concern is with the heirs of the Rosenbergs, the heirs of the political pessimism and paranoia of the early 1950's. The execution of his parents has not so much scarred Daniel's life as it has become the controlling framework of his existence, of his split perspective on himself and on the world.

Dodging between first- and third-person narration, Daniel tells two stories concurrently: how, in 1967, he tried to save his younger sister Susan from mental breakdown and suicide and, in an intricate series of flashbacks, the story of his parents' ordeal. Paul and Rochelle Isaacson, as Daniel sees them, were pathetic, useless people, consumed by rage and dogma, willing to use people to further Communism, which they thought would justify "their poverty, their failure, their unhappiness . . . they rushed after self-esteem." Communism allowed them to transform "envy into constructive outgoing hate"; like a religion, it was "some purchase on the future against the terrible life of the present."

Were the Isaacsons guilty? Doctorow taunts us, hinting both ways, but their legal guilt is not the point. If guilty, they were ineffective. "They *acted* guilty," a reporter said; they "had to have been into some goddamn thing." And they were: They were into their own joylessness and pious excuses for "wanting a new world of socialism without want." They were victims of a society that needed victims, and following family tradition, they were exquisitely able to make victims of their children. Above all, the Isaacsons were self-destructive. Daniel torments his wife and child—"We're not nice people," he says—and Susan torments Daniel, telling him that she remains true to the Isaacson cause; Daniel is the betrayer. Daniel, the victim, agrees.

It is a purgative book, angry and more deeply felt than all but a few contemporary American novels, a novel about defeat, impotent rage, the passing of the burden of suffering through generations and "the progress of madness inherited through the heart." It is a novel about Daniel's struggle for detachment, his need to put a distance between himself and his story. We know he will never make it, in spite of his taking fixes from history. Daniel's suffering is the matter of this story, though he hardly recognizes it, and Doctorow, in a ferocious feat of the imagination, makes that suffering appallingly real. There is no question here of our suspending disbelief, but rather how, when we have finished, we may regain stability.

So much of what Doctorow accomplishes might, with less skill, have been melodramatic or sentimental. He avoids, for instance, the trial scenes he might have made sensational; in fact, he refuses all our vulgar expectations. The Isaacsons might have been sweet martyrs, but Doctorow clearly does not like them: They are rich in humanity but poor in spirit, and the politics of Doctorow's book is far more complicated than is the kind of fictional propaganda that requires martyrs. The overriding tone of this contemporary book of Daniel is ironic. Irony is sometimes used to fend the reader off—of Paul Isaacson, stumbling into the electric chair, Doctorow writes: "the chair would kill him but at this moment it was his only support." Irony is also used to fix a position: The Isaacsons looked toward a future which rejected them; the New Left, bored by the Isaacsons, literally closes the book on them when SDS activists take over the library at Columbia where Daniel is writing his story.

The year is not half spent, and a better American novel may yet appear, but I wouldn't wait for it.

1971

Sex and the Serious Novelist

"Here," said my trusted friend, "you can take it home tonight." He slipped me a crumbly paper-covered book that explained what happened when thinly clad white women strolled too far into the Malayan jungle and (alas) into the horny hands of Japanese commandos. "Gee, thanks," I gulped. At thirteen or thereabouts, I had read *Ethan Frome, A Lost Lady,* even *Daisy Miller,* but what did the three old ladies who wrote them really *know*? "Be careful," warned my friend as I tucked this treasure beneath my shirt, "you read too much of that stuff and your mind begins to *rot.*"

He was right, of course. Readers are infinitely corruptible. Of what use are books if they do not affect the judgment of those who read them? What is disturbing, however, is to find that the rot seems now to be more of a problem for serious writers than for readers. Few writers today know how to write about sex in terms that convey artistically and accurately what they have to say about it. Since each past age has come to its own terms with the vocabulary of sex, it is time that our serious novelists created terms of their own. I don't want to return to the bad old days of crouching censorship; when the law plays literary critic, everybody loses. I don't even want to advocate Good Taste—which is what we call those tattered, agreeable attitudes that impede our understanding of art as a creative experience. But today, with censorship not only late but unlamented, good writers have an opportunity to write something both honest and significant about sex—and they are fudging the job.

The problem concerns our need to develop a sexual rhetoric suitable to our time—if by rhetoric we mean not only language, but a language vector: the words themselves plus the direction given them by the writer's intent. How the serious writer is going to develop an attitude toward sex that is worth our attention is problem enough, God knows. Hack writers everywhere are using the old words and the new sex studies for commercial gain and the sheer quantity of these exploitation books makes it harder for the serious writer to do his job. The bad books, and the commercial success that attends them, affect the climate in which every writer must work; they affect, too, our responses to similar themes and language when they are used by good writers. Moreover, the sudden rush of new information about sexual behavior and the rapid relaxation of old standards of what is fit to print have affected too many of our serious writers in much the same way that the first, often false, spurts of information about sex affect an adolescent. Confronted with so much new, fascinating, and above all *usable* material, some writers have come on with a pubescent cry: all giggles, snickers, and endless exploration of territories that have been thoroughly mapped before.

A large part of our problem of sexual rhetoric, however, is simply that of language. For the first time in history, literate men accept—even expect to find—on the printed page blunt obscenities and technicolor descriptions of sexual activity that they rarely allow themselves to express in conversation. This has never happened before; it has always been the other way around. A conscious effort is being made by many of our serious writers to legitimize as a proper language of love those stubby Anglo-Saxon terms that have, since their invention, been endowed by a mana of offensiveness. I am not sure that this movement is going to succeed. I don't think I want it to succeed. For one thing, I believe that the literary rhetoric of sex quite properly evolves, changing with the temper of the age, and I suspect that because no one is likely to make a more effective use of Anglo-Saxon terms in serious fiction than Henry Miller did in the thirties, no one, now that we are approaching the seventies, should want to try to imitate that particular rhetoric again. Miller's effectiveness was partly due to the ban on such words in books; with the ban lifted, the words seem curiously old-fashioned, or at least they do as long as they are being used pretty much as Miller used them.

More important, I lean away from the legitimization attempt because, as a writer, I like to have available as full an arsenal of words and literary usages, of nuances and shades of meaning, as possible. I like the offensiveness of the Anglo-Saxon terms for sex and its component parts, an offensiveness that results directly from our own human ambiguity about sex: part act of love and part act of aggression. Aggression is unpopular these days, and you will hear some who would like to see human beings mature to the point where aggression is no longer linked to love-making, and although I don't support that, either, I will agree that *if* it comes, *then* we can set about legitimizing the dirty words. Meanwhile, let us recognize that many writers use the more familiar obscenities to express, perhaps not always consciously, an aggressive dislike of women or of sex itself. We tend to assume that those who affront our sensibilities by language are more liberated, more freely responding to life than we—but the truth may be just the reverse. A reliance upon "dirty" words is—for writers, certainly—restrictive. Obscenity invariably involves a reduction of the complexity of emotion; by substituting clamor for intensity, we injure the variety of our responses to life. Even so, we must preserve, in writing, the possibility of this kind of deliberately reduced response, which we cannot do if we make obscenity the legitimate language of love. Let us use the bad words, by all means, but let us remember the tradition of emotion that they carry with them.

Finally, I suspect that the movement toward legitimization will fail simply because of the nature of the words themselves. Even discounting their quotient of offensiveness, the words are clear. You may not know what they mean until you are told, but once told you will have no further doubts: There is no ambiguity of *meaning* in any of them; no one has ever said, "Oh, I thought you meant that one another way." The words, then, are oddly rigid. Unlike such weak (though useful) words as "infer," "flout," and "disinterested," their meanings and usage do not shift (though the usage may increase) when they are used by those who are ignorant or insensitive to language.

All of which is prologue to fiction by two of our very best writers who have not yet, I think, solved the problem of contemporary sexual rhetoric:

Couples is John Updike's fifth novel and most ambitious literary endeavor. Because it contains an astonishing quantity and variety of sex, it has been received somewhat dubiously, but months before its publication, this same sex assured its commercial success. Knopf ordered 70,000 copies—enough for a fair-sized best seller—printed *before* publication; the Book-of-the-Month Club, which views serious fiction with suspicion, made it an alternate selection; Hollywood bought the film rights. None of this, of course, has anything to do with *Couples'* merits.

Couples has few merits: It is, both in conception and execution, a qualified disaster. Updike knows how people talk and how malicious, mean-spirited people gouge at each other's vitals. His book has an irritating, portentous air about it that suggests he knows *why* people behave this way, but nothing in the book gives us a clue to Updike's secret. For all its perfervid sex, *Couples* is an old-fashioned story. Like Galsworthy and Marquand, Updike creates an entire society, fussing over yesterday's news and his knowledge of specialized professional skills. But the idea behind the novel is more old-fashioned still: It is based on a corrupt conception of courtly love. Andreas Capellanus defined it, perhaps ironically, eight hundred years ago. He said that possession of a desired object destroys love; therefore, since love cannot survive marriage, it must seek fulfillment in extracurricular liaisons. Both Chaucer and Spenser disposed of courtly love—as far as literature was concerned—by confirming that marriage could indeed be combined with gallantry. Still, if the idea is a bit shabby, Updike believes in it and makes a pitch for reviving it in fiction.

The scene of the novel is a suburb of Boston, appropriately named Tarbox. Tarbox's moral architecture is based on the twelfth-century principle of groin-vaulting—or, to put it simply, Tarbox makes *Peyton Place* look like the Valley of the Jolly Green Giant. Piet Hanema, a builder, is both hero and victim; although married to a lovely woman, he takes on four mistresses before the book is done. The second of these, a pregnant woman socially superior to Piet, proves the cause of his un- doing. In all, ten couples are involved in Tarbox's sexual carousel, turning and tumbling to Updike's merry tune of contrapuntal cuckoldry.

Updike takes it all very seriously. "Man," he once wrote in a review of one of Denis de Rougemont's books about love, "is a spirit imprisoned in the darkness of the flesh." Well, the flesh is certainly willing, but the spirit looks a bit peaked these days; *Couples* is, in fact, a novel about the enervation of the spirit. Updike dealt with it all in that same review. The Don Juan figure (Piet Hanema) is, Updike insists, as much to be pitied as envied because he is slave, not master, to his talents of seduction. Furthermore, Tarbox's game of musical mating can be explained by man's fundamental anxiety that he will cease to exist—much is made in the story of the disasters that befall Kennedys, Popes, and nuclear submarines. "Only in being loved," Updike wrote in the review, "do we find external corroboration of the supremely high value each ego secretly assigns itself."

Philip Roth's story, "Civilization and Its Discontents," is as long as a short novel and occupies a good part of the third number of *New American Review*. Roth's story is not about sex, as I often had to remind myself. Alex Portnoy narrates it in a form that may one day be recognized as the archetype of our age: the long-winded confession to a silent psychoanalyst. Alex is, as those in his condition are wont to do, picking through the detritus of his existence, speaking plainly (very plainly indeed) of his obsession with sex and the troubles he still has with his smothering mother and his amorphous father. Alex is assistant human-rights commissioner of New York City, but the rights he wants to enforce at the moment are his own: "A Jewish man with his parents alive," he observes, "is half the time a helpless *infant*! . . . Free me from living my life in the middle of a Jewish joke!"

The story is more than another assault on Jewish mothers. Roth is genuinely concerned with relating Alex's obsessive sexual curiosity to his early life with his parents. Often scathing, usually hilarious, and always fantastically gross, the story might have been twice as good had it been half as long. Might have been, eccept for clear indications that Roth has lost control of his story.

Roth has written better about sex and about being Jewish before. Here, he is trying something different, but it doesn't work.* And as for Updike—for years, seeds of sexual discontent have blossomed more or less discreetly in his longer fiction; but now, in *Couples,* they blossom wildly, senselessly, like sick and ugly flowers. What went wrong?

Sex, like violence, is a part of life. Realistic writing about life properly, inevitably, requires realistic writing about sex. So much for realism. But there are other things to be done with sex in art than simply to report details of its climate and geography. Updike and Roth both know this. In these stories, they attempt to use sex as a metaphor to reach a truth about man that is larger than the truth about sex. All those genital gymnastics are not thrown in for their own sake; they are there because Updike and Roth—in very different ways—want to tell us that promiscuity of this sort, the enactment of fantasies most of us keep safely in our minds, is not in itself the sickness but the symptom of a deeper trouble. What they are saying about sex, then, may be true, but it is no longer realistic. And the truth of myth cannot effectively be expressed in the language of literalism.

These stories fail because Updike and Roth are using language suitable to one kind of writing to cope with the problems of another. Realistic description of sex serves marvelously well in pornographic or seriously realistic fiction, but it will not work when the reader is asked to consider sex as something more essential than the details upon which the author dwells. On the contrary, its use tends to deflate the significance of the characters involved. Moreover, Updike and Roth both ignore the distracting effect of such language, which, for all our purity of will, inevitably evokes from the reader reactions—erotic or antagonistic—that are irrelevant to the author's purpose.

We are, as I said above, in urgent need of a new rhetoric of sex, a rhetoric suitable to our time and sensibilities. If Updike and Roth were really bolder in the way they wrote about sex, they could help us develop it.

1968

*When this story was published as part of his novel *Portnoy's Complaint,* I changed my mind about what Roth had managed to achieve, as will be seen in the essay that follows.

* * *

Portnoy's Complaint, by Philip Roth, is a good novel, but it is also about as profane as a novel can get. It is *not* profane because it is about sex or because it floats on a tide of scatological offal. Doubtless, its rancid ambience will set the pornophiles to smacking their lips, but they will finish by grinding their gums. Whatever else it is, *Portnoy's Complaint* is not erotic: it contains too much sexual frustration, which is death to dirty books, and too much masturbation, which is unlikely to exercise the pornophiliac imagination.

True profanity comes not from the juices of the body but from dryness of the spirit; it is a loud and inefficient response to the crisis at hand. By this definition, Alexander Portnoy, the narrator of Roth's novel, is an expert: Repressed, frustrated, and exploited, he exposes his wounds to the reader and shrieks his story of pain, hatred, and despair. Nor is Roth, the presiding physician in the Portnoy case, any slouch at profanity himself: Where the treatment calls for transfusions of love, Roth offers exploding cigars; where grafts of tenderness might have cured disfigurement, Roth holds out the Band-Aid of low comedy. Laughter *heals*—you've heard that—and in these days of rising medical costs, high-quality healing materials are scarce. Alex's case is hopeless, anyway, so laugh at the funny man who suffers so very loudly!

Alex is afflicted by an acute case of Jewish parents. His father is constipated and clinging; his mother is fanatically self-righteous, a castrating mistress of intimidating rhetoric. The two combine their ignorance, bigotry, and consuming selfishness with the marvelously inhibiting qualities of kosher dietary laws to convince Alex that, from his earliest days, he has been a heartless criminal. At thirty-three, Alex still believes it. He is Assistant Human Opportunity Commissioner for New York City and a male nymphomaniac, but still he has no fun. Since puberty, he has fought back with his penis, "that battering ram to freedom," but masturbation is an unsatisfactory affirmation of the self, and even when he meets the girl of his dreams, the girl who would do *anything* in bed, Alex is left strung out; still living (as it were) from hand to mouth, because there is no security, even there; not when the girl is as illiterate as she is accommodating and when, like so many of her kind, she unreasonably asks for consideration as a human being.

This, of course, raises the question the book asks and does not answer: How does one become himself, a human being? At the very end, in a particularly devastating and cynical joke, Roth suggests we have not learned *how* to ask the question. The lamentations of A. Portnoy, who opposes duty to fun, Jewish misery to Gentile bliss, mothers and their laws to sons and their sexual perversions, are excruciatingly funny. But what sets this novel above all other comic novels about Jewish parents is the degree to which pain, hatred, and desperation curdle the story. This frenzy of pain and hilarity is remarkably effective and well suited to Roth's purpose. But it is, in the long view, profane (and therefore limiting) because the profane view of life recognizes little hope of redemption from any source.

Roth is a prodigiously talented writer, and *Portnoy's Complaint* is his best book since his first, *Goodbye, Columbus.* I hope he will soon write a better one. The present book lacks restraint and variety. Roth has apparently decided that nothing is beneath him—no joke too broad, no sexual conjunction too outrageous. His extravagance is usually effective, but not always. When it fails, it fails badly, and I have the uncomfortable feeling that Roth is too quick to forgive himself his excesses because he knows most critics will forgive him even more quickly. He knows, too, that what the critics acclaim as courage is often no more than commercialism; it may not be art, but it may sell better than art. As for variety, the book is, I think, too shrill for too long; it needs a greater variety of tone and emotion, thus creating a greater variety of reactions from the reader. Even so, if you are not appalled by the book, you will be amused by it.   1969

John Updike's talent is awesome, but his fondness for publication—thirteen books in thirteen years—has left him little time to bring his great skill to bear upon a great endeavor. His last novel, *Couples,* was a mitigated disaster, but his new collection of stories, *Bech: A Book,* is mellow, self-deprecating, and delightful—further evidence that Updike's success works in inverse ratio to his ambition.

Henry Bech, "the moderately well-known American author," is Jewish, in his forties, famous for his first novel, but blocked now, unable to write. In all other respects, however, Bech is a model writer. He travels, with our cultural-exchange program, to Eastern Europe. He experiments with pot, changes mistresses, lectures to female students, and, finally, when it seems certain that his muse has permanently retired, he is elected to the pantheon of American writers. The calcification of Henry Bech is not unnoticed by its victim. Bech is ironical; uneasily aware that *rigor artis* not only blocks his writing but blocks him from giving himself to others, he assumes teasing, defensive little postures. "You need something to sleep beside," a woman tells him. "An oxygen tent?" Bech asks.

The Bech stories show Updike at his best. They are dexterous, witty, urbane; little jokes fold over each other, and there is much precise observation of people and places. The prose is relaxed, the similes acute; there is none of the evident strain of writing that mars much of Updike's longer fiction. Bech himself is a delightful creation: a portrait of the writer as an institution, a movable monument, a smiling, public man of whom much is demanded, but not another book.   1970

* * *

Running came naturally to Harry "Rabbit" Angstrom. Throughout *Rabbit, Run,* John Updike's second novel, Harry fled the viscosity of living. At the end he thought: "Funny, how what makes you move is so simple and the field you must move in is so crowded." By then Harry knew he was trapped, but he ran anyway: from his wife and their daughter's funeral, and then from his mistress, pregnant with his child. It is a beautiful end to the novel, though some readers grumbled.

Harry is back again in *Rabbit Redux.* Ten years have passed. It is summer and then fall in 1969, and as is customary in Updike's novels, the news slides past the characters like a diorama: the moon landing, Chappaquiddick, riots in the cities. Harry is thirty-six now, a linotype operator. He has put on weight and patriotism; he and Janice, to whom he has returned, live in a tacky suburb of a Pennsylvania city. Harry has stopped running; he is self-contained now and bored, beset by a "nervousness that seeks to condense into anger." He is a hawk, has a flag decal on his car, prays on buses, and has lost interest in sex. As a rocket is launched on a television screen, Harry learns that his wife is unfaithful. He finds that he can live with it—which appalls Janice, who goes to live with her lover.

It is the other characters now who are desperate, who are looking to run. Harry cannot love people, but he has taken on some responsibility with his paunch and worries about others needing him: his son, the girl he picks up in a bar, the black dope pusher who hides out in Harry's house and reads him lectures on black history. Everyone looks to Harry to take decisive action—but he doesn't. Entropy sets in. Everything is touched by death or disintegration: Harry's mother is dying and the Disposall backs up, smelling sweet. "See no evil is the way I do it," says a fireman after the cataclysm toward the end. "That's the way I do it, too," Harry replies.

And so to numbness. Harry, though given to bigoted braying, can live with the ruins because he must be pricked to caring, his little metaphysical sojourns notwithstanding. In the end he can solve none of his problems, and Updike must do it all for him, ringing in death, fire, and seduction to get Harry back approximately where he started. The best, the most sharply observed episodes, are all in the front two sections of the book. A scene, for instance, in which Harry spars with the black pusher in a bar is far better than the scene in which the pusher comes to orgasm as Harry reads aloud from Frederick Douglass' autobiography. A bit strained, you will say, and it is true: The stagey machinations toward the back of the book, in which Updike can be too clearly seen tugging at the scenery, *are* unsatisfactory, but then Updike has for some years cared more for the architecture than the credibility of his longer fiction. An odd preference for a realistic writer, because Updike is unsurpassed at giving us the news, the details, even the ingredients of a TV Salisbury steak dinner, in his stories.

Rabbit Redux is too long. There are difficulties of tone as well as structure. Harry might, in his mind, support American militarism, but he could never think: "Beneath her patient bombers, paradise is possible." A lovely phrase, pure Updike, and there are many more like it. Updike has, I think, shown us a middle American and surprised us by making him more sympathetic than we might have expected—but that may be part of the trouble, part of the reason why Harry seems always slightly out of focus. Nothing he does seems necessarily tied in to what he did in the chapter before or what we may expect from him in chapters to come. Harry seems to be there, holding the novel's middle ground, only to be used. Not just used by the other characters (as he is), which is a legitimate device in fiction, but used by the author, too—we always see Updike's fingers wiggling through the cloth—for whatever purpose or point Updike has in mind at the moment.

Still, much of the book is funny and unpretentious, free of centaurs, shamans, and Don Juans. Updike is an excellent observer of spiritual death in family life. His women characters are as grotesque as the women in *Couples,* defining themselves only through their bodies or their bitchiness—an attitude that may reflect only a perceived disintegration in humanity, but an attitude nevertheless bound to draw harassing fire from the feminists. Updike's famous obsession with sexual encounters in which no one seems ever to have even a passably good time is present here, more broadly displayed than ever, and yet the petal similes and "ancient alleyway" metaphors have been retired. Sex, says Rabbit, "just makes me too sad."

Was the sequel a good idea? Perhaps not, though there is much that is the best and simplest of Updike in it. Believing, as I do, that although Updike has developed as an artist since writing *Rabbit, Run,* he has not yet written a novel to equal it, I approached this one nervously, thinking of the critics who had told him he had ended the earlier story badly and wondering whether something inside of him agreed with that judgment. "Perhaps Updike is not sufficiently ruthless," wrote Tony Tanner, an English critic, "in tracing out the inexorable end of Harry Angstrom." Well, Updike is not a ruthless writer—as if a writer should be or is obliged to provide inexorable ends to his characters. In this novel, Updike is still not ruthless, is perhaps (though I take the ending to be optimistic) not even finished. Look out for *Rabbit Resurgens.*

1971

............Here Comes Gore Vidal
with Charley's Aunt
in Modern Drag

Can it be only twenty years since Gore Vidal wrote *The City and the Pillar*? I read it recently, in both its original and revised versions. It seems dull enough now, not so much a novel as a stagnant and superficial tract by a writer who had not yet realized that fiction may contain, but must not be, an argument. Still, it was a scandal in its day, presumably because no one had previously traced with such apostolic determination the stations by which a young man approaches crucifixion on the cross of homosexuality.

Vidal's new book, *Myra Breckinridge,* is also a homosexual novel, but a much better one; it is an ingenious story, rich in wit, irony, and the crudest of comic invention. The book is about falsity and artifice, but nothing in it is false or artificial. Vidal has so carefully calculated his effects that the reader who guesses the book's Big Surprise need not congratulate himself: Vidal intended him to guess it.

Myra tells most of the story herself. From the beginning, it is clear that what Myra *is* is as important as what she does. She exclaims over her beauty and crows over her impermeability. "I am Myra Breckinridge whom no man will ever possess," she exults, "Myra, the self-creation . . . the new American woman who uses men the way they once used women." But Myra has a mission as well: "the destruction of the last vestigial traces of traditional manhood in the race in order to realign the sexes, thus reducing population while increasing human happiness and preparing humanity for its next stage." The next stage is "the fluidity of the sexes"—*i.e.,* everyone jumping at everyone. "The roof has fallen in on the male," Myra announces smugly, "and we now live in the dawn of the age of Woman Triumphant."

Beyond all this philosophizing, Myra has two matters on her mind. She comes to Hollywood waving the will of Myron Breckinridge, her homosexual husband, recently and mysteriously deceased. The will leaves to Myra half the land on which her Uncle Buck has built a school for hopeless actors, a school that teaches courses in Atavistic Rhythm and Empathy II. Myra wants her share in cash. She also wants to revenge Myron, who was most abominably used by undiscriminating men. Revenge of this sort requires the total submission, even the demolition of the male. Myra finds the victim she needs in a handsome stud of a boy, and, in what is certainly the most humiliating and probably the most

. . . . Ham on the Range:
Two More Excesses
of the American Dream

I was excited, for a while, by Kurt Vonnegut, Jr.'s new novel *Slaughterhouse-Five or The Children's Crusade.* Vonnegut had, I thought, worked toward this book for some time, blowing off the chaff from a lot of slick fiction, science fiction, arch and precious in-group fiction that he had written before, while he hoarded the grains for this story, a war novel that would appeal to the powerless, incipient alcoholic in us all. I could tell from the way he avoided his subject how strong his book would be as soon as he stopped playing footsie with it, stopped soft-shoeing over ironies of narration and perspective. But he never did stop, not really, and I had to read the book a second time to clear my mind.

The subject that Vonnegut never stopped avoiding is the bombing of Dresden—the fire raids of February, 1945, in which the British and the Americans leveled the most beautiful and defenseless of German cities for no reason, broiling 135,000 people in what may be the greatest single massacre in history. Naturally, few people know much about it; the Air Force hushed it up. And Vonnegut never meant to write about the actual disaster ("There is nothing intelligent to say about a massacre"); he meant instead to write about the way human beings collapse before such an event. "So it goes," Vonnegut keeps saying, to impress us with his fatalism, and so his novel goes, too, sliding fast off the ice at the end of the world because nobody, not the Air Force and not Vonnegut, knew where the brakes were. So, too, was I left clutching a handful of useless superlatives ("Tensile strength . . . contains more truth about war than any novel since *Catch-22*"), like a French *maréchal* holding medals he was about to pin on a balloon.

"All this happened, more or less," Vonnegut begins, meaning that he, Vonnegut, was a prisoner of war in Dresden at the time but that his confessional novel is written in that nervous vein in which our most intimate neuroses are made metaphor. Billy Pilgrim is the nonhero of this novel. Billy comes "unstuck in time," meaning that either he goes mad or he really is captured by little green aliens shaped like plumbers' friends, who take him in a flying saucer to the planet Tralfamadore, where he learns that all time exists at once and there is nothing we can do about anything. "So it goes," say the Tralfamadorians. Billy is also captured by the Germans; in Dresden, he helps to dig out the roasted skeletons. So it goes. For most of his adult life, Billy switches back and forth in time, foreseeing his death, his life in the womb. Toward the end of his career, he is rich and stupid and cries a lot.

What, from all this, is Vonnegut's gospel to the heathen? Men at war, he writes, are "listless playthings of enormous forces." Maybe, but if the best of us are as stupidly unmanned as Billy Pilgrim, and the worst of us are, well, villains, then the bombing can't matter much. Surely the author never meant *that* moral to leak from his story, and it would not have, had not Vonnegut seemed so deliberately determined to leave his reader unmoved, had he not concentrated on the foolishness, on the coarseness, and the thingness of people, thereby allowing the essence of his dilemma to escape him somewhere. *Slaughterhouse-Five* is often funny, and I enjoyed it, really, quite a lot, even when I found it mannered, so cute and buttoned-down that it leaves the reader no room to exercise his own responses.

Old bad books convey a fascination to which new bad books cannot aspire. An exception is John Redgate's *Barlow's Kingdom,* one of those "different Westerns," a book so misguided, so thoroughly outrageous, so skillfully achieved, that I read it breathlessly and recommend it to all students of "Hubris in the Novel" (classes meet Tuesday and Thursdays, at the discretion of Prof. Prescott). The plot is a retelling of *Hamlet,* set on a Montana ranch. Roy Barlow returns from the Civil War to find his father dead, his mother married to his uncle who has taken over the spread, and, well, you might risk a guess at what happens after that.

The point is, it can't be done. If you *could* attach *Hamlet* to your own brand of myth, you might get a better bloodbath, but *Hamlet* is an extremely literary artifact that cannot be bent to suit a myth already too encumbered by its own accumulation of conventions. Hamlet is articulate; the cowboy, stumble-mouthed. Hamlet is doubt-ridden; the cowboy, cretinously sure of duty. And with the reader muttering, "What about the gravedigger?" as he is bound to do, the novel has no chance to assume a life of its own. Still, it is smoothly written—better written, for instance, than *Shane,* which was a fine example of the Western myth played straight. Of course, the magnitude of its failure as fiction will assure its success as a film—suburban schoolmarms will herd their drama students by the busload to any town that shows it. Not The Thinking Man's Western, you understand: The *Educated* Man's Western. Lights! Culture! Action!

1969

. . . . A Genuinely
Dreadful Novel

That morning, as every morning, the soldiers sat around and discussed what they were doing in the war in Vietnam. Evans, as usual, did the talking—"I confess that as a dropout from American hysteria about Communism I think the whole problem is the usual one of generals and politicians seeing everything in terms of the last war"—while the boys, as you might expect, made jokes and told Evans to for God's sake shut up. A few pages later, Evans began to read aloud from an old magazine, and unless I looked very hard for those little quotes-within-quotes punctuation marks that tell you when someone speaks with words that are not his own, I could not tell the difference between Evans and the editorials. But that's the way it is in John Briley's novel, *The Traitors*: The characters are *not* soldiers, they are editorials. Nor can Briley prop up his soldiers' dialogue by leaning on that Anglo-Saxon term that American troops have made their own, because neither that nor any other pungent participle sprinkled about in what soldiers say can hide the truth about *The Traitors*: It is a sermon masquerading as a novel.

Bad wars make bad war novels. It should not be so. Leaving aside the question of whether there are any good wars, the self-righteousness, the piety and propaganda that overcome us in what we call our worthy wars ought to produce heroically tedious fiction. On the other hand, nasty, banal wars that kill off a little country and corrupt a big one, wars that find the traditional good guys fighting on the wrong side, ought to produce excellent fiction: unhappy allegories and agonizing fables, bitter comedies, and perhaps a few of those outsize epics that sum up war itself—the action and the characters, the landscape and ideas for which men fight and die.

And yet the good war fiction is about the two World Wars. People are still writing good novels about those wars, but no one, as far as I know, has written a good novel about the wars in Korea and Vietnam. Why not? For one thing, we live in a time when much of our most creative, most adventurous writing takes the form of journalism. Good fiction about the Vietnam War may emerge once we have left that country, but while we are there, journalism, being more argumentative, seems more apropos, and the war has produced much excellent reporting. For another, the war has not physically involved an entire generation. We resent having to think about the war as much as we do. Writers, and the boys who were to become writers, could not avoid the World Wars, but most of our writers today have fought neither in Korea nor in Vietnam. Finally, the experience of the war—the reaction of soldiers and civilians—does not seem to be the point of what is happening in Vietnam. That point can be found by studying the pathology of power and the rhetoric of self-deception; it must be sought in think tanks and in industries, in the skulls of men like Johnson, Rusk, and Nixon. Looking for it may be a task less suited to novelists than to politicians and psychiatrists, but if a writer tries to make a novel of it, he should remember his obligations to the genre.

Briley doesn't. In *The Traitors,* six American soldiers are captured by the Vietcong, who plan to convert them by kindness and argument to the thoughts of Uncle Ho. Impossible, I thought. What, no water torture? No drugs? No Chinese jackboots rammed into the prisoners' loins? Still, there is no point to the book if they are not converted—and the book runs long enough to persuade a Jesuit to swear by Allah's beard. Actually, Briley makes it easy, and for two reasons. It is easier to manipulate stereotypes than fully rounded characters. Briley gives us an idealistic Jew; a cynical Negro; a Negro sergeant of unbending principle (Briley doesn't want to offend anyone); an uptight Commie; a Vietnamese patriot; a bawdy buffoon; and some others less clearly defined because Briley seems ignorant of their racial and regional clichés. Then there is Evans, the renegade GI working for the Vietcong, who does the persuading. Evans is not a Communist, not even a peacenik; he just hates this particular war, and, hell, as soon as he opened his mouth, *I* was convinced because I had already read the articles and books that Briley has condensed for Evans' arguments. Hell again, by the time I realized *that,* there were still hundreds of pages of harangue remaining because these soldiers are pretty witless and have many stupid rebuttals to offer. In fact, I suspect they may know they're supposed to be in a *novel,* not a sermon, and the Fictional Characters' Guild takes a dim view of authors who make its members sit around and listen to lectures about fragmentation bombs and refugee camps when they should be out getting involved in such horrors, like characters in proper novels. There is some action, finally, after a lot more talk and a little silly sex (yes, a Vietcong girl falls for the Jewish lieutenant); there is a *Mission: Impossible* kind of impossible mission and a shoot-out between the converted and the reactionary patriots.

The Traitors is a genuinely dreadful novel, an interminable, ill-written affront to man's attempts over the years to make an art of fiction. The best that can be said for it is that it is ambitious, but whom is the author trying to convince? Some cretinous hawk as yet unexposed to Briley's borrowed arguments? Such people don't read books, and if they did, they wouldn't buy reason from a traitor. Briley suggests that Evans is not a traitor because passionate dissent justifies active treason. Sometimes, perhaps, it does, but Briley has not justified the transition here. *The Traitors* proves that good intentions are an inadequate substitute for intelligence, for imagination, for credibility, for wit, style, and technique—all qualities that this sorry novel lacks.

1969

. . . . The Crap Game
of Life

Joan Didion's *Play It as It Lays* is a short, consummately skillful novel, one of the very best of the year and as grim a fable for our time as anyone could ask for.

Maria is thirty-one and divorced; like her infant daughter, she is damaged and institutionalized as the novel begins—the question is, how did she get there? Her parents were compulsive gamblers, betting on races they never won; they left Maria "holding all the aces, but what," she asks, "was the game?" She made two films, married a director, confided in a homosexual producer. All the dead and desperate people. All the parties and liaisons when every human attachment had withered, and nothing—not marriage, motherhood, or sex—came up right. Play it as it lays, her father told her. Life is a crap game, and there are rattlesnakes under the rocks. Maria may live in corruption, but she is not herself corrupt. To be corrupt, as degenerate as everyone else in this novel, requires a control of one's life that Maria lacks. Maria never knew a good life, does not know what she wants, or what to ask for when people offer help. She is a victim; she knows, too, that she is unique and will endure.

Miss Didion knows that we have had this scene, in countless lousy novels, to the point of nausea. She brings it off better than anyone since Nathanael West. Reading this novel is like driving a Maserati flat out: It is technically superb, with dead-on dialogue and no quaver of false emotion; stripped to the bare essentials, it suggests the ruts that lie beyond the track. Most important, perhaps, is Miss Didion's skill in

writing about brutalized lives without contributing to the brutalization.
Few writers can do that.

1970

· · · · · · · · · · · · · · · · · · · Dark Laughter

The news about *The Vale of Laughter,* Peter de Vries' ninth novel
(excluding three that no one is supposed to talk about) is both good and
bad. The good news is that it is his best novel in half a dozen years. The
disappointment is that it is also basically the same novel that De Vries
has been writing for more than a dozen years.

Comic writers, virtuoso entertainers like P. G. Wodehouse, have small
but perfect talents. No one would ask them to change the scope or shape
of what they are uniquely suited to create: fragile, delicate, and her-
metically enclosed balloons which would, if more pressure were introduced, explode. De Vries, however, is not of this breed. Right now he
is the best comic writer we have. His books are far from fragile, far from
perfect. His plots are digressive, his sentiment plain; his humor has
hooks that catch and tear and make us bleed. Of him who has much,
much shall be required: It is not enough that De Vries squanders his
talents, nor is it sufficient that he has sharpened and darkened his Novel.
It is time he wrote another.

Consider what you will find in any De Vries novel:

1. A convulsively witty narrator, often more than one. Chicken
farmers, ministers, furniture movers, and investment counselors all talk
alike in the De Vriesian fields. They pop puns: "Love is an art," says Joe
Sandwich, hero of the present work, "I thought you might notice my
craft ebbing." They play on words, as when Joe considers his relationship
to his Creator: "Mirror my God to thee." They coin dazzling aphorisms:
"That a woman isn't appetizing doesn't mean she isn't hungry." They
crack wise: "He began to play on people's sympathies by contracting a
fatal disease." And they become lamely, metaphysically sentimental: "I
learned early that mystical solitude in which we all walk."

2. Three unvarying moral messages:

a. People must learn to live with each other. We rarely do learn,
but we can, and we begin by learning that life provides enough problems
without our needing to create a superfluity.

b. If the practice of religion is preposterous, the denial of God is
impossible.

c. Extracurricular sex is funny in fiction but disastrous in life.

3. A theory of wit: The wit that binds the novel divides the characters. Wit, the aggressive weapon that a writer uses to expose his characters, is also the defensive weapon that his characters use to shield themselves from human emotion.

All this will be found (again) in *The Vale of Laughter.* Joe Sandwich narrates two-thirds of the story. Joe begins his career as a buffoon by "clowning in the house of God"—rattling off his good deeds, not his sins, in the confessional. His cousin, studying for the new priesthood of psychoanalysis, lures him away from Catholicism, but immediately Joe falls victim to a kind of neurosis that compels him to do everything in multiples of three, seven, and twelve. Joe marries a girl and works in her father's investment house while fighting off the nausea that overcomes him while looking at the ticker tape. Clowning and practical jokes provide relief from marriage and from work: Joe is, his wife observes, the kind of man who puts lampshades on his head at home. Sex, too, is important to Joe and, in a parody of the Masters and Johnson electrode approach to sexual response, De Vries writes what is undoubtedly the funniest sex scene in all fiction. Joe's best friend and former teacher, Wally Hines, then takes up the narration of the final third of the novel, the part relating to Joe's seduction of Wally's wife.

The Vale of Laughter is better than De Vries' recent novels for two reasons. First, it is sharper, funnier, and more closely knit than either *Reuben, Reuben* or *Let Me Count the Ways.* Second, in this novel De Vries has posed for himself—and has surmounted—a formidable technical obstacle: He manages to be excruciatingly funny about Joe, a man who believes himself to be funny and isn't. In doing this, De Vries shows us not only the dark side of humor—which he has shown us before—but the frightening results of being funny, something I cannot remember any other humorist having attempted.

But if De Vries has brought together more successfully than in his recent novels the familiar elements of his fiction and his message, the elements remain familiar. He has said his piece on these subjects. The world provides other important concerns, equally worthy of satire. Please, Mr. De Vries, next time a *new* novel?

1967

. . . . .Disarrangement

Elia Kazan's first novel is dreadful. It is also a simple, sincere story, and it *ought* to have been a good book. It will please a lot of people, many of whom will think they have read a good book, and it will make a lot of money for its author and publisher. *The Arrangement* is three times as long as the average novel. It can, however, be read very quickly because the author has used a lot of zippy dialogue, and he hasn't messed around with distracting subplots. There are a great many carnal and carnivorous characters in it, all chewing, choking, slashing, and stabbing each other unmercifully—just the way we know such people do. There's a lot of real information, too: news about how the rich and powerful live and how much all of it costs. And the sex! And the rough-tough vulgarity! But all the frenetic groin-grinding has a moral purpose: Our hero, a middle-aged Siddhartha searching for his soul, staggers along the path to Buddhahood.

Eddie Anderson is both hero and narrator; Eddie is a Greek-American, forty-three, vice-president of a Los Angeles ad agency. He has spent his life lying to the public about products, lying to the people with whom he works, lying to his wife, lying with and to a succession of mistresses, and, of course, lying to himself. Eddie is the victim of The Arrangement many of us make with life: Don't make waves by saying what you really think or by doing what you really want. Abide by The Arrangement and your body will prosper, if not your soul. The Arrangement is our pretense to order in the chaos of living, the lie of civilization that keeps us from tearing each other apart.

By the beginning of the book Eddie (who moonlights for magazines as "Evans Arness," crusading journalist) has had it. He chucks over his mistress, Gwen. (Don't worry: Kazan shows us how their sex was in a clever flashback.) He tries suicide. He tries living in numb connubiality with his vapid wife. He goes back to Gwen. She leaves him. Eddie realizes that even as Evans Arness, crusading journalist, he is a fraud. He tries suicide again. He tries being Nothing At All. He starts to say what he thinks, to do what he wants. So the trouble begins. Searching for "the sanctity of selfishness," Eddie alienates everybody. He quits his jobs as ad man and journalist. He loses his wife; he loses Gwen. He raves like a maniac; then, accepted as a maniac, he is locked away in one of those institutions society reserves for people like Eddie. There, like Siddhartha, Eddie can sit under a tree and ponder the final steps to Buddhahood.

With all this moral indignation against the hypocrisy of the way we live, how can Kazan have gone wrong? The best thing that can be said about *The Arrangement* is that it is an honest book, but, like Henley's "Invictus" and Kilmer's "Trees," which are honest poems, *The Arrangement* is unintentionally phony. The truth that concerns Kazan is a complex truth, belied by the facility and sensationalism of the yarn that contains it. Kazan has come to an agonizing conclusion—that we suffer from dishonesty to ourselves—but he has come to it too easily. Kazan treats a primary truth as if it were a secondhand conclusion, as if he had grabbed a fashionable phrase and written a fashionable, crowd-pleasing novel around it.

As honest individuals, Kazan says, we are in trouble, but he hasn't the foggiest idea where the remedy lies. There may be no remedy; certainly Eddie's progress is irrelevant. Kazan might have written a better book if he had admitted that there is no answer to our dilemma. Instead, he seems to take Eddie seriously and—perhaps fearing *we* won't believe in Eddie—he has hinted at this pretentious parallel to the Siddhartha-Buddha legend.

To admit that there is no answer to our crisis of integrity requires either laughter or a genuine sense of anguish. *The Arrangement* lacks both. Eddie's revolt is not noble; it is silly. Eddie breaks The Arrangement (cheers), but then he has nothing to say or do (hiss); rather than embark on a glorious bender, he simply harasses his wife, mistress, and employers, all of whom try honorably to understand him (boo). Eddie, a selfish boor who graduates from the kind of selfishness society accepts to a monomaniac selfishness nobody can accept, is a pain in the neck. My sympathies are entirely with the squares and simpering boobs who have to put up with him. Buddha, indeed!

1967

· The Novel
as Old News

How can a serious novelist come to terms with actual events, the historical happenings of our immediate past? The historical novelist, writing about the Gracchi or the Medici, has no problem because few readers know or care much about the history he weaves into his fiction. But the novelist who writes about Kennedy's assassination or Eichmann's trial must contend not only with our memories, but with our emotions. Such memories and emotions are usually intrusive and irrelevant to the reader's experience of fiction, conflicting with what the novelist, the creator and instructor, is trying to accomplish. Most novelists avoid the conflict between their arguments and what the reader knows by outfitting a real event—a war, a Depression, a catastrophe—with imaginary characters and events, making at most no more than passing references to real people and occasions.

Still others, like Vance Bourjaily in *The Man Who Knew Kennedy,* give the history to us straight, asking us to care about how history affects imaginary people. But do we *really* care about how imaginary people reacted to the assassination? Do we *really* care how the narrator voted in Presidential elections from 1940 to 1960? How *we* reacted and how *we* voted spring to mind, crowding out whatever it is the author is trying to say. This conflict between reader and author is not unresolvable, but it imposes extraordinary problems on an author: His vision must prove more engrossing than our experience.

Bourjaily doesn't bring it off. In *The Man Who Knew Kennedy* he attempts to define the sensibilities of the sixties in terms of the fiction of the forties. He has written an old-fashioned novel, a moralistic novel which concludes unfortunately, while still in search of a moral. Kennedy's assassination, Bourjaily thinks, affected his generation as much as the Depression and the war. But it didn't, really; wars and depressions may rob us forever of our security, but few of us have found our lives permanently changed by Kennedy's death.

Bourjaily seems to believe that not only were we all changed by it, we would crush Kennedy again—as some people believe we would crucify Christ again. Dave Doremus, the man who knew Kennedy, is a man much like Kennedy—a poor man's Kennedy—popular, able, honest, determined, loyal, with a vision of the good life he was never allowed to achieve. The passive voice is important here: Bourjaily is whining a bit, suggesting that in this world we do not so much do as we are done unto.

Barney James tells the story. Like Dave, Barney is a good man, absurdly generous to those in distress. Both were best buddies in their youth, both as adults seem to have had the spark of life beaten out of them. Both were beaten by bad people: petty gangsters, business associates who did not share their idealism, and women, those bitchy beasts who are useful only as long as they don't *attach* themselves to men, spoiling the good old loyalty days, the masculine friendship days.

Dave is on his third marriage. Barney has had only one, but that's not going so well—the game of musical beds rings a sour note—and the only hope for both men is to get together on a boat again, in an attempt to relive the days just after World War II when they spent a summer floating around on the water, on endless martinis, and on a pair of willing broads. Dave, like Kennedy, was crippled by the war; Dave, like Kennedy, has made deep and not necessarily wise commitments; Dave, like Kennedy, will die under tragic circumstances.

The Man Who Knew Kennedy is a choked-up, sentimental novel which is at least as confused as the rest of us about the significance of violence, unhappiness, and compromised ideals. "It's all a part of the United States," Barney says in a less than memorable statement, "good and bad, and so am I, good and bad, but I feel that kind of thing too." Bourjaily is a professional novelist and works up several good scenes, but his effect is weakened by the soft thinking ("We all knew Kennedy") upon which his book rests, and by the atrocious writing ("There is something in a man that rocks more gladly with the wind womanless, I think") that crops up all too often. "What kind of people are we?" The question asked at the beginning of the book remains unanswered at the end.

The question, nevertheless, is central to all fiction concerned with yesterday's news. Robert Shaw asks it, too, in *The Man in the Glass Booth*, a far more imaginative and occasionally entertaining novel, but he doesn't have the answer either.

The title, of course, reminds us of Eichmann, and Shaw means us to keep Eichmann in mind as he teases us with his puzzle: Who is this horrible old man Arthur Goldman? Goldman is obscenely wealthy; he is almost certainly Jewish but virulently anti-Semitic as well. It is obvious that if Goldman were not filthy rich he would long ago have been dragged to the funny farm: Delusions (but *are* they delusions?) of persecution are only one manifestation of his madness.

Matters come to a head when we learn that Goldman likes to dress up in the uniform of a colonel of the *Einsatzgruppen*—the mobile killing units of the Nazi SS. And, of course, he is caught in the act, jibbering at the shrine of the Führer in his New York apartment, and, of course, he is hauled off to Israel to the glass booth. . . .

But Shaw is far from finished with his surprises. He has, in fact, a very neat and melodramatic denouement which is meant to make us all stop and think, "What kind of people are we?" It doesn't work, though. No matter how seriously we are supposed to take Goldman at the end, he is an objectional lunatic for too much of the book; his diatribes become quickly boring. The denouement, too, seems contrived; certainly it lacks credibility. As a morality play, *The Man in the Glass Booth* is a failure, but as a suspense novel, to be read quickly and forgotten, it works quite well.

1967

. . . . Wrong Turn

John O'Hara has published more pages of perishable prose than most writers who ask us to take them seriously, and the pages that he has preserved in *My Turn*, a collection of the columns he wrote for *Newsday*, are more perishable than most. O'Hara has published twenty-seven books, which is too many. Even Walter Scott, who wrote twenty-seven novels, is generally thought to have stretched his talent a bit. O'Hara may, and probably will, live to publish another.

It is not that O'Hara writes badly. He writes well enough. Brevity becomes him: His stories, on the whole, are better than his novels. But as a columnist he amounted to little more than a Robert Ruark with a flair for style. What is wrong with O'Hara—what has been wrong with his fiction for decades and is here carried over to his inconsequential essays—is his vulgarity and his absurd posturing as an anti-intellectual who knows better than anyone what anything is all about. In *My Turn* he poses as a gruff elder statesman of the republic of letters who must, because of his years, be forgiven the bluntness, even the inanity, of his opinions. But why? The brash vulgarity of age is surely more detestable than the innocent extremism of youth.

1966

. . . . Morality Novel

Let a good writer lie fallow for a few years and a strange chemical reaction occurs. Nothing else being equal to his talents, he breaks out in a rash intention to write a book about the Human Condition, about Modern Man. The symptoms are usually evident early on, as they are in Alan Harrington's new novel, *The Secret Swinger*. Carefully planted sentences tell the tale: "He had moved indecisively in neutral ground between the rebellious and the stodgy. . . . Amid terrible harmlessness, the years would wheel swiftly by. He could imagine her thinking: We'll grow old together. But he didn't want to age with anybody. . . . He was determined to avoid a genteel Anglo-Saxon middle age. . . . Warning flags were up all over the course."

Indeed they are. But the trouble with this kind of post-Herzog morality play is that its characters and situations are as rigidly controlled as in any Punch and Judy show. Authors who intend to write such a novel must cope with the following ingredients:

(1) A hero who is a trapped man, trapped into an unsuccessful marriage, a humiliating job, early middle age, and the habit of too much drinking. (2) He cannot have much sense of ambition or responsibility; he must, in fact, have failed his early promise. (3) He must have no idea where happiness lies, but he must pursue happiness so sturdily that he will do any kind of damfool thing to grasp at it. (4) Attempted happiness usually looms up in the shape of a whore, of amateur or professional status depending upon the author's whim. (5) The hero must make The Great Affirmation of Our Time: He throws over everything for a dream. (6) The Author never lets on whether he thinks this leap into the absurd is worthwhile, leaving a few intelligent readers to decide that the whole deal looks like a shabby enterprise.

There are some essential side effects as well. Such novels must include: (1) Negroes and/or Beatniks Who Know How to Live; (2) Psychiatrists Who Haven't a Clue How to Live; (3) Revelation of Truth Through Drugs; (4) at least one evil Mother Figure and one Kind & Understanding Woman; (5) a fatal fascination with the macabre.

And that's what *The Secret Swinger* offers. If it sounds like the warmed-over special from yesterday's menu, you have only the chef to blame. In all probability *The Secret Swinger* is a worse book than it first appears: Harrington writes well and can concoct a delightfully amusing scene which, for a while, distracts one from recognizing how stale a story he is serving up. Oh, yes: The hero's name is George Pectin and Webster says that pectin "(Gr. *pektos,* curdled, congealed) is white and amorphous. It yields viscous solutions with water, and, when combined with acid and sugar . . . , yields a jelly." That's our George. Recognize him anywhere.

1966

....................Hemingway:
The Last Wheeze

The theories developed in my learned article "Symbolic Combat & Ritual Chanting in the Puberty Rites of the Lesser Breeds" are much admired by anthropologists, but now that Ernest Hemingway's posthumous novel *Islands in the Stream* has been let loose among the bookstores, I feel obliged to share my discoveries with the public.

The Lesser Breeds, of course, are now extinct. Realizing that their seedy, artificial culture had become self-conscious, useless, and a mockery of itself, the Breeds packed up their idols, swore off reproduction, and sat around playing slapjack till they died. Once the Breeds had been vigorous chaps, living well and truly, drinking, fighting, fornicating, and catching fish as the puberty rites of their tribe required them to do. In fact, the Breeds came to like their puberty rites so much they never quite grew up, and when the anthropologists descended on their island to observe the colorful initiation ceremonies, the Breeds began to talk about the *philosophy* behind living well and truly, drinking, fighting, fornicating, and catching fish. They were never the same again. What had once been done with truth and grace lost its magic when it was staged for tourists, with printed programs to explain what it was all about.

An excess of talk about the rites of passage mars what I presume was Hemingway's last novel, his "big book about the sea," which he had brooded over for years and which he wrote, in a burst of creative energy, between December, 1950, and the late spring of 1951. At one time, the book was to consist of four independent novellas, but the last part was published separately as *The Old Man and the Sea*. The present book appears to contain the other three parts, somewhat cut but not otherwise edited by the author's widow and his publisher. Hemingway presumably would not have wanted the stories published in this form, but it is good to have them anyway. None is comparable to the story of the old fisherman and his giant marlin, but two of them are interesting and the dreadful middle story has some good scenes. What the stories lack as art they gain as autobiography. We must be careful here: This is *not* autobiography—though perhaps it is closer to it than any of Hemingway's other fiction—but it does show us Hemingway unrevised, almost naked. Amid the fussiness and gaseous banalities, the aging warrior finally is defeated.

The hero—and he *is* a hero—is Thomas Hudson, "a good painter" who is disciplined, works hard and well, and lives most of the time without women. There are two wives somewhere and three sons. In the first and best story, the time is the 1930's and Hudson is living on Bimini. His sons have come to spend a summer that takes its shape from isolated acts of violence. David, the middle boy, shows his courage when attacked by a shark and his endurance fighting a one-thousand-pound swordfish that, at last, he fails to catch. The ordeal, however, is clearly not a failure: David is initiated into manhood through pain and persistence, his determination, his love for his antagonist, and his faith in the men who advise him. "There is a time boys have to do things," Hudson says in one of the intruding interpretations that spoil many fine scenes but which show us exactly what Hemingway means, "if they are ever going to be men. . . . I know that if David catches this fish he'll have something inside him for all his life and it will make everything else easier." But David and the youngest son are killed in an accident. The summer idyll is over and, as Hudson remarks, "there are no terms to be made with sorrow."

The second episode, the sloppiest and least disciplined, shows Hudson during the war, mourning the death of his oldest son, playing with his cat (a fine scene) and then with his first wife (an even better scene), but there are interminable stretches of drinking and bantering with whores to yawn through in between. The final section is all chase, adventure, and the ceremony of battle. Hudson commands a queer ship and an even queerer crew on a secret mission: pursuing the crew of a Nazi U-boat through the offshore Cuban islands. Hemingway works up a good head of suspense. Even with their submachine guns, the good guys are outnumbered by the bad, but war can be fun, too, and Hudson drinks gin and coconut water while waiting for the Krauts to make their move. A paternalistic captain, he is confident about the battle, if gloomy about the ultimate meaning of it all. "No good will come of any of it," he muses. "But you have to do it. . . . But I don't have to be proud of it. I only have to do it well."

Open the book anywhere and the *nada* will fall into your lap: "There is only one thing you don't get over and that is death," Hudson says to his ex-wife. Wife: "And we just go on?" Hudson: "That's it." Wife: "With what?" Hudson: "With nothing." Or again, a whore asks him: "Tell me, Tom. What are you sad about?" and Hudson replies: "*El mundo entero.*" It is all part of the Hemingway mystique, which I find less attractive now than I did when I was younger. In this novel, Hemingway lectures the reader about rituals of manhood that I suspect cannot be talked about directly, at least not very much; instead, they must be perceived in action so that we may infer their significance for ourselves. Nor is Hudson, Hemingway's alter ego, a developed character. As an artist, he is unconvincing, but as a celebrity, accepting the deference due him, he has a presence that cannot be dismissed. Hudson's fatalism, if too much talked about, is real, as are his impotence and his unease. In middle age, he is content to drink less, to refrain from brawls and to remember the women he has had. His final battle kills him, but that seems all right: He was so very lonely at the end.

1970

......................John Hersey:
Another Parable

The good news about John Hersey's new novel *Too Far to Walk* is that it is far shorter than last year's *White Lotus*. It is therefore less tedious to read. The good news stops there. *White Lotus* was a grotesque attempt to wed the present to the improbable future; *Too Far to Walk* is an equally grotesque attempt to marry the present to the literary past. Both novels are so boring as to be virtually unreadable. What went wrong? Hersey lacks neither ambition nor skill. He always knows exactly what he is doing. What he did in *White Lotus* amounted to little more than what Sam Johnson called "the conspiracy against paper"; what he does in *Too Far to Walk* will never provoke the debate its obscurity invites.

In this novel Hersey forcibly yokes the concerns of the contemporary college generation to the story of Faust. John Fist, a brilliant student bored with the curriculum, decides it is just too far to walk to the hall where the bookish wisdom of the ages is being taught. A disciple of the orgasmic theory of maturation, Fist believes that experience should explode in noise and light like a fireworks display, with the truth, like sparks, fluttering down behind.

But if Fist cannot see the relevance of the history of civilization to his need for a "breakthrough" in living, Hersey can, and with heavy irony he trots out Marlowe's Mephistopheles in the form of a sophomore named Chum Breed, who smells of ozone and short circuits. Like Marlowe's devil, Breed is a disillusioned laborer dragging Hell along behind him. He winces at the banality of Fist's demands. He produces Margaret and, with the help of LSD, Helen of Troy, a witches' sabbath, and other more incoherent hallucinations. But, as in Marlowe's play, Fist's grand desires degenerate into frivolous pranks, and Fist, at the end, is willing to settle for the world as it is.

It doesn't work. Hersey intends his parable to be as wise as Time and as modern as 1965, but his book smells less of brimstone than the lamp. He has, for all his laborious research, failed to convey whatever it is that gnaws at young people today. He has all his references down pat, but his book lacks substance, conviction, and the lightness and wit that one uneasily suspects Hersey intends. Like any other man old enough to be father to this generation, he seems only to be doing the best he can to understand it. "Brother!" says Fist when confronted by the devil, but he might as well say it to Hersey who can conceive of no more interesting a devil than the spirit of negation, "the Spirit of Playing It Cool." Brother!

1966

. . . . Donleavy Declining

Have you noticed. Problems of even the most talented authors with second novels. Case in point, J. P. Donleavy. Acquired *Catch-22*-like cult with publication five years ago, *The Ginger Man*. Cause for general rejoicing, stamping of feet in honor of fierce talent, wonderful book, old-fashioned story in beguiling modern dress. Telegramese the style of.

> And sometimes
> little poems
> like this.

Which exactly suited the character of the book. Best of all. Exuberant love of life. Celebration of simplicity. Roguishness. Individualisticness.

Great success surprise to author. Surely. All the wild acclaim and well deserved. How to repeat. Simplest solution always best. Do same thing again. This time around use dream world, sterile, atavistic metropolis, like De Chirico painting where it is well known people lurk just behind the colonnade for some fell purpose withheld from viewer. Bring these people out. Running. George Smith, mystery multimillionaire, must move with care or lopsided statue in courtyard will extend foot and bring George down. Hard on his word George would only use to himself. Life full of unsuspected persecutions.

George Smith. Sensitive, likable, heel. Narrator when he can bring himself to talk about himself. All that money no one knows where or what from, but most of it budgeted for George's tomb to dwarf King Tut's. Two secretaries, both willing, George's sex life superb when he gets the chance unhampered by grasping wife he lives separated from. Story pretty plotless, everything like life up in the air at end, but obviously modern allegory and George modern man. Repressed. Impossibility of verbal communication. George running from world he cannot stand. Pungent moralizing throughout, but George has only half an ear available. Hands out deaf-mute cards or goes "Beep Beep" when cannot bear to talk. Good daydreams though. Everybody out to get George. Evil children. Earthy servants. Murderous strangers. Lawsuits and hilarious anonymous letters.

Author owes less to Joyce and Wodehouse. More to his own first book. Pity to see talent consumed in imitation. Donleavy flattering himself, success-to-failure ration roughly two to one. Fractured prose style works well sometimes less than in first novel. Maybe mannerism. Here. Can I show mechanical dialogue by dropping question marks. Asks Donleavy. Good-bye question marks many commas too. Much excellent writing despite. But overlong. Many wildly funny scenes, characters. Much that is moving in this comic bittersweet book. Some that is tired. Author working too hard.

A Singular Man does not advance author. Far as great writer. But glittering talent splashed all over the place. Vulgarities too. Oddly offensive, considering not so strong, seems like author feels obliged to stuff them in and that kind only inexcusable kind maybe. Uneven book but vastly entertaining.

> Mr. Donleavy
> we still
> love you
> write another
> book please.

1963

"Black comedy" is a term much bandied about by the fashionably literate these days. Among the semiliterate there is a wrinkling of noses at what is undeniably a whiff of sulfur, possibly brimstone: Black comedy is to be linked to Black masses, maybe even Underground movies. And yet a good number of our best writers are working this vein. Joseph Heller's *Catch-22* is one of the most talked about novels of the sixties, and when Bosley Crowther denounced the film *Dr. Strangelove* as unpatriotic and irresponsible one could almost hear a sigh: The center may not hold, but certain things are falling into place.

Irresponsibility and lack of patriotism are the black humorists' stock in trade. And so it has always been because black comedy is not, as some have suggested, as new as J. P. Donleavy's *The Ginger Man* or Terry Southern's *The Magic Christian,* but as old as the novel itself. The first novel of all, some scholars claim, was *Lazarillo de Tormes,* an early sixteenth-century Spanish romance about an unprincipled rogue who made asses of his betters. The book was immediately slapped on the Index by the responsible authorities of the day, with about as much effect as such attempts at literary suppression have always met with. A new genre was born, the novel, and with it certain elements of anarchistic, even nihilistic comedy that we now call black, as well as the picaresque tradition, which is still almost inextricably bound to the antics of black comedy. Later in the sixteenth century we have what may have been the first English novel, Thomas Nashe's *The Unfortunate Traveller,* another story of a rogue's peregrinations. In the climactic scene Nashe describes with lip-smacking gusto how a public executioner armed with a hammer breaks every bone in his victim's body. What could be more entertaining?

Black comedy today is simply old vinegar in new bottles, soured by shock, scurrilous satire, and an often heavy-handed reversal of American middle-class values. The hero in these novels is almost invariably stupid but cunning. As the story begins, he is stuck helplessly in the gum of modern civilization, a society so stupidly banal as to have lost whatever shreds of sanity and purpose it may have once possessed. Rather than fight back with reason, he adopts a guise of malice and determines, often with alarming logic, to outfox society at its own idiotic game. In a lunatic world, greater lunacy triumphs.

Donleavy's *The Ginger Man,* published in 1958, laid the foundation for a revival of this kind of story. It was a wise and wonderful novel, a hymn in praise of irresponsibility and the unspeakable joy of the flesh. To tell it, Donleavy invented his own prose style, creating a terse, nervous, inquisitive approach to syntax, with sentences left unfinished and punctuation as erratic as the hero himself. Five years later, when Donleavy wrote *A Singular Man,* black comedy was the fashion, so Donleavy (as it seemed to me) wrote his first novel over again, cashing in his early sensitivity in favor of his colleagues' insistence that modern man is divorced from life. The bittersweet comedy and some wildly funny scenes remained, but the whole seemed mannered and tired.

His third novel, *The Saddest Summer of Samuel S,* is hardly longer than a short story. Samuel S, an American hiding out in a sealed-up flat in Vienna, is, like Donleavy's other heroes, a stylish loser, but he recognizes the extent of his failures and, by keeping his integrity in the face of absurdity, manages to become something of a winner as well. Except for an occasional flirtatious bout, Samuel S has retired from life—but he has not altogether surrendered. He wants to be cured. He is searching for a sense of depth and permanence in his gray and meaningless existence. To this end, to escape from "standing alone in the middle of a great big zero," he has been seeing an analyst for so long that there seems to be a real danger that the analyst may go insane. Samuel S is a small cloud of incapability in the midst of a green and very capable world.

With each of his books, Donleavy becomes more concerned with man's insularity. Man is fragile, but the world is fertile. Man needs so little and has such a terrible time getting it; he moves through the world, which has so much to offer, as if it were enclosed behind glass. Looking out at the world through the glass, he sees only the mirror reflection of himself.

Shattering the glass and Samuel S's composure is Abigail, an American girl who comes to see him. Abigail is curious. She wants experience and excitement. She will never understand Vienna or Samuel S, but she offers him what she has, her body. The broad has come to conquer the deep, but it is clearly not enough.

The book is perplexing, not as well realized as it might have been. It seems to me clearly too close to what he has done before, although in this story he has stripped away the surplus fat of his second novel and the contagious exhilaration of his first. And yet this new story offers clear evidence that Donleavy is a master of understated *angst,* of the contrast between the world's fertility and man's sterility. It is a slick and skillful performance, funny as Donleavy's novels always are, poetic, tender, and strangely coarse, an admirable and repellent little parable.

1966

. . . . The Edge
of Fantasy

"The language of the heart either is a dead language or else nobody understands it the way you speak it. Very few." These words, spoken by one of the characters in Bernard Malamud's new collection of stories,

Idiots First, are underlined by the author in each of the dozen tales. Malamud's world is by no means tragic, yet it is filled with pity and terror. He observes it unflinchingly and with exacting integrity, generous with pathos and humor, quick to stress irony, occasionally precipitate in dumping his characters into despair. His people are invariably the lonely and the desperate. They are predominately Jewish (occasionally his Italian Catholics speak like his Brooklyn Jews); most of them are emotionally or financially bankrupt; nearly all are inarticulate. Lacking sophistication, poise, or the leisure good conversation requires, they come toward each other, touch, bump, join, or fall away, speaking only the language of the heart. It is to Malamud's credit that he can write so well about people who cannot use words, about emotions that other writers have articulated past all conviction.

Malamud is one of the best of America's younger writers, but since we belong to a generation astonishingly proficient in the art of the short story (Updike, Roth, Elliott, Powers, Cheever, the early Salinger, and others), our standards of comparison are necessarily high, and not all of the stories in *Idiots First* are as good as they might have been. They are all a good cut above average; they are all interesting, but many seem familiar and some fail because the author, having engaged our interest, settles for a hasty, tricky, or convenient ending, refusing to fulfill the potential of his material.

Two of these stories, however, are as exciting as any in recent years. The title story is nothing less than a small masterpiece, a taut and economical model of what contemporary short fiction at its very best can be, can say about the human condition. It defies summary because it itself is a summary of all that can be said about a beaten, dying Everyman who conducts the good fight to the very end, about the ultimate battle between the forces of light and darkness, corruption and charity, life and death. It is also, in its architecture, a superb example of how an author can move imperceptibly from realism to fantasy.

Nearly as good, and even more imaginative, is "The Jewbird," which compresses into a poignant allegory the whole story of Jews and Gentiles attempting to live together and how unreasonable hatred of Jews carries the day. The Gentiles are here ironically portrayed as a Jewish family and the Jew as a talking crow.

Malamud at his best is as good as they come; at his worst, he is still well worth reading.

1963

Several years ago, in *The Wapshot Chronicle,* John Cheever explored the character of that "ingenuous town," St. Botolphs, and its leading family the Wapshots. Now, in *The Wapshot Scandal,* Cheever looks in again on his own private preserve in a Never-Never New England suburbia to spin some more of his loosely connected and delightfully disingenuous fables. Here again is the atmosphere of gaiety, ghoulish gossip, and grotesque characters whose explicit lunacy is so evidently a mirror of our own. As in all his fiction, Cheever precisely observes the inarticulate agonies that lie just below the surface of ordinary lives. Relying little on the strenuous dialogue common to so much fiction, Mr. Cheever concentrates on the subtle tones of the author's own voice. Through the magic of his art, his mute and desperate characters obtain a wry eloquence; their passions and frustrations bubble up as if it were never customary for such to be concealed.

Honora Wapshot, eldest survivor of St. Botolph's patrician family, still presides over the affairs of Moses and Coverly Wapshot and their wives while neglecting, to her grief, her own. Honora never paid an income tax; dreading poorhouse and prison, she flees the country. Moses' wife Melissa succumbs to ungovernable lust, undertaking a surprisingly durable affair with the grocery boy. Coverly and Betsey live in a miserable missile town whose activities are so secret it is never mentioned in the news. In the book's most moving scene, Coverly's boss, the nation's leading nuclear physicist who has perfected an inexpensive method of blowing up the planet, is summoned before a Congressional committee that refuses to listen to his waffling about life on other planets, his defense of man's right to extinguish life on earth, but confronts him instead with the monstrous inhumanity of his private life and, as readers cheer, strips him of his security clearance. Mr. Cheever seems to be saying what many of us have long believed: Enough of this nonsense about educating humanity to the challenges of a scientific era; let us educate our scientists in basic humanity.

The ordinary stuff of humanity is the matter of Mr. Cheever's stories. *The Wapshot Scandal* is not a novel of ideas but rather an examination of fleeting figures in a landscape, their senses and emotions, their fears and desires, the furtive demands of the libido made plain, the ungovernable impulse translated into action. Nor is *Scandal* any more of a novel than *Chronicle* was. Most of the chapters could stand alone; indeed, some of them have, in the pages of *The New Yorker.* Mr. Cheever is plainly not a novelist, but as a writer of short stories, he has few peers; having no single story to tell in these pages, he tells a great many, varying in length from a few lines to a chapter. They are all expertly told, skillfully gathered into a skein his publishers generously call a novel. His methods of revealing the truth about his many characters vary sharply, but each is exactly right for the story he has to tell. Sometimes he is a narrator, one of the people of St. Botolphs, reporting on his neighbors;

sometimes he is the omniscient author, laying open the vital springs and cogwheels of his creations; another time he stands completely outside, relaying to us a single juicy story which characterizes a man or a family much as village gossip does, or again he can develop a series of related stories carrying a character through his entire lifetime.

Beyond his artistry as a teller of tales, Mr. Cheever displays two other conspicuous talents. He is a writer of marvelous prose; his measured sentences are fashioned with an eye for color, an ear for melody, bristling nerve ends in the skin which respond to a situation or an emotion that would be lost on realistic writers. Even more striking is his capacity to be both very funny and very sad. He is not occasionally funny, then sometimes sad; he is always funny and always sad, both at the same time. This effect, though not always completely convincing, is admirably sustained throughout the book.

The Wapshot Scandal is not a book entirely without faults. Not all of the stories are equally good. By choosing grotesque characters from one small town (as Sherwood Anderson, who had no sense of humor, did in *Winesburg, Ohio*) to illuminate his satirical comments on life, Mr. Cheever concentrates on telling us just enough about his people to make his points. Few of them survive this artistry to live and breathe for any length of time in their own right. The diffused narrative is also something of a drawback, making it, I think, a bit difficult to remember the *Wapshot* books once they have been put aside.

1964

Each year, our serious writers of fiction find it more difficult to cope with the human condition, particularly the condition of life in America today, without resorting to fantasy. By fantasy, I do not mean an author's temptation to build worlds of his own that he peoples with elves and leprechauns, or science fiction stories that examine our sexual mores as if seen through the bugged-out eyes of Martians, but fantasy used as a kind of artistic shorthand to avoid the tedium of exposition. More important (and this is what is new and alarming), many novelists use fantasy, or succumb to it, because it is the only way to deal with the absurdity of a world we no longer control, a world we can no longer describe efficiently in rational terms. What can one say that is coherent about a country that clubs its children, exterminates what might have been a nation, prefers to throw steel into space than feed stomachs on earth? What, except to say that it cannot be real, or that if it is, we are not? Like Lear's fool, we can only play a prank, hum a jig or two, and go to bed at noon.

Even the milder novelists, the satirists and realists, have taken to writing stories that begin straightforwardly enough, but then lurch, leap by necessity across the bounds of reason, because the only way these writers can say what is in their minds or hearts is to end their tales in realms of nightmare and allegory, with visions of holocaust and the disintegration of whatever it was that made us human. Hieronymus Bosch rides again.

John Cheever is such a writer. For years, he has written stories that slip almost imperceptibly from satiric realism to fantasy, the better to expose the lonely core and private vulnerability of man. Cheever's books do not differ much from one another; his affluent characters are much the same, beset by *angst, accidia, cafard,* that numbness of the heart that has no word in English. We have made our lives, Cheever seems to say, and insulated them with split-level ranches and country clubs, wrapped them around with automobiles and martinis on the patio, but the center is hollow—we lack love and conviction—and the whole elaborate structure is likely to implode. In Cheever's stories, the afflicted men and women recognize their desperation; out of touch with themselves and their environment, they become furtive creatures—thieves, voyeurs, addicts, alcoholics, lechers, and night crawlers—but somehow they maintain their purity. Cheever loves them, which is more than understanding, which is why his stories are so extraordinarily affecting.

His new novel, *Bullet Park,* tells the stories of two men who live in a prosperous suburb of New York. Eliot Nailles, a maker of mouthwash, is a good and normal man, happy in his unexamined life. He believes in purpose and order and that his marriage is a matter of life and death. He loves his family. But that is not enough: He can no longer get on the commuting train, that "portable abyss," without taking drugs, and one evening, he runs after his teen-age son with a golf club. His son takes to his bed and stays there. Nailles' life is crossed by that of Paul Hammer, a newcomer to Bullet Park, a man without love and therefore prone to obsessions. Hammer decides to assert himself by killing Nailles' son.

The end of the novel, freighted with symbolic melodrama, does not work because for once Cheever has not properly prepared his transition from a world of familiar signs and portents to one of darker significance. We can see where the transitions come, but they do not convince. No matter. If the novel as a whole is something less than the sum of its parts, it is because Cheever, author of three novels, is no novelist but an inspired writer of short and poignant stories. At its best, *Bullet Park* is a sequence of marvelous tales and anecdotes, some no longer than a page, in which people talk about their real frustrations and their imagined successes. I sometimes suspect that Cheever hoards his briefest, most fragile sketches, those he knows he can never develop to the length of his masterly short stories, for these occasional books that he calls novels, books that may lack the shape and cohesiveness of novels but which we should enjoy for their wit and their disturbance, and for Cheever's prose, unmatched in subtlety and precision by that of any other living writer of American fiction.

Bernard Malamud's *Pictures of Fidelman* is, I think, more successful than Cheever's book, though it is hardly more of a novel. Still, Malamud's use of fantasy is more integral to his purpose because the six episodes of this loosely jointed collection are designed as pictures in an exhibition, portraits of an artist learning if not how to paint then how to live. So we must not be surprised if one of these pictures is determinedly antirealistic, a gleeful mixture of religious symbolism and surrealism.

"Imagine all that history," says Arthur Fidelman, late of the Bronx, when he arrives in Rome. Fidelman is a failed painter who thinks he might write a study of Giotto. He cannot, of course, for the same reason he cannot paint: He has not learned passion; he has not learned how to live. In these six adventures, he learns. "Life is short if you don't hurry," Fidelman says. He is intense, nervous, and shy, the kind of man who is continually being used by others. He is also obsessive; in each story, he fixes on some person or some thing, so much so that all rational behavior deserts him. Then, of course, he is at his most vulnerable.

In one story, he is victimized by a fellow homeless Jew; in another, by a woman painter with whom he shares a garret and falls hopelessly in love. In another, he is held captive in a brothel and forced first to clean toilets and then to forge a Titian. Later, he becomes a pimp as he struggles with his "masterwork"—a painting of himself and his mother. Fidelman is never far from starvation or from suicide. "He considered jumping in the Tiber but it was full of ice that winter." Once, too poor to buy materials, he creates "sculptures" by digging holes in the ground.

It is inconceivable that Fidelman is a good artist, but, of course, we never know. More important is the act of creating, the single-mindedness of purpose (if you discount sexual distractions) that leads to the passionate and committed life. Someone is always destroying Fidelman's art, but it always seems the proper thing to do. More often than not, Fidelman escapes with a little victory of the spirit. He is a comic hero cut from the Quixote pattern: the resilient fool, the ridiculous man of noble aspirations. Malamud's stories about him are skillful in the extreme, often surprising, earthy, and funny, a delicate blend of pathos and irreverent humor.

1969

The ingredients of Bernard Malamud's new novel, *The Tenants*, are familiar. A parable rises from realistic details. The hero, a *shlemiel,* quests after a new life, after his salvation. Meanwhile, he denies his own humanity, cuts himself off from others, retreats to a prison of his own devising. Yet he yearns for contact: of the spirit, of the flesh. Malamud's heroes usually begin this way—as losers. Interlopers, clutching their anguish, assail them—"Take my problems!" these people insist, thrusting out their loads like so much dirty laundry. The loser accepts, recognizes that he is being used, but is somehow improved by the event. The way up is the way down. After much pummeling, the *shlemiel* finds his salvation where he least thought to look for it. What makes *The Tenants* so unnerving is that Malamud serves us his recipe again but with an appalling variation. The end this time is not redemption but destruction.

The *shlemiel* is Harry Lesser, thirty-six and Jewish, with two novels behind him (one good, one bad) and a third ten years in the works, the end not yet in sight. Lesser lives in a condemned brick tenement, a symbol, I assume, for our society at large; he is the only person there, fighting to finish his novel in the place where it began, though his landlord, pleading heart over art and offering increasing bribes, begs him to get out. Lesser refuses; he knows his rights. "Things could be worse and had been, but he was still a writer writing. Rewriting. That was his forte, he had lots to change—true, too, in his life." His novel is about "love, I guess"—Lesser knows he is ignorant of the subject, but he knows, too, that when he has figured out the end, he'll know what love is. All he has to do is follow the words—like some yellow-brick path to the Emerald City. Meanwhile, he seems to be writing against the end of the world.

What could disturb such single-minded concentration? Well, another writer: a poacher, a black man camping out in the next room, pecking away at *his* typewriter, a long rough semiautobiographical book about the brutalization of blacks. Willie Spearmint is perhaps a rival and certainly a crowd. He demands that Lesser criticize his book while insisting that the only course for blacks is to kill all the whites: Don't criticize my message, Willie says, criticize my style. Willie has his views on Jews, too.

Lesser stumbles: what to do? *His* novel is meant to help people understand and endure life; Willie's is to help the revolution. Lesser writes for immortality; Willie writes for freedom. Stereotypes, of course: Malamud means them to be, means to satirize them. His black characters and his quotations from black writing are both hilariously funny and unassailable because he has the wit to show them only as a white observer sees them. Willie works harder at his book—and Lesser steals his girl. "We're writers, Bill," Lesser says, hoping for accommodation. There is none. Snow, which is always bad news in Malamud's novels, falls continually, and Lesser dreams of consuming flames: "Where can I run with my paper manuscript?" The end is all irony, violence, and prayer.

The Tenants is the most formally designed novel that Malamud has written, and the most beautifully conceived—as narrative and parable. Tendrils of metaphor creep over every description, every scrap of conversation. Malamud is working with material he has used before: the confrontation of Jew and black man; the artist who is unable to work because true commitment must be made to men not to art. There is a Yin and Yang structure to Malamud's novels, a polarity that is one of the most attractive qualities in his fiction, but in this story the conjunction of opposites leads not to unity but to annihilation. An annihilation subtly and marvelously altered by irony, I should say. I should say also that *The Tenants* is Malamud's most comic novel yet—breathless, funny, and playful with words—and at the same time, it is his most mysterious.

1971

Two

.............Journey into the Interior

Better a worthy failure than a competent banality. Doris Lessing's new novel, *Briefing for a Descent into Hell,* is not, I think, particularly successful, but it is, in its conception and structure, so very imaginative that I found it far more intriguing than all but a few of the novels I have read in recent months. It is a visionary novel that hovers on the brink of traditional mysticism—by which I mean Mrs. Lessing looks for the annihilation of individual consciousness in some greater, pulsing stream of life. It is also a novel about The Meaning of It All, about the intervention of the gods in the affairs of men. It is a novel stuffed with allegory, metaphor, symbols, and quirky digressions—a novel that pauses at times for poetry, a novel that threatens at other times to let its prose congeal into poetic diction. It is, finally, a novel of conventional imagery that needed more intelligence (I am sorry to say this about Mrs. Lessing, who is reputed to be the most intelligent woman writing fiction in England today) and more intensity to make its vision and its symbolism bearable.

It begins well. An unknown man—he is later identified as Professor Charles Watkins—is picked up by the police and taken to a London hospital. He suffers from nervous collapse, remembers nothing, hallucinates about an ocean journey on a raft. He will stay in this hospital, out of touch with his physical environment, for more than two months while doctors feed him increasingly potent drugs—Librium and Sodium Amytal—hoping first to stop his hallucinations and then to restore his memory.

Most of the narrative takes place within Watkins' mind. Mrs. Lessing describes her novel as "inner space fiction: *For there is never anywhere to go but in,*" and she strives occasionally for what might be called interior similes: "the sky aflame with sunrise like the inside of a ripening peach." In his mind, Watkins goes out on a boat with some friends, searching for "Them," who will provide the searchers with aid and instruction. The sailors, however, are overtaken by a flying saucer, a crystal disc that sweeps all but Watkins off the boat. In despair, Watkins builds a raft, is wrecked on rocks, saved by a porpoise (more traditional symbolism here—but leading to what?), and finally cast upon an unknown shore where, Mrs. Lessing tells us dully, "hostility or dislike had not yet been born."

Even so, Watkins discovers a ruined city and witnesses a murderous war between some apes and some other creatures with dogs' heads and rats' tails. He escapes from this turmoil on the back of a white bird (Christ, perhaps?—it usually is, but in this story Mrs. Lessing's familiar symbols are divorced from any coherent reference). The bird carries him into space, where he is ingested by the disc that had spurned him earlier. Watkins is then taken to a point where he can see the world as a place where all contending elements are really one, where warring armies are in fact the same army and all judges one judge (an idea expressed somewhat better by Gerard Manley Hopkins), where radiant links of creation make "a shimmering web of fluid joyful being." The earth, it seems, is really surrounded by a singing light, a "finer air," that is funneled into the earth through certain human beings. Once, this fine air pervaded all the earth, but then a comet hit our planet, the air changed, and men, who had formerly understood the universal harmony, fell into error and began thinking of themselves as individuals. So much for Original Sin; through sloppy thinking, Mrs. Lessing suggests that our loss was imposed by an external cataclysm.

> *In Adam's Fall*
> *We sinned all*

has become—what?

> *With the comet's crunch*
> *We lost a bunch.*

It won't do. There is no point to a fallen world without a sense of moral significance. Now, as if Mrs. Lessing were determined to extinguish any interest we might have had in her allegory, she introduces us to the guardians of the earth, who include, unfortunately, such Roman deities as Minna Erve and Merk Ury, who speculate about the influence of the planets on what occurs below.

Up to the time Watkins is abducted by the crystal disc, the story is strange enough. It is symbolic and visionary, yes, and the tenses used in the narration shift unreasonably, but it is still a concrete and dramatic story. Not much time is wasted on third-rate thinking or shabby mystagogy. It is very much Professor Watkins' personal story, just as Edgar Rice Burroughs gave us Captain John Carter's adventures and not some philosophical discourse on the landscape of Mars. But at just this point of abduction, Mrs. Lessing's story swerves grievously off course. She removes Watkins from her story for a while—just when she should

not have done so—precisely because she does not want her book confused with fantasy (though it will be—the science-fiction freaks will
embrace it as an example of what can be done with their sterile and
limited genre). She wants us to take what she says seriously, to believe in
what she evidently thinks is a serious statement about the nature of life
and universal harmony. But we cannot. What she has to say is neither
interesting nor moving, neither original nor wise. It is, in fact, rather
stupid, wordy, and abstract, and also embarrassingly didactic. "For we
may suppose, I am sure," she writes, "that Planets are altogether gentler
and more humane than poor beast Man." Who would suppose any such
thing? It is bilge, nothing less, and reads like all the uncounted, un-
solicited manuscripts that flood book publishers' offices the world over—
all the books by halfwits who have had a vision of harmony much like
Mrs. Lessing's. The embarrassment here is that Mrs. Lessing is intelligent; only her book is stupid.

Anyway, the guardians of the earth form a "descent team" to spread
the word among men that they must love one another. Team members
are warned that they must be born again as human beings and may find
it difficult to remember their mission. Briefly, the book revives: Watkins
is a member of the team. In the hospital, we now realize, he is trying to
remember not the trivia of his family existence—which is what the
devilish doctors care about—but the real importance of his existence.
Or—the question cannot be ducked—is Watkins' mental turmoil no
more than a mad fantasy, brought on by the cumulative effects of the
doctors' drugs? Mrs. Lessing never says, but her sympathies are clear.
She began writing about such improbabilities at the end of the preceding
novel, *The Four-Gated City,* when, with England lying in ruins, survivors
talked of transparent spaceships; some even talked to visitors from
another world. What existed externally in that novel exists internally
here.

There is considerable drama in Watkins' struggle to remember his
mission and in his doctors' determination to make him normal. But in
the second half of her book, Mrs. Lessing introduces new characters and
subplots, all of them unfortunate, as if to remind the reader that for all
her fanciful speculation she is still concerned with the home truths of her
previous novels, Marxism and feminism. "At last love had come to birth
in man," she writes at one point. "Communism and its Red Star of hope
shone out for all the working poor, for all the suffering everywhere, to see
and to follow. Within that general Love," and so on, and it is hard to
believe that one is actually *reading* this stuff, that a woman who has the
brains to create a complex and generally interesting novel could think so
badly.

But she can, she does. Mrs. Lessing is unable to maintain the pressure of her principle narrative; she can't keep her mind on what she is doing and so she launches out on an episode, develops it further than need be, and keeps pausing to hare after private demons. Archaeology, for instance: She doesn't seem to like it—there were "profound doubts about what was going on in archaeology" she writes at one point—although archaeology, to most of her readers, will hardly seem a controversial subject. I cannot believe that a writer of Mrs. Lessing's intelligence has not the skill to write a visionary novel, but she apparently lacks the discipline to keep it short and intense, as all such novels must be if anyone with anything more than a high school diploma is to read them at all. Offhand, I can think of only two recent novels that have succeeded in this very special genre. One is William Golding's *Pincher Martin,* which appears to be the story of a man's struggle to survive and is in fact an allegory of man's insatiable greed for life, a whole novelful of tenacity that, ironically, occurs entirely after its protagonist is dead. The other is Michel Bernanos' *The Other Side of the Mountain,* a truly terrifying vision of an ascent into Hell expressed through symbols that seem strange but are, somewhere low on our brainstems, distressingly familiar. Both these novels create their own frames of reference—which Mrs. Lessing's never does.

Her vision of Ultimate Meaning will provoke giggles of delight from the weak-minded, from the devotees of Hermann Hesse and Kurt Vonnegut, but from no one else. Her symbols are shopworn, her thinking sentimental. The most effective visionary stories reject her conventional morality and her fondness for generalization in favor of a sense of otherness, of remoteness from anything that man can understand in a literal, or easily definable, symbolical way. Earlier writers knew enough to stop short of final explanations—Dante, for instance, says toward the end of his *Comedy,* "To the high fantasy here power failed"—they knew enough to maintain a sense of awe, and to admit (as Mrs. Lessing does not) that they wrote in metaphor.

1971

....................Irrational Man:
The Nineteenth Century
as a Mirror
of Our Own

In my attic, I keep a cardboard box stuffed with my college lecture notes. On one page, a diagram of the sonata form; on another, "Boyle, Robert—His Problems with Gas"; and so it goes, through "What Is Comedy?" and "Economic Reasons for Enclosure" to the real name of the Green Knight. I have forgotten it all, of course (except for Bercilak, the Green Knight), but like an alcoholic who keeps a spare fifth tucked beneath his floorboards, I get a secure feeling knowing it is there: my college education disintegrating gently within its three-ring binders. In times of great stress, I can run to it, riffle through it, and—*Shazam!*—The Critic's Armed Again.

So, when I read John Fowles' new novel, *The French Lieutenant's Woman,* I ran to the cardboard box. I knew what I was looking for: my notes on "Twentieth Century Sensibility." There, nestling under such headings as "Renaissance of the Irrational" and "Problem of Unity and Fragmentation," lay the explanation of what made twentieth-century novels different from their nineteenth-century predecessors, and, perhaps, a clue to Fowles' extraordinary tale, which seems to combine the best of both traditions.

Much of the shape and all of the materials of the story come straight from Victorian England. The year is 1867. The setting, for the most part, is Lyme Regis, a resort on England's southern coast. Two lovers promenade beside the ocean, engaged in a proper, formal banter designed to keep each other at a distance, just as their clothes and attitudes envelop, conceal, and constrict the human animal within. A few yards away, a dark and ravaged woman broods intensely at the sea. She, of course, is *not* proper, but dark and brooding women properly belong to Victorian novels; they break up courtships and the comforts of convention and, for their troubles, are annihilated at the end. This woman—we will never know her well—might be Hardy's Eustacia Vye down from Egdon Heath to cast a little melancholy on the waters, but whoever she is, the reader knows from the opening chapter that she will distract our hero from his fiancée. That is the way it is with Victorian fiction; we can only wait and turn the pages.

The man's name is Charles. He is thirty-two, a gentleman, heir to a title and estate. Charles meddles in paleontology; it is only one of the many ironies in Fowles' narration that Charles searches in rocks for evidence of life that died a million years ago. Charles is also a prig and, like his beloved fossils, a bit calcified, but that does not bother Ernestina, his fiancée. Ernestina is twenty-one, heiress to a business fortune and, by her own description, "a horrid spoiled child." Her playfulness and irony conceal her shallowness and lack of human feeling. Her money and Charles' rank should be very happy together, but there is Sarah, the dark and brooding woman, a warm-blooded governess who, they say, was ruined by a French lieutenant. Condemned by the proper Victorians for losing "a woman's most precious possession"—and that, dear reader, is her *reputation*—she embraces the life of an outcast. "I married shame," she says, but nobody grasps what she means. Sarah is a joke—"Poor Tragedy" they call her—and a scandal; they offer her cruelty and charity, which any Victorian outcast should gladly accept, but Sarah wants neither. She wants Charles. Charles doesn't understand. "I am not to be understood," Sarah tells him, but that doesn't help. She gets Charles, of course, just as I began to wonder whether anything would ever *happen* in this most leisurely of Victorian novels, but, as you will have guessed, the story is not the point of *The French Lieutenant's Woman*.

Fowles' point is, I think, that our lives, echoed by our art, are full of contradictions that isolate us from each other, that cannot in any way be reconciled. To prove it, he has written a novel that seems to be Victorian but is not, a novel complete with chatty digressions and didactic essays on the fashions of 1867, changing social mores, Victorian sexuality, the work of Lyell, Darwin, Marx, and the precursors of Freud. With considerable erudition, Fowles shows us Victorian society at its middle point and reminds us of revolutions in the making. Through a perspective no Victorian novelist could have mustered, Fowles indicates how the conformity of the age, the veneer of civilization, is threatened, though no one in Lyme Regis knows it. Charles, for instance, has read Darwin, considers himself an unfettered modern man capable of saving Sarah from the bondage of convention. But Charles no more understands Sarah than does the local doctor who suggests that she is hysterical. Lacking sexual fulfillment, the doctor says, she behaves irrationally to attract sympathy and attention. Sarah, in fact, is more complex than this. Accustomed to playing roles defined for her by others, she will in time be freer, more modern in her views, than Charles. Sarah is Fowles' principal triumph: From a distance, as the characters see her, she seems to be not one but a succession of women; we can never anticipate her. But we can, like Charles, always believe in what she says she is.

Art reflects life; both deceive us. Fowles, intent upon demonstrating that Charles and Sarah are much like ourselves, turns to the ironies and ambiguities of modern fiction. Modern literature—according to the notes in my cardboard box—began with a discovery of the hold that the past has on the present. Fowles, too, plays with time: Look, he says, at how the present is alive in the past. Modern literature (my notes inform me) is obsessed with the appearance of truth, with how we pass off what we *wish* to be true as if it *were* true. It won't work, of course; there is always the Dark Other which we find convenient to deny, and which in modern literature is no longer denied. One cannot both possess and enjoy a thing, Fowles says. He made the point in his first novel, *The Collector,* and makes it here again. Fowles is fascinated by these contradictions that have no resolution. What a man is, his novel says, is probably not what he himself thinks he is and is certainly not what anyone else thinks he is. We are locked in ignorance, in isolation from each other. Matthew Arnold said as much in a famous poem that Fowles quotes. In fact, many Victorians said as much, and this is what is strange about Fowles' conclusion: Why should a man who understands the Victorians so profoundly, who has taken such pains to provide a modern view of Victorian concerns, settle for the facile pessimism of which the Victorians were so fond, improving it only with the hope that man may endure and acquire through defeat a shred or two of wisdom?

Fowles' approach to his story is, I think, not always wise. He strikes poses, offers his readers alternative conclusions, appears onstage himself to flip a coin or to admit that, after all, his characters are invented and he really does not know them well. Such playful forays into existentialist narration seem to me a gratuitous sleight of hand, entertaining but irrelevant. No matter: *The French Lieutenant's Woman* is a unique and intelligent novel. Fowles' faults, if they are faults, may be extensions of his strengths and, with the exception of those in Nabokov's *Ada,* no greater strengths in fiction have been exposed to view this year.

1969

. . . . Another
Snow Job

"Look at this," said my eight-year-old son, pointing to the story he was reading. "On page 29, the teacher tells Johnny he is going to get his comeuppance, and"—he riffled over most of the book's pages—"on page

156, she's still talking about it." Poor kid: Like his father, he was stuck with a novel that was long on moralizing and short on plot. *Why do they write such stuff for children?* But as soon as I asked, I knew the answer: to train them to grow up to read novels by C. P. Snow.

I was, at the moment, dozing over the 205th page of *The Sleep of Reason,* the tenth volume in Snow's seemingly interminable sequence of novels, *Strangers and Brothers.* The plot had not yet begun. This is more serious than it sounds, because Snow's novels *need* plots. Snow has, for thirty-four years, been writing about the life and adventures of Lewis Eliot, a poor provincial English boy who does very well for himself in the worlds of law, university, and government. Since the purpose of these novels is to teach the reader what it's like up there in Powerland, Snow shows little concern for the *art* of fiction. He is, in fact, a realist who seems to believe that fiction may well profit from being as dull and difficult to follow as life itself. He also cares more for his series than for its component novels: Like some Druid engineer, Snow shoves and bullies his individual slabs of fiction; he is clearly less interested in seeing how each will look when propped upright in its own pit than he is in seeing how all of his slabs contribute to the improbable architecture of the whole.

So, with each volume, there is more news about more characters to pass on to the reader, an accumulation that obstructs the plot. Snow exhumes scores of such characters in the present book; he dusts them off to blow a brief flush of life into their cheeks, then casts them aside to await another resurrection in still another novel.

This nonsense occupies about half of *The Sleep of Reason.* To be fair, the same half also includes some secondary stories, which, with all the understatement of a tuba voluntary, introduce themes of free will and sexual responsibility that will occupy Snow when he does get around to the plot. Lewis Eliot is now a pragmatic, public man, measuring his life by the drinks and deference due him as he potters around dispensing advice and comfort to those less fortunate than he. He visits his old father, who remains fiercely independent. He intervenes on behalf of four students about to be expelled from his old college for staging a mini-orgy. He helps a lovesick girl and then, for many pages, worries about his eye: He has a detached retina that eventually reattaches itself.

By this time, the reader, stunned by so much dullness, is either nodding his head in sleep or shaking it in disbelief. And yet, halfway past the novel, a story *does* develop. An old friend asks Eliot to see that his niece, a lesbian, is treated fairly when she and her lover stand trial for torturing and murdering a young boy. There's little Eliot can do, of course, except attend the trial, visit the niece, and talk to the family of the other girl involved. But, as no gentleman would normally get involved in such a sordid mess, the appeal for help is necessary to allow Snow to ruminate on the Important Questions that this trial, so much like the Moors Murder Trial, provokes. If man is not guilty of his greatest crimes, can he claim credit for his greatest virtues? If the guilt of one of us is diminished by mental aberration, are any of us guilty at all? There are no answers to such questions, and Snow provides none. But then Snow, who is good at describing the way these girls behave, cannot come close to the metaphysical horror of what these girls *are*.

Snow is more at ease in the rational world, reporting on the politics of success and the intense satisfaction a man can derive from the struggle upward. Probably no writer alive better understands the jungle behavior of civilized men approaching the peaks of their professions. But, as Lewis Eliot plods on to greater successes, and as the novels he narrates grow puffy and flaccid, a kind of Snovian snobbery intrudes: the middle-class exultation of the self-made man who is never "more interested in people than in the job they had to do." That is a chilling phrase, but Snow tops it with what is perhaps the clearest statement of his ethic when he writes off a scientist who "wasted his creative life" because he took part in research that would not be completed for a generation. In the world of Lewis Eliot, Snow's alter ego, success is the only tangible reality. A man's abilities exist only in comparison to those of others, and his achievement in life must be constantly reevaluated.

Eliot seems to believe that these evaluations can be made in terms of exact statistics, that a man's chances for success can be measured precisely *and/in advance*. Seeking to tame the most uncontrollable human variables with percentages won't work, of course, but there are always fools who think it will. Perhaps this explains why Snow's recent novels, so shapeless, humorless, and insensitive to prose, are his most popular.

1969

My grandfather-in-law, a British professor and theologian, tended to waffle away from the facts into the thin air of theory. When a student once rebuked him for this, he replied: "I may not know the facts, but God, can I interpret them!" Miss Pamela Hansford Johnson, the wife of C. P. Snow and a civilized British novelist lately alarmed by the more unattractive novelties of our civilization, would have sympathized entirely.

Her progress from facts to theory is outlined in *On Iniquity,* a very short book in which very little is said about a very important subject. The catalyst is the Moors Murder Trial in which a young man and a young woman, both sane but incapable of human feeling or decency, were convicted of the sexual assault, torture, and murder of three children. Photographs and a tape recording of the agony of a ten-year-old girl made the case that much more alarming. Miss Johnson wrote about the trial for a newspaper but stayed on to write a book about the society that produced the murderers.

"We all too readily comfort ourselves," she says, "by believing there can be no such thing as wickedness: that there is only 'sickness' . . . I believe that some of us are, or can be, pretty wicked."

She believes also that through ignorance and greed we permit, even encourage, people to act wickedly, that we have become an "affectless" society in which human feeling is denied, in which our sensibilities have become coarsened through exposure to evil.

Part of the blame, as she sees it, must rest on the recent permissiveness of publishing: Titillating and sadistic books are now generally available and such books were found (among others) in the home of one of the murderers. Miss Johnson feels we should ban such books. She doesn't come out and say so directly. She knows she doesn't have the facts; nobody has.

She is right, I think, about the affectlessness of much of our society, but she mistakes one symptom of it (dirty books) as the cause of another symptom (torture and murder). She does not prove her case. She doesn't really try. Still, while she is extremely critical about the availability of books dealing with sex and sadism, it is difficult to determine how much she knows about those that she would ban. She seems to have read some of De Sade, but she lumps *The Kama Sutra*, perhaps the best and loveliest book we have which describes the secular life of a vanished civilization, with *Pleasures of the Torture Chamber*. The combination does not inspire confidence.

Her question is: Is the death of one small child by torture too high a price for making all books available to all men? She feels it is. Ivan Karamazov (to whom she refers) asked a similar question: If you were God, could you let a child suffer? The answer is no, but we are not God, and Miss Johnson's question is illegitimate. Freedom and the compulsion to virtue are, as the Old Testament tells us, incompatible. The Grand Inquisitor would have eliminated pain by eliminating freedom; so, now would Miss Johnson.

There is more than a hint of paternalism in Miss Johnson's indignation. By stressing that she is one of an intellectual and moral elite which can safely absorb ideas that prove indigestible to the masses, she seems to oppose the egalitarianism of vice. As a paternalist, she believes that this diffusion of vice among the plain people is the result of our society's "permissiveness." Surely this permissiveness is illusory. We may be more permissive than our ancestors about what we do in bed and we may publish books describing it, but this is small potatoes compared to how much less permissive we are about regulating our economy. We may *talk* more about vice than we once did, but we *tolerate* it less. Wellington's extraordinary sex life was long suppressed from public view; he got away with it. Profumo's wasn't; he didn't. The Moors Murders, symptom of our "permissive" society, were talked about and the degenerates brought to court; white slavery, symptom of an "inhibited" society, prospered.

On Iniquity is emotional and thoughtful, always intensely personal. When its author speaks of the trial or her own reaction to the murderers—the spiritual fear such people generate—she is both astute and eloquent. The result is a courageous and inadequate book, precise in small affairs and fuzzy in large, a book concerned with the right problems, even if it asks few of the right questions and offers answers to none.

1967

. . . . Wodehouse Preferred

The Prescott Clapping Palms Award, an irregular recognition of meritorious service to the republic of letters, goes this month to Simon & Schuster for its decision to reissue three novels by P. G. Wodehouse: *The Code of the Woosters, Fish Preferred,* and *Uncle Fred in the Springtime.* They first appeared in that cheery decade that began with the Depression and ended with World War II—without them (who knows?) we might have fallen into something worse—and now, here they are again, as we wallow in a new Time of Troubles, for a new generation that does not know these books. I wonder whether anyone will pay them any mind.

Those who have read them are a little richer than those who have not. They are not, I suppose, the funniest novels ever written, but only because the greatest comedy is always somewhat sad—look at Shakespeare and Dickens, at Chaplin and Marceau—and Wodehouse is never sad, never sentimental. He doesn't write about noble whores or cuddly junkies. He hasn't cringed before any of our century's pieties, hasn't suggested that Bertie Wooster would be improved by gainful employment, or that the boiled-shirt façade of British clubs, and country castles where prize pigs graze upon the greensward, be pulled down. On the contrary, Wodehouse writes hard comedy—the comedy of Congreve and Sheridan, of Wilde and Gilbert, and he is as good at it as they were. His plots don't vary much: Young men set snares for girls or try to fend them off; they study the anger of aunts and plot ways to touch uncles for loans. If they suffer while they're at it, that's because they haven't learned, as someone, probably Wodehouse, has said, that the pain of one girl's refusal is drowned in the pain of the next.*

Wodehouse's stories are literate, stylized, and urbane. They take place indoors and on well-groomed lawns, with no hint of darker elements attending. Evelyn Waugh once said that for Wodehouse "there has been no fall of Man," and in fact Wodehouse has created a new Eden, a world quite independent of ours—though tied to it by geography and literary references—a world that will never go out of date because it never existed, though we wish it had. For these reasons, Wodehouse will be read for generations, but he deserves to be read forever because of his style. His prose is remarkable: There is no fat, no superfluous phrase, in it. He coins his own metaphors and similes in such a way that no one can ever use them again. And, like all great comedians, his sense of timing is perfect—as anyone who has ever looked at the first page of the best of his novels, *The Code of the Woosters,* can see.

Strangely, our serious critics, a humorless lot who try on scowls before their mirrors, have neglected Wodehouse. Ever since Plato expelled the poets from his republic, critics have been trying to justify the literary enterprise. They usually fail without recourse to some larger claim: Literature is *good* for you because it makes you good; because it can be used as a substitute for religion, you must be very careful about what you deign to read. Literature holds society together, they say; it is the unacknowledged legislature of the world, and so on, and there is some truth to all of this hyperbole. But it leaves Wodehouse, a useless writer if there ever was one, standing in the cold of critical neglect because his books are simply hilarious. Critics dismiss Wodehouse because he has no moral relevance, and if, in this century, we feel uneasy about having a good time, what can we do about Wodehouse except ignore him? Castelvetro, a critic who lived four hundred years ago, was, as far as I know, the first to say that literature is primarily for *joy.* Its ultimate function is delight. Not many people believe it, but it is in this spirit that I recommend these novels to you.

1969

---

*A reader in Florida corrected me, citing Kipling's "Certain Maxims of Hafiz": "The pain of one maiden's refusal is drowned in the pain of the next."

Suffering Fools
Gladly*

"The production of the supreme effect through means the least extravagant"—so wrote Max Beerbohm of Beau Brummell's sartorial style. Beerbohm is contemptuous of this fop who could not have matched IQ's with any peacock on any lawn in England, and yet there is a glint of admiration in these words. They apply to Beerbohm's own work as well—his caricatures, essays, and short stories. If a dandy can be intelligent, perceptive, and humane, Beerbohm was the dandy of Edwardian and Georgian letters. His prose is elegant, combining an urbane levity and a cultivation of the *mot juste*. His aphorisms seem negligent, his insights carelessly achieved—and yet how long must he (like Beau Brummell adjusting his cuffs before his mirror) have sat at his desk, crumpling up his pages and starting in again? The throwaway effect that Beerbohm worked for is never attained until much has been thrown away.

Irony is the informing character of his work, parody the essence of his skill. So it is with other writers. What sets Beerbohm apart is his compassion—his unique combination of wit, insight, and gentleness. Think for a moment. Wit + surfaces = P. G. Wodehouse. Wit + insight = Thackeray. Like Henry Fielding's and Jane Austen's, Beerbohm's comedy has a serious edge to it, but even Jane Austen is nastier than he. Most comedy is at least partly cruel, which is why we like it so much, and most comic writers of intelligence have let some disenchantment with humanity filter through their work, but Beerbohm, who mocks men's pretensions ("Too intense contemplation of his own genius had begun to undermine his health"), seems quite fond of his fools. As he extends his foot to trip a man, his hand goes out to help him up.

In the introduction to this collection, Lord David Cecil, Beerbohm's biographer, writes: "For me, his work is the finest, richest expression of the spirit of comedy in all twentieth-century English literature, and the most varied." These essays and stories support his judgment. There are the parodies, for instance, of Conrad, James, and Chesterton that mimic the substance as well as the style of their originals. Parody is always popping up in Beerbohm's work: parodies of sample letters—what the well-bred blackmailer should write and how a young man should refuse

*A review of *Max Beerbohm: Selected Prose,* edited by David Cecil.

to pay his tailor's bill—and, in the marvelous story " 'Savonarola' Brown," a full-dress parody of Jacobean tragedies that plays such havoc with blank verse that I doubt if I can ever read the stuff again.

Then there is the theater criticism—mild fare by comparison, but good examples of its kind—and three excerpts from *Zuleika Dobson,* Beerbohm's burlesque novel. There are short, light essays on the joys of not being a schoolboy and of not going out for walks: "Even while I trotted prattling by my nurse's side I regretted the good old days when I had, and wasn't, a perambulator." There are more substantial essays, too, such as "No. 2 The Pines," a portrait of Swinburne as an old man which, for its affection, its self-mocking perspective, and its complex structure, is one of the greatest essays in English.

Finally, there are the short stories with their common theme: how something that did not exist—a work of art or a reputation—is created. In "Argallo and Ledgett," Beerbohm conceives of a hoax by which a famous writer will lend his name to make a minor, despised writer famous. In "Enoch Soames," a dismally aesthetic poet—"the lower one's vitality, the more sensitive one is to great art," he says—makes a bargain with the devil to see what his reputation will be like a century hence. He discovers that not only is his work forgotten, but he himself is thought to be fictitious. "So far from being able to imagine a thing and make it seem true," he says to Beerbohm, who narrates the story, "you're going to make even a true thing seem as if you'd made it up. You're a miserable bungler."

Such conceits enchanted Beerbohm. He was, he said, one of life's "guests," a man of small gifts that he used perfectly. If he ever kicked a dog or cursed a politician, we will never know. He was not only witty, he had the wit to know he could not write seriously about serious matters. Like Vivaldi, he has no message for us—which is not to say that either he or Vivaldi is beneath our notice.

1971

. . . . How Much Shape
Does a Novel Need?

It is extremely difficult to fake a novel. Unlike painters and composers, novelists cannot very well say, "To hell with content, I care only for form." There is no such thing as an abstract novel. Fiction must always be *about* something, and that something should relate to some aspect of the human condition. I do not mean that fiction must necessarily aim at rational discourse; it can, instead, strike at our groins or at some preliterate pocket in our subconscious. But the concern remains the same: who we are and why; how we live and what we think about it. Nothing else will do. I know there is a fluctuating vogue for novels about our furry forest friends and that French writers fool around with stories about coffee pots and mirrors. But such stuff is less than fiction; it may be no more than journalism.

Form, however, *is* expendable. By form I do not mean beginnings and endings and gettings from here to there—these are necessary to any verbal communication—but rather an imposition of a design that shapes everything in a book: its structure, what the characters think and do, and the language the author chooses to describe them. This kind of form, far from being necessary, can be injurious. It would do no good, for instance, for a novelist who has written a big sprawling story involving four generations, thirty-seven characters, and an acre of costumes and furniture, to tell his wife: "They will call me an impeccable wordsmith, a subtle architect of narrative." Not likely. They may call him a grand, boozy storyteller, but the restraints and disciplines of a well-made novel would have ruined his book. The need for discernible form and the possibility of achieving it increase as the author steers his story inward, away from the familiarity of the external world and toward dangerous, uncharted realms of intellect and imagination.

Thomas Williams' *Whipple's Castle* is a good example of the shapeless novel. It is a huge, old-fashioned book, a conventional family chronicle that wrings from the reader all the conventional emotions: pity and fear, admiration and (perhaps) a little conventional lust. As a novel, it neither engages the mind nor extends the art of fiction. It wasn't meant to. It is, indeed, a novel for the reader to wallow in, a *fun* book that, if I could, I would invest money in, because it will sell scores of thousands of copies and inevitably it will shake many shekels from the money tree that grows in Movieland.

The story is about the Whipple family, which in the 1940's lived in a big and ugly house in a small New Hampshire town. Like so many American families, the Whipples are community leaders, sexually precocious and violence prone, with a streak of madness in their lineage. The father, permanently crippled by an accident, yells at his children, who think him a bit insane. There are three sons: The eldest is kind, grave, and weighed down with unwanted responsibility; the middle boy is well-meaning but feckless; and the youngest, the most desperate, is a boy who stumbles and breaks things and fears the dark that unleashes a galaxy of scaled and hairless monsters. There is a thirteen-year-old girl, too, almost too beautiful to believe, and a mother of peasant stock who really cannot cope with her "strange, precariously balanced" family.

In 1942, America was losing the war, and an atmosphere of vulnerability and expectancy hangs over the Whipple clan; they are waiting to grow up, to be drafted, waiting to lose their virginity, their limbs, or their lives. In time, all of this happens, as we watch the children and their friends undergoing the inevitable rites of passage—getting drunk or getting a girl for the first time, fighting, working, worrying, and changing quite perceptibly as they mature. We get to know and like them very much. The story staggers badly toward the middle of the book, but Williams gets it in hand again, inflicting some kind of violent crisis on each of the Whipple children and their lovers. A majority survives, but scars remain.

Just as in life. If truth to an uncomplicated view of life is the purpose of this kind of fiction, *Whipple's Castle* succeeds better than most. Never underestimate the kind of audience that exists for novels like this. As far as I can determine, there are hordes of women across the country who berate their librarians for recommending "good novels" when what they want is "a novel I can read for *pleasure.*" These women feel threatened by irony; they are tired of wit, moral ambiguity, and the kind of cosmic desperation that obsess most good writers today. Their girdles are tight, and their teen-age offspring are loose, and *what they don't need from fiction is more problems.*

Williams will give them what they want. He plays for nostalgia, adroitly re-creating the details they have forgotten about American life in the 1940's and the details they have certainly not forgotten about the anguish of growing up. Williams tells them that most people are pretty good—the Whipple children *are* good, and they love each other—and that, although life can be horrible, some sort of happiness is not an abnormal condition of man. He includes a lot of extracurricular sex (but *nice* sex, the kind women can enjoy without feeling like perverts), and great dollops of Dickensian sentiment, with never a trace of irony. It may *sound* terrible, but Williams brings it off with a great skill. I enjoyed it and recommend it to all but the most arrogant of critical readers.

Irony is, however, the controlling force behind the form of Nicholas Mosley's *Impossible Object,* an odd and intriguing book that seems to have begun as a collection of short stories before Mosley discovered how he could link the themes and language together and declare it to be a novel. I still think there is a loose short story floating about in it, but otherwise it is a marvelous piece of work, taut and aphoristic, combining a rather appalling wit with questions about the instability of love and a recognition of man's impotence in the face of the forces that control him.

An English writer, well married and father of three sons, falls in love with an unhappily married girl. They meet to argue in a London pub; they occasionally make love in a bed-sitting-room; they separate, then meet in Italy and North Africa, where the child born of their affair will die. It is a deliberately banal story in which Mosley, by concentrating on a shifting perspective of narrative, discovers disturbing depths.

The novel consists of eight stories about the malaise of love. Love, as Mosley sees it, is a harnessing of opposing qualities; it will not rest, and it will not stay the same; it sucks life from that which will destroy it. Martial images abound; "Their love-making was a change of battle," Mosley says of one couple. "You make love like war," the girl says to her lover in another story, "like horses on the Parthenon." The centaur is the central symbol in these stories: Half-man, half-beast, it is both the brain and the crotch of sexual love.

Each story exists on several levels, with staccato bursts of symbols exploding everywhere. Different narrators tell the stories. In one, the lover splits in two: Half of him becomes the ironic observer who perceives the inevitable pattern of his affair, while the other half remains involved and hurting because he does not. The stories are not told in order, but they hang together by common incident, common language, and common themes. One of these themes involves the hurt people do to each other in the name of love. "It is by pain," Mosley writes, "that caring is demonstrated: we were taught this in Sunday School." Another is that man does not control either his actions, which tend to grow as ritualized as games, or his life, which always seems more suited to a story, reaching ahead to God or behind to antique myth.

I admire this novel very much. Mosley works with a limited range of incident, but by making everything he says about this narrow affair point several ways at once, and by hooking all his metaphors so neatly together, he drives very deep indeed. Mosley's is a vertical novel, as deep as a well, whereas Williams' novel is horizontal, as broad as a church door. Mosley's requires more art; Williams', more energy. Most readers will enjoy one or the other, but few will like both.

1969

. . . . A Perishable
Pyramid

Why change a winning game? Too many novelists seem to think that writing fiction is like playing roulette: You find a winning formula and stick with it for as long as your luck lasts. But not William Golding. With his sixth novel, *The Pyramid,* Golding perseveres in his compulsion to write stories which at first glance seem totally dissimilar. Any gimmick, however, will fail in time and *The Pyramid,* Golding's worst novel to date, fails because this time Golding is trying to be different in what he says as well as in how he says it. Ironically, the result is a surprisingly conventional story.

Why should the author of a first novel as successful as *Lord of the Flies* try to reinvent the form of the novel every time he writes one? I don't think we know enough about Golding's purposes as yet to do more than stab at some suggestions. Part of the answer may be that Golding's first novel did not become successful until he had written three more—that is a rather trying time for any author. I suspect, though, that Golding must have felt that by making his novels different in form he could attract more attention to his unvarying theme: the primordial violence and corruption inherent in the nature of man. It is a black and compelling theme, a theme that should be more roundly recognized than it is, and just the kind of thing that teen-agers, surfeited with J. D. Salinger's sentimental views of man corrupted by society, might clasp to their pubescent, palpitating bosoms. But in *The Pyramid* all this dark ferocity is gone, replaced by pathos, home-fried nostalgia, and the dreary, thrice-repeated revelation that loneliness leads to sexual abnormality.

Oliver, the narrator, now a successful man, looks back at his boyhood and adolescence in a stupid, pulsing English town that appears to be a cross between Winesburg, Ohio, and Peyton Place. In the first of three connecting vignettes Oliver lays seige to, and finally storms, the local teen-age slut. In the second he strikes a rapport with, but fails to understand the intentions of, a visiting homosexual theater director. In the third he endures the eccentricities of a spinster music teacher.

Three familiar, even comfy stories, each with its Maupassant twist at the end, but which fail to add up to a novel. Humor is an excellent thing in fiction, but when Golding experiments with it for the first time here the result is much like a cement mixer suddenly inspired to cough up a plateful of *petits fours*. More troublesome is the question of why Golding chose to narrate these stories as he did. Oliver Old relates the tribulations of Oliver Young and this, I suppose, is the pyramid: three cornerstones of life viewed from life's summit. The design is less impressive than it appears because Golding tells us nothing of Oliver as an adult (perhaps that is because the point of a pyramid is so tiny) and his perspective on his youth—at times acute, at others thickly coy—contributes nothing to the story. Since Golding is a writer of superior imagination, able to sustain a cruel and distressing metaphor of man's endeavor, it is a pity to see him write and think so conventionally here, cashing in, it would seem, his youthful pessimism for the toothless benevolence of middle age.

1967

. . . . Amis Cold . . .

A few hardy masochists still read each new novel by Kingsley Amis. I count myself one of these, but, as I read *I Want It Now,* I wondered why. First, there is *Lucky Jim* of blessed memory, one of the funniest novels written since the war; and, second, there is the hope that Amis will somehow manage another as good. Third, there is Amis' dead-on dialogue, his flippant prose, his rude invective. But lately, Amis has been writing weak and eventually sentimental stories about thoroughly detestable people: *I Want It Now* is the kind of novel P. G. Wodehouse might write if Wodehouse thought about sex all the time, had a bleeding ulcer, and wore shoes that pinched his toes.

The plot is not worth describing, but it concerns a British television personality on the make, the girl he thinks is both a nymphomaniac and rich (she is only rich), and their troubles coping with her rich parents and even richer friends. Amis manages to unload some very witty cracks about the canny stinginess of people so rich they have lost touch with the world around them, and he is here, as in his other books, funny about food: "local so-called spinach which Ronnie could have sworn he had seen doing its level best to grow out of the garden wall." You can pick up quite a bit of that kind of thing before the story gets hooked on tenderness and dissolves in sentiment.

1969

. . . . And Amis Hot

Lurking about Kingsley Amis' fiction is a civilized urbanity that is both fashionably sour and more than a little slick. The narrators of his recent novels are dyspeptic, alcoholic, oversexed men who know about food and wine and therefore tend to obesity. For example: the narrator of *The Green Man*. Maurice Allington is equally disenchanted by life and the prospect of death. Proprietor of an English country inn, he puts back a quart of Scotch a day and tells us of his ailments: cancer and Huntington's chorea, which he has managed to arrest, and hallucinations of parts of human bodies, which he hasn't. Maurice is hardly surprised when, just before he goes to tell his guests of the ghosts that haunt his fourteenth-century inn, he sees a red-haired lady in old-fashioned dress running from his private quarters.

A ghost story from Kingsley Amis? Yes, but not like any you have ever read. I don't know of any ghost story ever written that combines real ghosts with such mundane humor and acidulous detail. Most ghost stories work toward an atmosphere of horror, but Amis, who means us to believe in his ghosts—and we do, we do!—is interested in his fleshly characters, in Maurice's determination to seduce his doctor's wife and then to get her and him and his own wife into bed together. The ambience of horror that any unionized ghost writer would have wanted is continually deflated by Amis' fussing over wines, artichokes, and two of the best comic sex scenes I have seen in modern fiction. Can Amis pull it all together when the secret of the evil ghost of Dr. Underhill and his creation, a thing of branches and leaves that tears people to pieces, is revealed? Yes, and very neatly, too. *The Green Man* is easily Amis' best book since the immortal *Lucky Jim*.

1970

..........................A Lean and
Hungry Novel

The nature of truth, the existence of God, man's responsibility to his fellowmen in a ravaged world where appalling suffering is the most important fact of life to most of humanity—these are the questions which concern Richard E. Kim, a young Korean living in this country, in his astonishing first novel. *The Martyred* is a lean, ascetic story; it seems almost hungry for the fleshy roundness of conventional fiction. In this novel of ideas, everything not essential to advancing the involved debate between a small handful of characters, who themselves are reduced to little more than the ideas they hold, is ruthlessly swept away.

The scene is Pyongyang, capital of North Korea, from the time the UN drove the Communists north to the Yalu until the Chinese advance recaptured the city. The narrator, a young officer in Korean Intelligence, is assigned the investigation of the murder of twelve Christian ministers by the Communists. Captain Lee's commanding officer is anxious to establish these men as martyrs, thus rallying the support of Korean Christians and pleasing that strange Christian ally of Korea, the United States. Two ministers survived the murders; one of them is mad and the other, Mr. Shin, is an enigma: He refuses to talk about the matter. Then a captured Communist officer reveals that many of the ministers "died like dogs," renouncing their faith. Soon the question becomes, did Mr. Shin betray his colleagues?

Violence, suffering, and man's inhumanity to man are the usual background to philosophical novels which attempt to delve to the agonized core of the human condition. The central question, whether put by Job, Raskolnikov, Ivan Karamazov, Dr. Rieux, or Captain Lee is usually the same: Does God know or care about the suffering of men? Ivan Karamazov condemned a God who could listen to the cries of a single child; Rieux, in plague-ridden Oran, said that if he believed in an all-powerful God, he would leave the healing of the sick to Him. In all these books there is the disquieting thought that man must sacrifice himself for his fellows because God, if He exists, has defaulted.

The ideas in Mr. Kim's novel develop as layer after layer is peeled away from the mystery surrounding Mr. Shin who, at various times, appears to be a Judas, a coward, a hypocrite, a saint, a martyr, perhaps even Christ himself. What *is* the truth about the "martyrs"? If the truth is sickening, must it be revealed? Man may not be able to live with the truth, but has any man the right to suppress it? Even if the truth hurts, is it not all we have? By withholding or falsifying the truth, man attempts to make it his own. But the truth belongs to no man. How can we ever *know* that people want or need a lie? This is Captain Lee's position. He is an atheist with a certain honest simplicity to his beliefs, and he has tormented Mr. Shin with his challenge of God's indifference to human suffering. Mr. Shin, tortured by more conflicts than it would be fair to reveal here, holds firmly to his conviction that despair reduced weary sufferers beyond endurance. The mass of men must be allowed to hope for meaning in their lives.

"All we need consider is the answer given to men's hopes"—the line is not from *The Martyred,* though it might serve to sum up the problems that the book presents. It is part of the truth that Rieux manages to attain toward the end of Camus' *The Plague.* Mr. Kim acknowledges his debt to the late French writer in his dedication—and perhaps *The Martyred* would be even more impressive if much of the same argument, tending toward much the same conclusions, had not been advanced first by Camus. Both novels are existentialist in outlook, celebrating the doubting man. Granted the condition of universal human suffering, what can men do to make life bearable? Although suffering, like the poor, we have always with us, and although on occasion—the Lisbon earthquake of 1755 comes to mind—suffering has given rise to philosophical and religious speculation, only in this century have men been much concerned with man's responsibility for his fellows' suffering. Formerly, atheism—at least the kind of atheism that attained any kind of notice—took the form of such confident boasts as LaPlace's: *Je n'ai pas besoin de cette hypothèse.* In this century, however, some men have tried God and found Him wanting in His own terms. It may be no longer decent to believe in God; we may have to reject Him for ethical, even Christian, reasons.

And yet, the existentialist answer is always disturbing. Rieux and Shin, the good existentialist heroes, are like Dostoyevski's Grand Inquisitor not only humanitarians but snobs and cynics, too. For all their good works they are elitist; they have appointed themselves the guardians of the souls of other men, and they are quite prepared to deceive the masses for the masses' own good. Such attitudes, as we have learned from spokesmen of other persuasions, have brought untold grief to our time. *The Martyred* answers no questions, but it debates a great many with vigor and some subtlety. It is a modern novel in the best sense of the word.

1964

..................."What Is Our Innocence, What Is Our Guilt?"

You will be glad to hear that I have at last come up with two debatable generalizations rashly intended to summarize what most serious current fiction is all about. Among the more beautiful book people, they are known as Prescott's Principles of Innocence and Contingency:

1. Innocence is an attractive quality—as long as it is limited to infants and the mentally defective. In adults, innocence is always less than the occasion requires. Life is real, life is earnest, the novelists tell us; it is often quite smelly and sometimes bloody as well. When the going gets rough, we will be betrayed both by our ethical reflexes and by our need to tidy up our lives. "You want all the lines joined up and all the colors flat," says a woman in John Le Carré's new novel, *A Small Town in Germany.* "You haven't got the guts to face the halftones." It is an old idea: facing the halftones was the concern of both Homer and Henry James. But perhaps only in our own day has the terrifying destructive potential of innocence so consistently haunted our fiction.

2. Contingency, once an argument used to prove the existence of God, is now used to describe the condition of man in a world in which God is either silent, dead, or a dangerous delusion. In olden times, when Aristotle invented it and Aquinas applied it to theology, contingency meant simply that because man is ragged, incomplete, and an insufficient cause unto himself, something else—a First Cause or God—must have started him. Characters in contemporary fiction recognize their contingency well enough: They talk endlessly about how ragged, incomplete, and insufficient they are, but they generally agree that there will be no help from God. "No," says one character in Richard E. Kim's second novel, *The Innocent,* "there is nothing out there." Another agrees: "We have only ourselves." It is important to note that the presence of such an argument in a novel is not *prima facie* evidence of the author's own convictions; today, believing and skeptical writers alike find it convenient to have their characters talk that way.

Both novels make much of both principles, but of the two books, Le Carré's is the better. Like his other novels, *A Small Town in Germany* resembles a spy story, but if a spy story is what his readers expect, they are going to be disappointed. *The Spy Who Came in from the Cold,* Le Carré's first popular success, *was* a spy story—the best ever written—

which, like all good spy stories, subordinated every element it contained to the requirements of its deceptive plot. Admirers of that book found Le Carré's next novel, *The Looking Glass War,* an unsettling experience. "Too confusing," said one book club in declining it. But it was not confusing; in fact, it was not even a spy novel—it was a novel about spies. Without warning, Le Carré had moved from the realm of entertainment to the realm of serious fiction, where character and commentary take precedence over plot. Now, he has done it again. Spy and counterspy hunt their quarries with all the cataclysmic urgency found in a thousand lesser tales, but that is not what the book is about. It is about the walking wounded that Le Carré, in his black and polished pessimism, believes us all to be.

The time is 1970, and the scene is Bonn. In Brussels, the British are once again being considered for membership in the Common Market, but they will need Germany's vote to get in, and Germany is torn by dissent. A popular movement, mixing farmers and students and led by a man of "flatulent sincerity," insists that Germany turn to Russia in the future. So busy are the diplomats in the British Embassy at Bonn that they almost overlook the disappearance of one of their members, who has taken a carload of secret files with him. One of the files, in fact, could turn the tide against Britain's entry into the Common Market.

Alan Turner, "clever, predatory and vulgar, with hard eye of the upstart" and a tendency to destroy those whom he investigates, is rushed from the security department of Britain's Foreign Office to track down Leo Harting. Harting, as a child in the war, had fled Germany for Britain; now, he has returned as a temporary and slightly tawdry diplomat to wangle his way into every file the British possess. He has vanished, of course, by the time Turner arrives, but he has left his track. As Turner tightens the screws on the men and women connected with the Embassy's political section, he discovers that Harting had somehow turned the weaknesses and romantic illusions of each to his own advantage—not because Harting was skillful at this kind of exploitation, but because men and women, poor wounded creatures that they are, are anxious to offer trust and love where they are ill advised to do so, recklessly exposing their vulnerabilities even when they know that the consequences are bound to prove disastrous.

This cheerless message is one of three unvarying themes that extend through all of Le Carré's fiction. Another is the depreciation of the human organism and the institutions it is capable of creating. A sense of attenuation, of enervation, hangs over all his books; his buildings and cities are cold and damp, and his characters are aging, facing retirement without having discovered a meaning in their dull and sometimes dangerous lives. Finally, there is the theme of the hunt, which, in Le

Carré's stories, expresses the kinship of two dedicated people—the hunter and the hunted—in an alienated society, a kinship that is a kind of love in a world where the opposite of love is not hatred but apathy. "That's how we spend our lives, isn't it?" Turner asks. "Looking for people we'll never find."

Le Carré began his career with good stories that were too easy for him. The necessity of showing that a manhunt is more than a scuffle in a dark and European alley, and that the corruption of man is endemic, and not just a matter of bribery and politics, forced Le Carré to switch from thrillers to serious fiction. The result, combining the best elements of both, seems still in the process of developing, but it is something very special in fiction, and it is altogether fascinating.

The Innocent is a sequel of sorts to Richard Kim's extraordinary first novel, *The Martyred*. It doesn't much matter. One or two characters overlap, and the narrator is the same Korean Army officer, promoted to major now, but no wiser than he was before, in spite of all the moral ambiguity he had to cope with in the earlier book. What does matter is that this is essentially the same story told over again with rather too many words this time.

Major Lee is the theoretical strategist of an army coup aimed at ridding South Korea of the corrupt government that emerged from the Korean War. Lee lost his religious faith in the earlier novel; not the nature of God, but the nature of social justice is what is argued in the present book. Must every coup degenerate into "an act of blood-stained violence?" Lee insists that if the new government is to be better than the old, it must not murder the opposition. Lee's opponents insist that you cannot be honorable if you don't survive.

The leader of the coup is Lee's old friend, Colonel Min. Min is a magnificently shady character—rather like Mr. Shin, the shady saint of Kim's previous novel. Min is charged, with having fought with the Japanese and then with the Communists, with murdering a Russian, a Japanese, and an entire company of North Koreans. Hardly the kind of man to lead a bloodless coup, as Major Lee slowly comes to understand. But Min has a reasonable explanation for each act of horrifying violence. As generals defect and the coup progresses, Min and Lee find time to meet in darkened rooms to argue whether the evil in society will be expunged by the good or the evil in men. Both, it turns out, are fatalists, insisting they have "no other choice" in what they do, but Lee is the innocent, the rigid man who nearly ruins the coup by his impotent idealism.

The Martyred was a lean, ascetic story; one could almost see the holes where superfluous words had been stripped away. *The Innocent* is an intriguing novel, better than most, but nevertheless overburdened with contrived dialogue and underburdened with onstage action. Major Lee is unsatisfactory as a narrator; lacking sophistication and self-doubt, he is less than morally obtuse—he is an uninteresting man. The arguments seem windy and polarized, not integrated into the course of action as they were in the previous novel, and the whole story should have been shorter by a third.

1968

.... Muriel Spark:
Short Takes

Muriel Spark is a miniaturist and a fantasist, a clever writer who combines style with wit and grace with sophistication to write thin and rather bloodless exercises in atmosphere and tone—detached and ironic comedies designed to skewer a frustrated spinster on the twin horns of sex and dogma. She has a delightful trick of telling her readers what happened to her characters after her stories end; she is, in fact, the most omniscient author around. Brevity was the soul of her wit.

Vaulting ambition, however, causes *The Mandelbaum Gate* to fall. Everything, and more, that made her early novels delicious has been assembled here, except the brevity, except the brevity, except the brevity. We have a British spinster, half Jew, half Gentile, and entirely Catholic, off to the Holy Land on pilgrimage, looking for her fiancé. She is hounded by the Arabs as an Israeli spy, rescued from a nunnery by a witless oaf who has a bit more iron in him than anyone would have thought.

Mrs. Spark couldn't care less about a conventional plot, but her novel fairly seethes with event: espionage, amnesia, murder, insanity, sex, double-crossing, misfired revenge, even the reformation of a lesbian. The characters are fully drawn, meaning that one almost recognizes them. The spinster's spiritual alienation is straight from Rose Macaulay's *The Towers of Trebizond* and the superbly unfathomable Arab family might have come from E. M. Forster. Israel, Jordan, and divided Jerusalem are realized in all their convincing detail. And, if that isn't enough, Mrs. Spark chucks in considerable repetition, a standard device of hers: excerpts from the testimony at the Eichmann trial and even a complete sermon to bulk the pages and stress the significance she intends her novel to attain. *The Mandelbaum Gate* is nearly as good as what Mrs. Spark has done before. The trouble is that it takes twice as long to read.

1965

Reading Muriel Spark, her novels or her short stories, I say to myself two times out of three: Here is the cleverest writer at work in the world today. The third time I say, no; she is just very good and sometimes better than that. Now that some of her short stories have been brought together in *Collected Stories: 1,* I find myself in the same dilemma, hopping twice on my right leg and once on my left.

At their worst, Mrs. Spark's stories have substance; at their best, they are all fluff and style, a formal elegance of prose deliciously juxtaposed to foolishness of subject. Mrs. Spark writes about ghosts and visitors from space as if they were natural men. Like Saki and A. E. Coppard, she compresses her stories most marvelously, pulling in the reader immediately, as if he had been intimate with her characters for pages. More often than not, something extraordinary happens. More often than not, the stories are extraordinarily funny. Two times out of three. The third time, not.

1968

. . . . A Wanting Novel

Writers of serious fantasy or futuristic fiction are generally impatient with the paucity of moralizing that realistic writers are permitted in their novels. In fantasy, and its kissing cousin allegory, the author is permitted sweeping didacticism on the progress of the soul or the problems of society. In the last few decades, Zamiatin, Orwell, and Huxley, by projecting present social trends into the future, created recognizably unbalanced worlds especially designed to prove their authors' points. As long as totalitarianism, left and right, is a threat to our society, novels presenting such dystopias will appeal to many because, as they stress the need of the state to reduce individualism to a seedless pulp, they show how a renascent, if often ineffective, individual tries to thwart the trend.

Anthony Burgess, in *The Wanting Seed,* attempts to join this select group by speculating on a world in the comfortably distant future consumed by the problem of overpopulation. London, a city of monstrous skyscrapers, now covers the better part of England. One child to a family is all the law allows, and better if it die and its little corpse be returned to replenish the famished soil. Food is synthetic, the multitudes work in shifts around the clock, and a giggling population police shoots at random into crowds. A curiously benign government, having managed to eliminate war (a contradiction of Malthus, on whose theories this nightmare is based), insists on contraceptives and abortion. Homosexuality, not only official policy, is a key to advancement second only to voluntary gelding.

For all his excellent material—an unnatural crop blight, cannibalism, a new theory of cyclical historical change, an army designed solely to murder its own—Mr. Burgess has written an inferior novel. Most of what is worth having in *The Wanting Seed* is developed in thirty pages; after that, the story groans under the stupidities of the plot construction and the unrealized potential of the author's horrific fictional prophecies.

The generic weakness of such fiction seems to lie in its authors' inability to create characters as interesting as the hellish worlds in which they live. Mr. Burgess' two nonconforming individuals are more insufferable than most. The hero matures from a sniveling, gutless cuckold to a nondescript cipher just smart enough to survive. The heroine is a fleshly earth mother, attracted by the fertility of the sea. An often lively and sardonic style is sabotaged by the author's fondness for inkhorn vocabulary, unfathomable medical terms, and mongrelized words of his own invention. He ignores the cardinal precepts for such fiction by prematurely revealing the poor surprises of his plot and by neglecting to develop both a crescendo of terror through the inevitability of the events he sets in motion and perhaps a sophisticated irony, which might have made more plausible the motivation of those who run his terrifying society.

1964

...............The Ancient Greece
of Mary Renault

A dull novel is bad enough, a long dull novel considerably worse, but the worst experience for one who loves fiction is a long dull novel by one who has written with vigor and imagination in the same vein before. *The Mask of Apollo* is such a book; any college writing instructor could have shown Mary Renault why it would not work.

It is not one story but two. In the first, Nikeratos, an Athenian tragic actor, discourses at length and with formidable erudition on the nature of the Greek theater and its connection with religion in the fourth century B.C. In the second, Plato and his aristocratic disciple Dion attempt to bring to Syracuse, a miserable city oppressed by a decadent tyrant, the philosophy of government outlined in *The Republic*.

Running two stories together is no great problem for a competent novelist. Miss Renault's mistake lies in making Niko not only the narrator of his own affairs, but the narrator of Plato's and Dion's as well. Niko is an all-Athenian boy, one who (if homosexuality were not condoned in ancient Athens) would have delighted Lord Baden-Powell and served as a model for the *Boy Scouts' Manual*. Niko is courageous, resourceful, magnanimous, modest, loyal, and reverent; a nimble but entirely humorless creation, he possesses just enough wit to forge ahead in his career. Naturally, he is insufferably dull. Confessing his ignorance of philosophy, he is, understandably, barely tolerated by such luminaries as Plato and Dion, who use him only as a messenger.

The result is not so much a story as a slack and protracted series of reports, delivered at secondhand, of what the interesting characters, whom the author has ruthlessly resolved to keep offstage as much as possible, are doing. To make matters worse, Miss Renault succumbs to the cheapest trick of historical fiction: The man whose name is not remembered is Aristotle; the man whose name is not caught is Plato; Aeschylus is described as a playwright "who has been with us a hundred years and looks good for another hundred."

At the very end Niko is introduced to Alexander. Suddenly the reader comes awake: Will Miss Renault's next novel tell Alexander's story? Will some youthful Macedonian narrator play Robin to Alexander's Batman? Great Zeus preserve us! *The Mask of Apollo* is proof that when Miss

Renault deals with history she is on shaky ground. ·When she deals with myth, as she did with the story of Theseus in *The King Must Die* and *The Bull from the Sea,* she is superb.

1966

Mary Renault sets her better fiction in Archaic and Hellenic Greece. None of her antique and myth-believing heroes is immune to the Sirens' singing. In the best of her novels, *The King Must Die,* Miss Renault carved from myth and archaeology the boyhood of Theseus; in the latest, *Fire from Heaven,* she works with history to reconstruct the apprenticeship of Alexander the Great. To do so, she combines two mythic inventions: the story of Achilles, which Alexander would have recognized (he thought he was a new Achilles, come to conquer Asian Greece), and the tangled demonology of Freud.

At the age of five, Alexander was precocious and something of a fanatic. Faster than most boys and a handler of horses, he planned to marry Olympias, his mother. Olympias is one of Miss Renault's most successful creations. A foreigner and a devotee of Dionysos, she detests her husband; plotting and railing against King Philip, she hints to her son that his father is really Zeus. Miss Renault does equally well with Philip, drawing a sympathetic portrayal of a barbarian king on the brink of culture, a one-eyed man who, in an age of perpetual war, lives by war and trains his armies himself.

These characterizations are true to history and are the best part of the book. To support them, Miss Renault moves her story at a regular pace through a series of set episodes: Alexander wins his manhood in battle at the age of twelve; Alexander calms the untamable horse Bucephalus; Alexander meets and loves the boy Hephaestion; an unknown philosopher named Aristotle comes to Macedon to teach the prince; Philip and Alexander win the battle that unifies all Hellas—and so on, with plenty of action and intrigue. Each episode, however, can be predicted even by readers who know nothing of Alexander's life, and Alexander himself is cast in too rigid a heroical mold to achieve much individuality. For all his chastity, anguish, and brooding sense of destiny, he seems as smooth and perplexing as his effigy, the famous marble head that was found at Pergamum.

Miss Renault ends her story with Alexander's accession to the throne. This seems strange. When we think of Alexander, we think of the famous march through western Asia, with Alexander conquering all the cities of the known world, cities with such haunting names as Ecbatana, Gaugamela, and Persepolis, while founding cities of his own—each of them named Alexandria. Has Miss Renault realized that her story is done, because fiction is more reliably tied to character than to motion, or is she saving the great progress to the steppes of Russia and the Indus River for a sequel?

1969

.......................Crossing
the Water

An excellent novel—and one I suspect will receive little attention—is Brian Burland's *A Fall from Aloft,* a stark, appalling and utterly convincing story of a young adolescent's initiation into the world of men.

James Berkeley, almost thirteen, is sent by his upper-class family in Bermuda to a fashionable school in England. "If you miss your public school education," his father said, "you miss everything," and so it seemed worthwhile to send James out, even though the year is 1942 and the only way James can get to England is to live and work with the crew of a Liberty ship, which, as part of a convoy harassed by German submarines, makes a torturous progress across the Atlantic. James, of course, is desperately seasick. The ship's sirens honk; the crew torments him; he cannot stop vomiting or bring himself to sit on an open toilet where anyone might see him. For James, the thought of dropping his pants in a public place is even worse than his fear of the enemy torpedoes.

Absurd? Certainly. What we forget too easily is how real such shame can be at age thirteen. Before the U.S. Marines unkindly usurped it, Death Before Dishonor was the private, unspoken rallying cry of every adolescent. The external physical threats to James are sickeningly real, eternally present, but they are as nothing compared to what James, in the torment of his own mind, is doing to himself. He is caught in the sick desperation of one who has lost control of his life; the comfortable world he knew has been replaced by a frightening unknown world in which a different breed of men speak an almost incomprehensible language composed almost entirely of sexual terms—and sex is what worries James. "It was with him all the time." Just the sight of women disturbs James, sends his imagination reeling, provokes memories of solitary sins. James fears he is rotten, a criminal about to be justly punished for his crimes. He is a liar, he knows, and a juvenile delinquent, but he cannot stop lying, even though he is sick with anguish about what God thinks. James concludes that he is basically evil, a sinful boy sent from the warm Bermuda waters into the cold and dangerous unknown; everyone else on the ship is going home, but he alone is leaving home, and if the Germans don't get him, vomiting and constipation will.

Burland's book is lean and powerful, creating great beauty from ugly elements, but, more than that, it is a totally believable story, a short book with no flaws, no trace of pity or wavering toward sentimentality, no phony literary devices or intrusions of adult perspectives. Every writer is tempted to write such a book and most do, but few can bring it off. There are temptations on every hand: toward romanticism, condescension, superior knowledge and a literary tone of voice, any one of which is death to fiction about children.

Burland, who has been writing for years without a discernible sign of success, had the guts to write this book honestly. He shows sailors as they are and as they talk, no better and no worse, and he shows, but does not emphasize, the failure of James' parents. More important, he reminds us of what James lacks—and what we as adults have acquired—a life that includes routine, perspective, humor, and an enjoyment of leisure. James may become a tired, toothless man, but Burland has caught him as a boy and caught him live.

1970

·················· A Woman's Novel

In the bad old days, before I took the pledge for Women's Liberation— when I was drunk on bigotry and a falling-down sexist of the most embarrassing kind, I would have said that Shirley Hazzard's *The Bay of Noon* was a novel that only a woman could write. By this I would have meant that it is an intelligent, cultured, well-written novel of the kind that women from various ports in the British Empire have written, virtually unchanged, for forty years. In women's fiction, no attempt is made to work out man's relation to the universe, but astute, even beautiful perceptions of human relationships are developed in a minor key amid thickly detailed textures of clothing, landscapes, and the weather. Women, so long denied a chance to shape society, observe it well; their novels define the games adults play—with words, with sparring encounters before the emotions can become entangled. Intense as these novels always are, they tend to fade from the memory even as they are read.

Jenny, Miss Hazzard's narrator, is an unawakened girl, in flight from a love that scares her and England's "life of indignation and Sunday roasts." A girl accustomed to playing roles defined for her by others, she goes to Naples as a translator, and there, under Vesuvius (ready to blow again and sweep all before it), she is herself translated into a warmer temperament. Jenny is all primness and reserve, but Gioconda, her glamorous Italian friend, is an open, long-suffering woman, personifying commitment and experience. Gioconda's lover Gianni, quick to tears and an insufferable egotist—"he was kind in order to be cruel"—provides the unlikely fulcrum by which Miss Hazzard moves Jenny to a kind of self-discovery.

What happens is predictable; what is said about what happens is not. I think Miss Hazzard cheats us at the end, but her graceful and civilized discourse, her descriptions of the atmosphere of Naples—"the history and geography of calamity"—with its assets concealed in malodorous streets and its past visibly woven into the fabric of its present, will endear her novel to educated women everywhere who do not demand distinction or innovation in their fiction, but who do like good writing and are *tired* of "modern novels."

1970

................Is Graham Greene a Burnt-Out Case?

The basic difference between tragedy and comedy is that tragic heroes bring to the occasion something less than what is required, comic heroes something more. Graham Greene's new novel *The Comedians* is far from a comedy; its characters have difficulty coming to terms with the responsibility life imposes. Greene, in fact, seems to be using the word in its French sense: *comédiens*—actors and hypocrites. As one character in the novel says, "As long as we pretend, we escape."

The chief pretender is the narrator, a sixty-year-old Englishman with no other name than Brown. Greene cannot allow the symbolism to pass unnoticed: "What a Brown world you live in," Brown's mistress says to him, reminding us that wit, or even bubbly good humor, has never been Greene's forte. Brown owns a hotel in Port-au-Prince, the Haiti of Dr. Duvalier's dictatorship and the terror of the *Tontons Macoute,* the Bogeymen in sunglasses whose skill in mayhem and extortion cows the populace into mute submission. Brown is a lapsed Catholic, as are most of Greene's heroes, and, like most of them, he is weathering an excruciatingly unsatisfactory love affair.

But if Brown's identity, property, faith, and love are questionable assets, Jones' position is worse. Jones (who also lacks a first name) is a liar, a soldier of fortune, in trouble with the police. Also on hand are Smith, an American vegetarian armed with the dignity of foolish innocence, and a Haitian doctor in revolt against the regime, a committed Marxist whom Greene has failed to develop as a foil to his *comédiens.* This Dr. Magiot is, in fact, very much like Camus' Dr. Rieux. "You cannot stop martyrs," Magiot says, "you can only try to reduce their number."

Accidie, that splenetic sense of uselessness and alienation, is the hallmark of all of Greene's fiction; in this novel it is identified as acidity, which Smith says is the result of eating meat and the cause of all the world's woes. Nevertheless, the acidity of life is not here brought into focus, as it is in Greene's most memorable fiction, by contrasting it to the desperation and commitment of others who achieve a tragic stature. We are used to shabby heroes in Greene's novels, but Brown, whose only vision of a lost and better world is a naked girl in a swimming pool, is positively tattered, without any redeeming qualities at all.

1966

Something embarrassing happened last night to Richard Burton and Alec Guinness. Well into the third hour of their Metrocolor disaster *The Comedians,* they found themselves occupying a quarter acre of screen with nothing to do and with precious little to say.

The script writer was snoozing and the director was dozing, but the camera, presumably working at union scale, was willing to run on, so there they were, two of the most highly trained and exciting talents in acting today, hunkering on their heels, remembering when each of them played Hamlet, and trying very hard not to look at each other. I know how they felt. If I could have avoided it, I would not have been looking at them either.

All three of us were impatiently awaiting the end of *The Comedians,* once a flaccid novel by Graham Greene and now an outrageous film produced and directed by Peter Glenville. Since Greene claims credit for the screenplay, he also must accept much of the blame for translating his novel's curious atmosphere of depletion and hypocrisy, religious impotence and sexual enervation, into banal episodes of grossness and vulgarity.

Glenville, who is capable of better work, capped the fiasco by deciding that Greene's tawdry, nearly anonymous characters should be played by Richard and Elizabeth Burton (that's $2,000,000 in casting right there, and wasted, too, if you don't allow them time for at least five clinch scenes), by Guinness, Peter Ustinov, Paul Ford, and Lillian Gish. Ford, I suppose, could waffle contentedly through any role assigned him, but the rest of the cast is obviously having a hell of an awful time. The Burtons have never been worse and even Ustinov, who can usually smirk his way past any part, nearly suffocates under his lines.

Glenville and Greene, disinclined to weave two plots together, switch back and forth between Story A, which concerns the Burtons, and Story B, which concerns the Haiti of Papa Doc Duvalier, his *Tontons Macoute*, or secret police in sunglasses, and the rest of the unfortunate actors. Burton is a down-and-out Britisher who owns a hotel in Port-au-Prince. Tourism is slim because everybody in Haiti lives in fear of the regime, so Burton has nothing better to do than sleep with Elizabeth Taylor, who is married to an ambassador, Peter Ustinov. The rest of Story A involves the Burtons asking each other: Whom else have you been sleeping with?

Story B involves Guinness, a seedy mercenary who cheats Papa Doc's army by way of a bogus weapons deal, Paul Ford and Lillian Gish, who try to sell Haiti on vegetarianism, and some Haitians ("Haiti means Hate!" they shout), who are brewing a revolution in the distant hills. The vegetarians, their idealism somewhat shredded, retire in disarray, and Guinness is exposed and hunted down.

There is plenty of sadism—shootings, beatings, and throat cuttings—and a little panoply: a voodoo orgy, an execution witnessed by schoolchildren, and Liz Taylor's unfettered bosom bouncing behind a transparent nightgown. Whenever Glenville takes his story outside, into the horror of the Haitian streets, it becomes believable, but whenever he moves it inside, and the characters talk for more than sixty seconds, it isn't. Greene's dialogue is more tortured than anything the *Tontons* can devise:

"We meet tonight at the Voodoo Temple," a Haitian says. "Come and join us." "I sometimes think," says Ustinov, looking very thoughtful indeed, "that Haiti's no different from life anywhere."

Liz Taylor: "Does it hurt your mouth when we kiss?"

Dick Burton: "It's a good hurt."

Later Liz says: "You can't be jealous of the past."

Dick replies: "Oh, yes, I can. One day I'll be the past."

Later still, Dick says: "Your belly is like a heap of wheat," but Liz has the answer to that one: "I think you're a defrocked priest." Could Graham Greene have seen *The Sandpiper*?

1967

It takes a great deal of talent to become a Famous Author, but it doesn't take much talent to remain one. Think of Tennessee Williams and Edward Albee, of James Gould Cozzens and C. P. Snow. To assure a warmly comfortable senescence, a writer need only generate a great blast of heat at the beginning of his career; then, when he turns fifty or so, he can turn his burners back to medium low, warm up a few leftovers every couple of years, and rest assured no one will notice. Not the Book-of-the-Month Club, which will continue to select whatever he writes, and not (alas) the critics, who will continue to review his books as if they were still important.

Take, for example, Graham Greene. The facts in his case are clear: no living British author has written as much good fiction as Greene; still, he has not written any good fiction in nine years. Greene's stature as a major writer is assured because his novels once presented a coherent and alarming vision of man's role in the universe. The world is racked by pain, Greene said, and man is irresistibly drawn toward sin, but pain teaches men to understand the world, and as for sin—those who understand it understand salvation, too. Priest and atheist are equally eligible for redemption as long as they are committed men, engaged in the nasty, brutal, and often banal, business of living. To be saved, one must—as Revelation has it—be either hot or cold; it was the lukewarm men that Greene spewed from his mouth. In his last two novels, however, Greene himself shows signs of the enervation he once deplored in other men. His vision is crumbling; the fight no longer seems worth the trouble; the shabby people with tacky lives of whom he has always written seem incapable of genuine anguish or despair—they are simply shabby people with tacky lives and, as such, are no more than figures of fun. The tragedy is gone; the banality remains, and the lukewarm man whom Greene would have once despised becomes the narrator of the latest novel, *Travels with My Aunt*.

Henry Pulling, a bachelor in his fifties, accepted early retirement from his bank. Having spent most of his life looking after other peoples' money, he plans to spend the rest looking after his dahlias. Then his mother dies and, at the cremation, Henry meets her sister, his Aunt Augusta, a woman in her seventies. "I was present once at a premature cremation" are Augusta's opening words, and it is not long before we take her measure: a British Auntie Mame, with more respect for the libido than for the law; an imperious free spirit who has escaped from a brothel and now sleeps with a black dope runner while waiting for her ancient lover to return. Greene, I fear, thinks she has style. Augusta immediately takes Henry in hand. She tells him that the ashes in the urn are not those of his real mother—guess, reader, who his real mother is— and she pulls him protesting on a series of trips: to the seacoast, where she tells him how she helped run a church for dogs; to Istanbul, where she flummoxes the chief of police; to Paraguay, where she joins her lover in a life of crime. For Henry, it is a journey of the soul—"I discovered in myself a streak of anarchy"—and the easiest thing for the reader to do, short of not reading the book at all, is to agree that Henry is saved in the end.

The book, of course, is intended as self-parody. Greene includes most of the accidentals of his fiction—tattered cabs and battered trains, innocent and ambiguous Americans, incompetent police and persistent spies, a tropical landscape, cranky minor characters, and religious nuts—but none of the substance of his fiction. Here, everything is laughable, which would be all right if what Greene wrote were really funny. But it isn't. Admittedly, the British are fond of a kind of damp, drab, understated humor that is good for an occasional curl of the lip or a snort through a wrinkled nose, but this kind of humor, eminently suited to Britain's fogs and chilly drizzles, doesn't travel well. "I sometimes believe in a Higher Power," Augusta says, "even though I am a Catholic." It takes great determination to laugh at that, but a grimace is in order.

To be fair, there is better humor in the stories Augusta tells, stories I will not retell because they would lose something in translation. The book is, in fact, a collection of jokes and anecdotes that I suspect Greene has hoarded for years—bits and scraps that occur to him at cocktail parties or after he turns out the light at night—knowing he could not develop them beyond a paragraph or a page or two, but determined not to waste them, planning all along to write a book into which he could squeeze them, each and every one.

Travels with My Aunt is the sputtering confession of an unredeemably uninteresting man. We are enjoined to hate the sin and love the sinner, but it is impossible to hate a book so pleasantly, so inanely inconsequential as this. The sinner, though, must take some blame: for letting his talent disintegrate into mellow tastelessness. Greene was a strong man, a tiger in fiction, but he seems toothless now and—what's worse—glad of it.

1970

*   *   *

Where should an autobiography end? With the author's death, of course, if that is possible, and Graham Greene, by defining failure as a kind of death, ends his account of his early life with the failure that beset him after the publication of his first novel. Very neat: the kind of pessimism we expect from Greene. Notice the title: *A Sort of Life*; the pessimism has already begun. Notice his first memory: "The first thing I remember is sitting in a pram at the top of a hill with a dead dog lying at my feet." Some years ago, Greene entered and lost a contest for the best opening line of a new Graham Greene thriller. He is not about to lose here. What did we expect? Browning's "roses, roses, all the way"? Hardly. Though Greene admires Browning, stressing the sensuality of the verse, his early recollections are of a man who slit his throat and a witch in a linen closet. He learned terror early and distinguished it from fear: "From terror one escapes screaming, but fear has an odd seduction."

His childhood was ordinary enough: eccentric aunts, perishing pets, toys and collections, games and books. He "particularly liked the dull historical parts" in G. A. Henty's novels and still admires Beatrix Potter's books. "Early reading," he writes, "has more influence on conduct than any religious teaching." In the school where his father was headmaster, he recognized that he belonged to "the side of the victims, not of the torturers . . . I had left civilization behind and entered a savage country of strange customs and inexplicable cruelties." He dodged sports to read in private, takes a dim view of those who were sympathetic: "Kindness, alas! is often false kindness, enabling one to endure a little longer an almost unbearable situation." It is that famous pessimism again, in this book wed to the kind of aphorism old men favor in their memoirs—the kind young men dare not use.

In school, Greene tried to injure himself; at sixteen, he went into psychoanalysis. Manic-depressive tendencies persisted: throughout his life Greene has tried to stave off what he calls boredom, the same affliction that Baudelaire called spleen. For kicks, he played Russian roulette by himself with his brother's pistol. The effect was like that of a drug: "I remember an extraordinary sense of jubilation." And yet it was not enough: Because the odds were five to one for survival, he played the game six times. Then, because boredom continually threatened, he tried drink. "For nearly one term I went to bed drunk every night and began drinking again immediately when I woke." Because danger was the best remedy, he volunteered to spy for the Germans—and very nearly did so.

An unsettled beginning to a life, surely. Greene tried and abandoned several occupations, wrote two unpublished novels, but was not entirely discouraged: "There is a splinter of ice in the heart of a writer. I watched and listened." His first published novel, *The Man Within,* sold well, but his success dwindled until his tenth novel, *The Power and the Glory,* drew a first printing of only 3,500 copies. "For a writer," Greene insists, ". . . success is always temporary, success is only a delayed failure." If Graham Greene says so, what are lesser writers to expect? Because Greene's good fiction is long behind him, *A Sort of Life* is his best book since *A Burnt-Out Case.* Because it only suggests the perils and intrigue that he courted in later life, a sequel is very much in order, but I doubt that we will see one. The present volume has an air of finality about it.

1971

Three

. . . . Here
There Be Dragons

There was a Dragon or winged Serpent brought unto Francis the French king, by a certain Countryman, who had slain the same Serpent himself with a Spade, when it set upon him in the fields to kill him. And this thing was witnessed by many learned and credible men who saw the same: and they thought it was not bred in that Country, but rather driven by the wind thither from some foreign Nation. For France was never known to breed any such Monsters.

I have always liked that story. It comes from Edward Topsell, who, three and a half centuries ago, published an encyclopedia containing all that men then knew about the animal world. Topsell had never seen a dragon, but he was not a bigot and had no reason to doubt their existence; in his chapters on dragons, he reported what he believed to be true. The story charms me because of its suggestion of banality. The French sages approach the incident with disdain, as if it were already an anachronism, as if it were bad taste for such a beast to wander into France.

Brueghel might have painted such a scene: rolling farmlands and a stormy sky; some barns here, cows there, and trees beyond; a child with buckets in the foreground; and, off in a corner, in a half-dug turnip field, a peasant turns from his labors to swat a winged serpent. Once, twice, and again with the edge of his shovel across its neck, just behind its ear. The dragon dies, exuding a stale smell. No flames, no smoke, just a small beast with tattered scales and leather wings that bore it on a gale from Transylvania. No need for a knight with lance and armor; any farmer and his spade will do. The Great Days are gone forever.

Topsell may be the only authority on monsters not quoted in *The Book of Imaginary Beings,* a marvelous miscellany written and assembled by the great Argentinean writer Jorge Luis Borges, with the help of Margarita Guerrero. In the most important sense, Borges is a believer. He does not believe, of course, in the literal existence of the monsters he describes but in their necessity, in the way they enlarge man's perspective on himself. "We are ignorant of the meaning of the dragon," he writes, "in the same way that we are ignorant of the meaning of the universe, but there is something in the dragon's image that fits man's imagination."

Something that fits, that man needs: This is why we have monsters. According to Genesis, God gave man dominion over the animals, and ever since, man has exploited animals, labeled animals, and put them behind bars in zoos. But man has needs for beasts. We need beasts to make sense of the world, beasts like the Calchona, which snatches lunch baskets from travelers and mutters sullen threats, and the Remora, a sucking fish that holds back ships, lawsuits, and expected babies. Most importantly, we need beasts that have nothing to do with man, that are of no use to a utilitarian society. We need beasts safe from man's relentless denaturing of nature—centaurs, gnomes, and unicorns— which we can only contemplate, which in themselves are invitations to joy, to fear, and to delight. "Teach me," wrote John Donne, "to hear mermaids singing, Or to keep off envy's stinging."

Borges is critical; he introduces us only to the best beasts that man's imagination has created, presenting each with grace and gravity. His entries are short, supple and erudite. Borges draws his stories from Norse, Greek, and Egyptian sources; he quotes Arab zoologists and Byzantine grammarians, Vedic tales and Buddhist philosophers; he seems equally familiar with Mazdaism, Zarathustrianism, and the Cabala.

And what animals he gives us! The Basilisk with its deadly stare is the most horrible of beasts; it makes its own desert wherever it goes. The Celestial Stag lives in mines and begs miners to take it to the light. The Squonk, with its ill-fitting skin, can be hunted by the tears it leaves in its track. The Chinese Fox lives eight hundred to one thousand years, sets fires with its tail, looks into the future, and changes at will into an old man, a young lady, or a scholar. Zaratan, the sea turtle, sleeps with his shell above the water; sailors landing on him suppose him to be an island, but when they set their fires, Zaratan awakes.

Brownies and Carbuncles, Golems and Griffons, Hydras, Harpies, Krakens, and Satyrs—it is hard to think of any superior creature Borges has barred from his enchanting bestiary. He passes on whatever precise information he has heard: Plutarch, for instance, says that nymphs live more than 9,720 years, and Tacitus reports that the Phoenix returns every 1,461 years. Such information must be preserved; we are not likely to come by it again.

Borges is an alchemist, transmuting wonder into words. His genius lies in his ability to distill from many base sources the essence of these awesome creatures. The best of his accounts—like that of the day to come when the creatures who live in mirrors will revolt against the men who locked them there—are as disquieting as his remarkable short stories; like mythical worms, they burrow beneath our skins to gnaw at some nerve we have not yet discovered.

Strangely, the young seem least convinced by the necessity of myth. "The Sirens of Greek mythology," a college freshman wrote this fall, "were associated with enticing men and carrying them off to meet their doom. The times warranted such beliefs, but with new values there is no place for such fantasies. The hardships of reality make men immune to these powers." Do they, indeed? *The Book of Imaginary Beings,* adroitly translated by Norman Thomas di Giovanni in collaboration with the author, is a short book, but I doubt there is a limit to what it contains.

1969

An imitation of life, that's what Aristotle tells us art must be: Stories of heroes and the fall of kings will educate the common man to heightened moral sensibility. True enough, I guess. Most of the best art—and nearly all of the worst—to which we Westerners have been exposed adheres to this tradition. But Aristotle is practically a kissing cousin of ours. He laid down the law for art a mere 2,400 years ago in a society secure enough, rational enough, to argue about its own validity.

Art is older than that. The other tradition, the anti-Aristotelian tradition, goes back 22,000 years to the caves at Altamira, and perhaps even beyond that to some dim dawn when man first acquired more calories than he needed to survive. With his extra energy, he picked up a chalk, held it in the same grip he used for fine work on his flints, and sketched a buffalo—not a real buffalo posing for its portrait, but a buffalo of the mind, the idea of the beast that he would like to eat that night.

So we have the oldest of all traditions of art: the artist as maker, as magician, the conscious expert at artifice who never shows us how the trick is done, never admits to trickery at all. Jorge Luis Borges is such a magician. Blind now, he rejoices in his interior vision, weaving symbols, as he says, of "the unimaginable universe." He has taken on creation, the universe seen as a whole, the transmigration of souls, dual identities, the nature of reality and of incarnations, and the trick that history has of repeating itself. "A maker of dreams" is the description Borges once offered of himself, which places him precisely among the ranks of those who have used art as magic. The caveman used art to subdue nature and the spirit world. Later, the magicians—Pygmalion is the mythical example—introduced into the so-called real world, the world of the senses and experience, something that had not been there before. Later still, the artist as magician found he could do better: He could make another world.

This is what Borges does. Like Lewis Carroll, Borges is skeptical of man's ability to understand himself or the tracks he leaves across a world whose boundaries he cannot guess. Lacking a world of certainties, Borges seems to say, let us create a world that at least asks one proper question. There is a handsome selection of Borges' worlds and questions in his new collection, *The Aleph and Other Stories 1933-1969.* The stories, written originally in Spanish, have not so much been translated as rethought into English by Borges himself and his collaborator, Norman Thomas di Giovanni.

Several are among the finest any writer in this century has produced. In the title story, for instance, Borges discovers, in the home of a tedious friend who has been trying to set down a description of the entire world, an aleph, which is to space what eternity is to time. An aleph contains in one point in space—a tiny, shining sphere barely an inch across—*all* points in space seen at once from all angles, in undiminished size, without transparency or overlapping. Borges leads us to his aleph gently, but his description of what he finds there is a poem worth brooding on. In another story, a man dreams into existence another man, only to find, to his relief, that he himself is dreamed of by another. Two of Borges' detective stories are included: In one, the detective is lured by his own cleverness to his destruction. "You'll say reality is under no obligation to be interesting," he says before he is caught. "To which I'd reply that reality may disregard the obligation but that we may not." There it is: We do not imitate reality; we create a world that cannot fail to hold our interest. Borges the magician: He writes of knife duels by night, of a fugitive turned hunter who recognizes his quarry as himself. In his best story, he tells of a man who died a coward, but not before he had, through the power of his will, reversed his role in a long-forgotten battle to that of heroism—and reversed the memory of those who were there as well. Perhaps I made him up, Borges suggests, or then perhaps I made up a man who really did exist.

Fashions in fiction change. For the moment, the Aristotelian idea of fiction as an imitation of life seems exhausted. While it pants by the sidelines, waiting to catch its breath, writers who create worlds of their own, writers like Beckett, Borges, Nabokov, Gass, and Barthelme, hold our attention. They are the heirs of the Pleistocene magicians.

1970

.... Radical Innocence

By Act I, Scene 4, Shakespeare had lost whatever chance he might have had to make a comedy of *Hamlet*. It is at that point, you remember, during the ghost-watch, that Horatio asks about the noise of revelry coming from the clean, well-lighted part of the castle. Hamlet replies with an ill-tempered diatribe against the king's wassail and the kettledrums and trumpets that accompany the drinking. It sounds like fun to me (when I want to drink to drums, I must put a record on), and in a comedy it *would* be fun: We'd leave Hamlet to his damp debating and join Claudius and the boys, slapping our thighs and downing Rhenish wine.

Both tragedy and comedy are concerned with excess. Tragedy takes a dim view of it—it is, as Hamlet says, the fault that corrupts virtue—but some of our greatest comedy extols it. There are, after all, only four elements, but we have five senses with which to celebrate them; why should we be so well-equipped if we were not meant to taste the food and drink, to touch the cloths and women? Great comedy reveals not only the vanity of human endeavor but also its exhilaration. Intensity is what counts; we should all die spent and out of breath.

The exhilaration of excess, which wrings the juice and joy from life, and the loneliness of excess, which is ultimately fatal either to our bodies or our spirits, are the twin themes of Gabriel García Márquez's masterly comic novel *One Hundred Years of Solitude*. The story concerns the history of Macondo, an imaginary town in the interior of Colombia, and six generations of the Buendía family, the leaders of the town from its birth until its destruction. If you look sideways at Macondo, you may see in it the story of all of South America—a story of dreams and adventure, of corruption, war, and decadence, all in a dramatic landscape—but if you open both eyes wide in wonder, Macondo's story becomes that of the world itself, a world that begins with the fresh innocence of Genesis and ends with the windy plagues of Revelation.

"The world was so recent," García Márquez writes in his third sentence, "that many things lacked names, and in order to indicate them it was necessary to point." It is an enchanting idea, and the first indication that García Marquez is up to something very different and very much his own. "Macondo was already a fearful whirlwind of dust and rubble being spun about by the wrath of the biblical hurricane," García Márquez writes in the third sentence from the end of his book, but by then, his pattern is clear. Like most great writers, García Márquez dismisses the dreary idea that art is an imitation of life. Instead, he creates a world of his own, a world that in some ways resembles the one we know but joyously ignores the laws of time and probability. It is a significant world, full of signs and messages. The excesses of one of the Buendías with his concubine make the domestic animals fertile. When the first Buendía dies, yellow flowers rain all night; when his son dies, his blood runs through the streets of Macondo and into his parents' house where, avoiding the rugs, it stops at the feet of his mother.

José Arcadio Buendía founded Macondo because, after twenty-six months of marching with his friends and their families cross-jungle through Colombia, they had not found the sea and it was too much trouble to return. They settled in a torrid swamp, not far from a place where a landlocked Spanish galleon rotted among the flowers. For some time, their only contact with the world was with gypsies. José Arcadio, a dreamer, thought that with the magnets the gypsies brought he might draw gold from the ground; with their magnifying glass, he might revolutionize warfare; and with the ice they also brought—"This is the great invention of our time," José Arcadio says—he might build cool cities if, of course, ice could someday be made from a common material like water. He died mad, as you might expect, tied to a tree as he planned, with the ghost of a man he had killed, ways to pass "the tedious Sundays of death."

The male Buendías are named either José Arcadio or Aureliano. The former are introverts who lock themselves into an alchemist's laboratory to knock at the foundations of existence, and the latter, like Colonel Aureliano Buendía, who started and lost thirty-two wars and became a corrupt fanatic in the name of the liberal cause, are men of drastic and disastrous action, rattling at the foundations of society. The female Buendías are almost as interesting: One, after encouraging and rejecting several lovers, died a virgin; another, the most beautiful woman the world had ever seen, was lifted to heaven one day as she stood shaking a sheet on the lawn. And so it goes in Macondo, a town that has no need for a magistrate because there is no disorder, no need for a priest because everyone has made his own arrangements with God and has lost the evil of original sin. It cannot last, of course: The rot, the decay, the cruelty and violence set in as the community collapses, but one is left at the end with the impression of a kind of radical innocence. The woman who bleeds to death because her "passionate blood was insensible to any artifice that did not come from love" is somehow typical of all the Buendías.

Solitude is one of the best novels to be published in this country in several years. It deserves a great success, a success it may not attain because in this country there has long been an unfortunate resistance to Latin-American literature. Some readers may be put off by its length, by its quantity of characters with similar names, or by its episodic quality. Still, *Solitude* is a rich and inventive book, one of the rare novels that can continually surprise the reader. The surge of life in García Márquez's characters is so great that even if we have known them for no more than a few score pages, we are astonished when they die, or go insane, or are corrupted, or wither away. García Márquez is a consummate comic writer. He knows that in his kind of story, transitions are not necessary; that in the comic tradition, a writer can play on what the reader already knows or assumes about human behavior—no explanation of actions or motives is necessary.

To one who knows no Spanish, Gregory Rabassa's translation seems inspired.

1970

..........................The Artist as Moral Hero

One is enough to change a man's life, but anyone who cares for reading remembers a few more: novels that seem to contain the truth about man and his endeavors. We must be young to respond to them properly. In our flat-stomach, single-chin years, when we switch philosophies as often as our shirts, we are excited by novels of ideas, novels in which characters talk of suffering, self-doubt, and what, if anything, a man must do. Later, when certainty becomes less of a possibility, we may still admire these books, but they may not seem as *right*. I cannot be sure what I would think of them today, but I cannot forget my first encounter with novels like *Man's Fate, The Stranger,* and *The Plague.*

When I was in college, I knew that André Malraux and Albert Camus were the most exciting living novelists. They wrote violent and difficult stories, affirming the dignity of man by proclaiming the necessity of action. Their ideas were aphoristic and argumentative; their prose was somehow both sensuous and lean. Moreover, both men were *engaged*. Writing was not enough, they had risked their necks, they were moralists turned heroes. They had not only written about pain, despair, and death; they had confronted them and found them wanting. "The great courage," Camus wrote, "is still to gaze as squarely at the light as at death." What Camus once wrote of Malraux applies equally well to himself: "This secret fusion of experience and thought, of life and reflection on the meaning of life, is what makes the great novelist."

For Camus, life was a struggle toward humility; for Malraux, it is a struggle against humiliation. It comes to nearly the same thing, as we can see from Camus' *Lyrical and Critical Essays* and Malraux's *Anti-Memoirs*. Camus, in his essays, tried on ideas he later worked into his major books, while Malraux, in a rather guarded way, sums up in his memoir much of what his novels and his books on art have said.

Malraux's peculiar title is not only a play on his initials, it is an announcement that this strange and noble book is not what we expected. It is, in fact, all kinds of books at once. There is fiction: a section of an abandoned novel bearing upon Malraux's family history, and a novelette touching upon the author's principal theme. There is history: Malraux, much moved by Gandhi's Salt March and by the Long March of the Chinese Communists, retells both stories. There is a great deal of smoky travel writing in which the author puffs over Vedic nights and Merovingian dawns as he spins through time and space, from the Queen of Sheba's desert capital to the caves of Lascaux and the crypts of Guatemala. There is a lot of talk, too, about art and the ancient gods, and even more talk, already out of date, about French and American foreign policy. There are some grand war scenes: Malraux trapped in a tank, waiting for the shell that would annihilate him; Malraux, laughing as a firing squad raised its rifles toward his chest. But something, in all of this riot of color, philosophy, and rich prose, is missing.

What is missing is André Malraux. There are few facts about his life that he cares to reveal—nothing about the rumors that, as a young man, he stole Khmerian sculpture from the Orient and worked for Chiang Kai-shek, nothing about his early sympathy for Communism, and only passing mention of his role as chief of the Loyalist air force in the Spanish Civil War, or about how, as commander of an Alsatian partisan brigade, he liberated the Grünewald altarpiece from a cellar where the Germans hid it. Clearly, Malraux enjoys watching the mystery attending his career solidify as myth, though sometimes it is hard not to believe that both he and it are no more than figments of the French imagination.

"Art and death are all I hope to rediscover here," he writes, warning the reader that there will be no confessions in this book, none of the nickel-and-dime particulars that make men human. It will be, all the way, Major Issues like justice and endurance and Big Questions, because a man can be defined only by the questions that he asks. It is almost too much, all this palaver of eternal concerns. Not by such abstractions do we get to know a man; only by knowing the man do the abstractions take on meaning.

Anti-Memoirs is a magisterial and very public book that is finally redeemed as a personal testament by its author's admission that, after all, it is not death that matters but the possibility that a man be degraded before he dies. How, Malraux asks, can a man know that he can remain a man unless he has stood up under torture? Malraux, who had written much about the question, was nearly tortured by the Germans. Because of a bureaucratic mix-up, he was spared. The secret these memoirs reveal, the chink in Malraux's armor that shows the flesh beneath the iron, is his regret that he was *not* tortured, that he had not had a chance to prove his manhood in this way. "My experience," he writes, "is almost valueless." Here the man and not the monument is speaking.

Otherwise, the book is valuable for its portraits of world leaders. That of Malraux's master, Charles de Gaulle, is unexceptional; his authority emerges, but nothing of his stubborn arrogance or his malicious meddling. There are remarkable portraits of Chou En-lai and Mao Tse-tung talking about what matters most to them—China and its future in the world. Most extraordinary of all, however, is a sequence of conversations Malraux had with Nehru in which they discussed the philosophies of prison and of art, the differences between Eastern and Western approaches to life, and, finally, the difficulties involved in creating a state that is both strong and just. Malraux tends, in reconstructing these dialogues, to make everyone talk as Malraux writes. But if the result is stiff and stagy, rather like Shaw's *Don Juan in Hell* without the wit, it is informed, provocative, and, since no one else has had such conversations with such people, unique.

Resistance, Rebellion, and Death, published by Knopf eight years ago, contained Camus' most important essays on political and social concerns. Those in *Lyrical and Critical Essays* deal with landscapes and literature. Some are disarming, most are discerning; all should appeal to anyone who cares for Camus, but none should doubt that this is a collection of the writer's lesser work.

The first selection contains three short volumes of essays, *The Wrong Side and the Right Side, Nuptials,* and *Summer.* In them, Camus celebrates his childhood on the Algerian coast with a sensual appreciation of the sun, the sea, and "this heat-soaked sky"—the stilling effect upon a man that nature has when it has become a part of one's inmost self. There is, in the early essays, a surprisingly anti-intellectual note—a belief in the predominance of body over mind—but there is also the first stirring of the joyful pessimism that marks Camus' mature work, and that was perhaps best expressed in his late essay on the novelist Roger Martin du Gard. "To be certain only of men," Camus wrote, "and to know that men have little worth, is the cry of pain that runs through the whole of this work . . . this fundamental doubt is the same doubt that is hidden in every love and that gives it its tenderest vibration."

In the later essays on Gide, Faulkner, Sartre, and Melville, Camus more closely defined the artist's role as a revolt against the human condition, a "refusal to despair" at the absurdity of a life without God, without a meaning other than man can provide. "The key words, the final secrets," he wrote, "are not in man's possession. . . . The community of joy and reconciliation."

A bleak message, perhaps. One has only to look at pictures of Camus or to read his letter to an acquaintance who made impertinent demands upon his time to think that life *was* bleak for him—and is, for the rest of us, bleaker than we realize. But Camus did not think so. In his own life, he avoided envy and bitterness, felt a closer connection to the physical world than most of us, who live in cruel northern climes, will ever know. He believed in what man could become and in what the artist could do to better the lot of others. He wrote the best prose of his generation. In an interview given toward the end of his life, he said: "At the center of my work there is an invisible sun."

1968

. . . . An Overcooked Novel

The Frenchman, as any Frenchman will tell you, cannot exactly be said to have a monopoly on intelligence, but he will admit to a better understanding of the elements of intelligence: *la raison* (sense, judgment, and proportion) and *la clarté* (limpidity, perspicuity, and clearness). Since he uses what Kate Simon calls "the language that expresses emotion and thought more precisely and clearly than any other," how can an intelligent French novelist go wrong?

It may not be easy, but Françoise Mallet-Joris has done it. She left her new novel in the oven too long; its ironies and effects emerge gray and overdone, and its juices have disappeared altogether. *Signs and Wonders* suffers from an excess of intelligence and craftsmanship as well as from a deficiency of genius and passion. If it offers little dialogue and less plot, it runs twice as long as it should have done and involves more characters than can possibly hold a reader's attention.

The situation (one can hardly call it a plot) is complex. The hero, Nicolas Léclusier, is a metaphysical cripple, "afflicted with the malady of the Absolute, the malady of God." At thirty-five he flees the significance of life, the little signs and portents which seem to point to meaning but which actually contradict each other, in an attempt to find a choice other than "to live a lie or not to live." Nicolas has outlived one mistress who proved "purity can only die" and has abandoned another, an opium addict, who seems to prove that corruption can only live.

In the summer of 1962, Nicolas takes Marcelle, the girl who is to become his third mistress, to the south of France. For a new magazine controlled by the O.A.S. they interview French refugees flooding in from Algeria. Marcelle, at twenty-eight, has had many men. Gauche and unthinking, quite the opposite of Nicolas, she takes life as she finds it until Nicolas offers her his; *then* she begins to worry. Meanwhile Mme. Mallet-Joris distracts us with other characters. Paul, Nicolas' father, is a proper and progressive man who comes alive only when he assumes the care of Nicolas' abandoned mistress. Wanda, Nicolas' mother, long thought dead, survives a Nazi concentration camp to marry the German guard who saved her. Simon, Nicolas' brother, is a priest whose life is wasted because he has "caught this leprosy of misery and erosion of the soul."

Even as her novel reaches its closing pages, Mme. Mallet-Joris is busy introducing new characters: A general, a singer, a ballet dancer, a whore, a deputy, a homosexual, émigrés, mothers, and magazine executives—all hold the stage for a while and treat us to detailed examinations of their inner *angsts*. Each has tried to put his life in order; each is crucified by his failure to do so. In fact, Mme. Mallet-Joris often introduces her characters in contrasting pairs to show us how neatly she is covering every condition of life.

Where does it all lead, "this eternal quest, this eternal suffering and absurd torture that is life?" Mme. Mallet-Joris doesn't tell us. A pity, because she is an intelligent writer who, with her concern for individuals, issues, and ideas, has the courage to buck the trend of the *nouveau roman*. Some of her scenes and characters come alive, but in general her artifice is too evident. Her characters' problems are not developed but stated only in abstract terms; they touch the reader no more than they seem to touch their author. *Signs and Wonders* is a handsome failure.

1967

................A Dreamer's
Novel

The Other Side of the Mountain, a very short novel by the late Michel Bernanos, begins as a boy's adventure story and ends as nightmare. An eighteen-year-old boy on a galleon bound for Peru makes friends with the ship's cook. Later, when the ship is becalmed, and the food and water are exhausted, the crew turns to murder and cannibalism. The ship sinks in a whirlpool, but the two escape (or do they?), to be cast on a deserted shore where the sky is red, the stars are strange, carnivorous plants grow among trees that bow each night to a singing mountain, and statues in human form show faces frozen in fear. "Death," as the cook observes, "is on the prowl alongside of life—here as everywhere else, only a little more so, that's all." Stubbornly, the boy and the man struggle to stay alive, but it is clear they will not succeed.

An allegory, a vision of hell, or a parable of a trip on LSD? Probably, the book is none of these. It *is* fantasy, and it may point toward a vision of the world as a voyage through blood and fear with only the struggle, and perhaps friendship, to sustain us. What happens to these two on land may be, in fact, a repetition of what happened to them at sea. In any event, this kind of story, like surrealist painting, cannot be taken on any other than its own terms; it appeals not to our reason but to some obscure subcortical nerve. It is a book for those who enjoy, and are a bit frightened by, their dreams.

1969

. . . . Italo Calvino:
Cosmicomics

Somewhat diffidently, I offer my favorite book in many months: *Cosmicomics,* a collection of short stories by Italo Calvino. These are not great or even important stories, but they are *rare* and witty tales, told with such beauty and imagination that I am convinced that those who read them are richer than those who do not.

Each story begins with a scientific theory, correct or otherwise, of what took place in the early days when time and space began. Then Qfwfq, narrator of all the stories, agrees and tells us what it was really like before the sun was born, or when the universe was compressed into a single dot, or the fun of using the first hydrogen atoms to play marbles in curved space. How did the sun look when seen through a still gelatinous earth? What did one do in a flat nebula before matter existed? How did one see in a world without an atmosphere to break light up into its colored rays?

Does it sound corny? It isn't. These are a poet's conceptions, not a storyteller's collection of characters and action. Four of the stories are exceptionally fine. In one, Qfwfq recalls when the moon was still so close to earth that adventurous souls could pole-vault to its surface. In another, he circles at the edge of our galaxy, making signs he hopes to find when he returns in 200,000,000 years, signs "created before the beginning of forms," but which nevertheless have much to do with the idea of a man's identity. Later, Qfwfq emigrates from the sea to the land, leaving an uncle who remained a fish in the old country, an uncle convinced that the emergence of land was a temporary phenomenon. Later still, Qfwfq becomes the last of the dinosaurs, returning to a new race that has discovered both disbelief and racial prejudice.

Awe, splendor, delight, and laughter—these are the substance of Calvino's curious tales. *Cosmicomics* is a slim book, but the kind you will want to put in that slim bookcase of books to be read sometime again. William Weaver's translation, to one who knows no Italian, seems about as good as they come.

1968

.... An Early
Modern Master

If you come in close and squint a bit, you'll see the parts you recognize: a torpid, bourgeois town. Men mumbling over politics and flags flying on birthdays. A pretty waitress at the inn. A cripple, jeered at by the citizenry, and a pure and plucky spinster (has she a secret after all?). The schoolmaster drinks, of course. And a ravishingly lovely girl: One man has died of love for her, and another, her fiancé, is conveniently off at sea. The town is in Norway. We must forgive this eccentricity because the novel is Norwegian, but it is not such an impediment to recognition as it might seem: All the big nineteenth-century novels have interchangeable furniture. Enter the hero, to traditional themes: He is nervous, articulate, romantic; his life is poetry and his behavior a scandal. He is attractive and probably wealthy; before the book is done he will be waiting for poison to convulse his entrails as he tears at the turf in the midnight woods, and that's all right, too. We remember Julien Sorel and Anna Karenina. *Mysteries,* Knut Hamsun's second major novel, was written in 1892.

But now, if you step back, you will see that *Mysteries* is not a nineteenth-century novel at all. A novel's furniture is there to be shoved around; it is the eye of the decorator that counts and Hamsun, perhaps more than any other writer at work in the 1890's, prefigured techniques and attitudes that became familiar thirty or forty years later. By the time the age caught up with his innovations, he was already in his decline; he won the Nobel Prize in 1920, after his best work was long past, and in his old age Hamsun endorsed Hitler. Now, in a series of lively new translations, Hamsun's early novels have been made available to Americans who are familiar not only with modernism, which Hamsun helped to create, but with such brilliantly deceptive parodies of nineteenth-century novels as John Fowles' *The French Lieutenant's Woman.*

We must look again at what Hamsun does. Johan Nagel, the romantic intruder who falls desperately in love with Dagny, the beautiful and thoroughly engaged girl, is inquisitive, intuitive, quick to lie and to contradict himself. His romantic effusions embarrass others. He dreams of suicide and then "said yes to life once more and listened, but no one came." Nagel has a compelling neurotic imagination—the kind that none of these dull burghers has ever encountered—he prods the townsfolk into fantasy, into reversals, into a realization of what they might have been by talking of angels and demons and dreams. He offers each what he needs most: dignity and clothing to the cripple, romance and love to the beautiful girl, money and marriage to the spinster. But, in doing so, he brings each to a crisis, makes each less happy, more tormented, than before. At the same time, he denigrates himself; he wants only to be honest, he says, but the reader can never quite believe him.

"I wonder if you are rational," asks Dagny, the beautiful girl to whom Nagel has lost his soul. "Every time I meet you I feel more disturbed, more confused . . . Why? I've never in my life met anyone who contradicts my basic beliefs as you do." "I'm a living contradiction," Nagel replies. "I don't understand it myself." In fact, each exercises power over the other. Nagel is indeed half mad, on the verge of breakdown, but he suggests to Dagny the possibility of life; Dagny, beautiful beyond bearing, is sexually hypnotic. She has the power to break Nagel and we know she will. And thus far, everything proceeds in the fashion of nineteenth-century fiction.

What makes *Mysteries* seem so curiously modern is Hamsun's unsettling perspective on his plot and on his characters. The narrative doesn't mean much, serving only as a design, and yet it moves briskly, in clipped sentences of the kind that Hemingway made popular. There are lengthy interior monologues, swift switches of tone, digressions and addresses to the reader. Not one of the characters has a credible past— everything we learn about Nagel's history is called into question— because each exists only for the passion and confusion of the moment. Our understanding of these people, Hamsun insists, must be ambiguous. The novel ends ambiguously, suggesting further links between the characters.

And so we are left with a story that refuses explanations, that is content to leave irrational behavior quite irrational. Nagel, we know, does not quite mean to be so kind to the cripple, cannot be applauded for his proposal to the spinster. He may outrage the dull, boring citizens of this provincial Norwegian town, but he is not quite in control of the forces he unleashes. We do not like him; we do not like Dagny or any of the others; we cannot become involved in the action of this novel because we cannot care—and this is what is so extraordinary, because in every novel of similar plot and situation we have always cared: about Raskolnikov and Emma Bovary. Hamsun, a cynic and a pessimist, thinks none of it matters a damn. There is no moral base here, nothing to work from or against, except the stupidity of the burghers and (for

Hamsun) their absurd concern with liberalism. Blast them all, Hamsun implies, except insofar as they serve my design, which should surprise and please—and it does. *Mysteries* may not be as good a novel as *Hunger* or *Pan,* but it is a disturbing experience.

1971

· Africa
of the Mind

Few African novels have attracted much attention here. The novel is a middle-class invention, spawned by general literacy in societies generally at ease with themselves—which is why, perhaps, there have been few African novels at all, and why Yambo Ouologuem, in his very fine novel *Bound to Violence,* has practically reinvented the genre.

He begins in a minstrel's voice—we must remember that African literature is oral—telling stories, transmitting and ornamenting legends and scraps of history. Like all good minstrels, Ouologuem twists dexterously through time and groups of characters, condensing centuries in a phrase, but—if there is a good murder or mutilation to relate—he flattens out his narrative so that no detail is overlooked: "On the twelfth day of Ramadan the worms began to eat him alive." Who can resist that? Ouologuem's story is the kind we have always liked: a story of lust, madness, and treachery; of drugs, incest, and suicide; of torture, slavery, and assassination—a story, in short, that makes Rider Haggard's novels read like the League of Women Voters' annual budget.

It begins in Nakem (a mythical West African kingdom much like Mali, the author's country), which in the thirteenth century was unified under the tyranny of the Saifs, who slaughtered their enemies or sold them into slavery. The Saifs, or black nobility, claimed descent from the Jews; they had only contempt for the "niggertrash," the rabble blacks "who unlike God have arms but no soul." In his minstrel voice, Ouologuem tells of the Saifs' atrocities, but because the minstrel style, for all its cadences and compactness, is inimical to irony and satire, Ouologuem abandons it when he comes to the modern part of his tale. From the turn of the century, Nakem was ruled by Saif ben Isaac al-Heit, a man of "meticulously organized cruelty," who kept twenty-seven wives and the French government at bay. Saif was skilled in training vipers to attack his enemies—the French governor and his family were among the first to be dispatched, all accidentally bitten, as it was said.

Saif was a slaver, trading in zombies. He thought his white oppressors no worse than the blacks who had sold slaves before the white man came. "Man *is* evil," Saif said. "We are wanderers in disaster," he told a white bishop, "but we fall, we are humble, we gargle with poison from the bloody cup of violence, the chipped glass of values; we are sick, degraded; but that's because the world *is* odd." He is the realist; the white bishop sees all the torture, the sadism and murder as something grander. Violence, the bishop says, "becomes a prophetic illumination, a manner of questioning and answering. . . ."

Perhaps. Ouologuem's story is as violent as any ever written, but he has used violence as a metaphor to re-create in concentrated and fictional form the history of his continent. Like the greatest writers, Ouologuem has created a world that suits his purpose—a world less actual than true, free from the wishful hypotheses of some blacks in Africa and America, too. Proponents of the white-devil theory will grind their teeth over Ouologuem's stories of black genocide and slave-mongering, but his book will survive all attempts to deny it or make use of it because in the joyful way with which it makes legend of history it assumes the truth and invulnerability of art. The people in it, rutting under the sun and dying from swords and snakebites, live for their brief moment. Ouologuem impresses their lives keenly upon us by the strength, intensity, and freshness of his language.

1971

. . . . "Oh, My Lolita, I Have Only Words to Play With."

Vladimir Nabokov's new novel, *Ada, or Ardor,* is extraordinary for so many reasons that I hardly know how to write (or be right) about it. Let's start, as most of us did, with sex—that noun or conjunction necessary to the mass reproduction of best-selling books of fiction.

Our good writers today seem to hate sex; our incompetent writers know nothing about it. John Updike and Philip Roth have recently written about sex as if it were a prison from which we should want to escape, or as if it were a scourge, a sickness of the spirit aggravated by the contact of one person's epidermis with another's. Someone, perhaps the man Nabokov calls "Dr. Froid of Signy-Mondieu," has told them that sex is a Marxist condition that determines what we are, but from which there is no escape and certainly no joy (*Freude*). Hack writers like Jacqueline Susann only pretend to write about sex; because they are secret prudes who don't seem to know what it is that makes sex fun, they are unable to write indecent pornography. I am sorry to say that about Miss Susann because she sent me a Christmas card with her name rubber-stamped on it, but it is still a sad situation—all this fear and revulsion and ignorance about sex. Like the increase in overt homosexuality and overt child-beating, it is perhaps part of an angry, nationwide reaction against the overpeopling of our globe. Even so, I am sorry to see our writers showing sex as a force that somehow makes us something less than human.

Nabokov's *Ada* (to get back to where I started) is entirely different, a novel about (among other things) sex—elegant sex, literary sex that would disturb no one if it were not also incestuous sex. Ada Veen, you see, is in love with her brother Ivan, called Van, and when he isn't there, she makes love to their sister Lucette, who is hopelessly in love with Van. "Purr-version!" cry the ladies of the Lawful Literature League (tax deductible contributions may be sent to Box Six, Tecumseh, Idaho). "But what did you expect from the author of *Lolita*? The Supreme Court has banned all preyers but those who prey on decency." Not so. In spite of the consanguinity of the lovers, there is an erotic incandescence about Nabokov's novel that is one of its principal triumphs. Nabokov is a sensualist, a master of language and observation who scorns (as he himself has said) the tedium of copulating clichés. He returns erotic writing to its first principles: details of sight and touch, a gesture caught before it is completed, a movement of clothes, the warmth of sunlight striking the back of a woman's arm. The effect upon the reader is electric because—surprise!—sex is fun again. Nor are the good ladies from Tecumseh likely to object: For all its puns and pleasantries, its diversions and digressions, *Ada* is Nabokov's longest and most difficult novel.

Its architecture alone is of baroque complexity. At the age of ninety-seven, Ivan Veen, writing about himself in the third person and in a tone of voice like that of his own author, tells the history of his affair with Ada, an affair that began when she was twelve and he fifteen, and lasted, with lengthy intermissions, throughout their lives. Ada, reading the manuscript, makes marginal comments of her own. They fell in love in the summer of 1884, believing at that time that they were only cousins. Van was visiting Ada's family estate, called Ardis Hall, in a country that might have been America if, say, there had been some kind of warp in time and continental shelves, and Louis XVI had fled to England, Paris had an Avenue Guillaume Pitt and, all along, America had been a province of Russia instead of a British colony. Nabokov, who described America so acutely in *Lolita,* clearly delights in his vision of a Russified America where the servants speak French and the aristocrats speak Russian, where tea, served alfresco in the summer afternoons, is emphatically a Russian, not an English tea. Nabokov pretends to offer clues to this act of his imagination, but I prefer to take it as an act of faith: like Alice's rabbit hole, it is simply there. The reader must hold his breath, pop through it, and believe.

At Ardis, with its "Ardors and Arbors," Van and Ada make love in the bushes, shadows, and ferny ravines to the delight of the servants and their half-sister Lucette. Lucette, three years younger than Ada, develops into an "impeccable paranymph," but Van resists her seductiveness (though Ada does not). Van is anxious to avoid further incestuous complications as he comes to realize what the reader has always known: that Ada is his father's illegitimate daughter and finally, though the family tree printed at the front of the book is deceptive on this point, that Ada's mother is also his.

Although *Ada* is often at its best when at its simplest, telling this story of familial love, the plot serves primarily to launch Nabokov's full range of fictional fireworks, most of which will be familiar to those who have read his other books. Themes of exile, suicide, the love that kills, memory, and the recapturing of time past are explored in *Ada* as they have been explored elsewhere in Nabokov's work. He places particular emphasis on the problem of identity (a constant Nabokovian preoccupation): If, as they say, it is a wise child who knows his own father, how long will it take a child prodigy to discover his mother? And, in the tradition of great Russian novelists who hope to be known also as great Russian thinkers, Nabokov includes a lot of talk more sensuous than profound about the nature of time: time as rhythm, the pulse of the blood; time as memory in the making, a constantly developing present that denies the reality of the future.

More important is Nabokov's verbal artifice, more complicated and hilarious in this novel than in any since *Finnegans Wake.* Nobody can get everything *Ada* has to offer from a single reading; perhaps there is no single reader who can decipher it all. But if I return to it, and it is worth coming back to, it will be not for its plot or its theories, but for Nabokov's unexcelled genius in playing with words in many languages. In *Ada,* he parodies everything from Tolstoi to publishers' blurbs, twisting names together by sound as well as by literary and historical association. He plays with anagrams, anachronisms, inkhorn terms, and neologisms, with grammar and sentence structure, with slang and colloquialisms. But his most spectacular effects are made with puns: pedantic puns, naïve puns, bawdy puns, phonetic puns, puns in foreign languages (*"Ça va seins durs,"* quips a man who was asked how he liked his French wife), and even bilingual puns (the French *"n'est vert"* for the English "never").

Ada, of course, is not for everyone. A knowledge of French is almost essential and a knowledge of Russian would help. Readers who find the following phrase funny (it is not even a complete sentence) will probably like the entire book: "the peasant-bare footprint of Tolstoy preserved in the clay of a motor court in Utah where he had written the tale of Murat, the Navaho chieftain, a French general's bastard, shot by Cora Day in his swimming pool." It is typical Nabokovian foolery, requiring no more than a knowledge of Tolstoi's biography, a familiarity with the antics of film stars, and enough French history to know the difference between Marat and Murat and that the latter lived in this country for a while. It is fair to say, I think, that there are arid, virtually inaccessible stretches in *Ada* and there is an almost onanistic quality about all of Nabokov's writing: the author admiring himself a bit too much as he sweeps his wit into dusty corners where no one else can follow, wheezing and guffawing, perhaps, as he thinks of Milton's phrase: "Fit audience find, though few."

But, with that said, all the rest must be praise. Most novels are easily judged because they are kissing cousins of novels any critic has read before; all one needs to know is the conventions. Nabokov's books, however, are not so easily evaluated. He is an authentic genius, the literary heir (if not the equal) of the nineteenth-century Russians, of Lewis Carroll and James Joyce. His novels are unlike anyone else's not only in the originality of their style, which Van Veen (speaking perhaps as Nabokov) says is "the only real honesty of a writer," but because they are not (like most novels) primarily stories *about* something else. They simply are. They exist as complete and triumphant aesthetic experiences in themselves, and *Ada,* more delightful than irritating, seems to me an overwhelming performance.

1969

................Russian Realism:
The Prison World
of Aleksandr Solzhenitsyn

Ten years ago, a diplomat from a Soviet cultural mission sat in an American publisher's office. He was unhappy. The year before, the American had brought out a translation of *Not by Bread Alone,* a tedious novel, yet remarkable because, for the first time in a generation, a book critical of conditions in the People's Paradise had been published openly in Russia. Since the book was denounced by the People's Press, the diplomat wondered why the American had published it. To make matters worse, another American publisher had, just months before, published *Doctor Zhivago,* a novel so reactionary that the People's Publishers had suppressed it.

"Why do you Americans not publish our *progressive* fiction?" the diplomat asked. "In *our* country, we publish all your great writers: Steinbeck, Farrell, Upton Sinclair Lewis." The publisher nodded toward his Youngest Editor. "Send your progressive fiction to Prescott, there," he said amiably. "Prescott will be glad to read it."

The Youngest Editor no longer works for that publisher, but in the months immediately following, he soaked up a skinful of Socialist Realism. Nearly every day, bundles tied sloppily with string arrived, disgorging stubby, ill-printed volumes with cardboard covers whose red dye left stains upon the fingers. Clumsily translated into English, these pudgy novels were, apparently, meant to be fed to American prisoners in North Korea.

The novels of Soviet Socialist Realism—that is, the fiction that hews to the party line—fall roughly into three categories. First, and most common, are those dealing with *Reasonably Current Events.* In one stirring tale of seven hundred and thirty-six pages, the hard life of Okhotsk fishermen in 1920 is described. They were humble peasants all, their women raped by the White Army and their fish stolen by Anglo-American interventionists until, one day, a youthful Komsomol instructor arrived to teach the community to rejoice in Lenin, to roll back its oppressors, its past, and its poverty.

Next come *Military Myths Relating to the Great Patriotic War.* A long epic, entirely in blank verse, tells how Vasilii Terkin, a soldier wounded by the Hun in 1916, volunteered to fight the Nazis in 1941. He laughed and sang and killed the Krauts, exhorting his younger comrades to acts of unheard-of heroism. For his fearless sacrifice, he was made a party member. Finally, there is *Historical Fiction Proving the Inevitability of Bolshevism.* In Part 2 (we never received parts 1 and 3) of an historical novel about Albai Kunanbayev (1845-1904), "the prominent poet and enlightener of the Kazakh people" insists that these disorderly children of the steppes will never straighten out their unhappy, nomadic, polygamous tribe until they are assimilated by a wise and revolutionary neighbor. Too bad Kunanbayev did not live to see how happy and straightened out the Kazakhs are today.

Needless to say, none of these novels was published in this country—which is perhaps a pity because only in contrast to this government-endorsed drivel can we appreciate both the honesty and literary achievement of a handful of postwar Soviet novels published here in recent years. Most of them are about prison life, which is not surprising: Most of their authors, bucking the official trend, know what they are talking about.

Aleksandr Solzhenitsyn's *One Day in the Life of Ivan Denisovich* was, as an experiment, allowed to be published in Russia. In a rough and artless prose, Solzhenitsyn detailed everything that happened to a political prisoner during a single day in a Siberian labor camp, developing a neat, ironic gap between the author's outrage and Ivan's fondness for the freedom he finds in his situation. The Russians didn't like the result of their experiment—there was too much interest in it—and refused to let Lydia Chukovskaya publish her even more remarkable novel, *The Deserted House,* a thinly disguised autobiography of what happens to a woman whose son is packed off to a Siberian camp. And when Valeriy Tarsis allowed his novel, *Ward 7*—relating his experiences as a political prisoner incarcerated in an insane asylum—to be published abroad, he was stripped of his citizenship.

All of which is prologue to Solzhenitsyn's *The First Circle,* a book that has not been, and is not likely to be, published in the Soviet Union, but which nonetheless strikes me as the best novel that postwar Russia has produced. It is a mammoth novel, probably a great novel, and certainly—because it lacks both plot and principal characters—an unconventional novel; a novel lacking the suspense and continuity Western readers expect from fiction, and therefore a novel that, while easy to read, is difficult to keep on reading.

Its focus of interest is a *sharashka,* a scientific institute that, in 1949, was staffed with two hundred and eighty-one political prisoners, so-called enemies of the state. The institute *is* a prison, and the prisoners, though well-fed and lucky to be in only "the first circle" of the hell of Soviet prisons, are working off lengthy, sometimes indefinite, sentences.

They know that, at the whim of the warden, they can be transferred to Siberian camps where they are likely to die. But in the *sharashka*, the prisoners work twelve hours a day, seven days a week, on secret, scientific projects: the development of a scrambler telephone with an "absolute encoder" for Stalin's personal use, and the refinement of voice prints so that other "enemies" can be identified from tapped telephones.

The strange thing about the *sharashka* is that the prisoners don't mind it much. Nearly all of them like their work. Many have been in prison most of their adult lives; others have discovered that "freedom itself was quite often lacking in freedom," that only in prison can one learn to know others and oneself. Prison *becomes* the world, and these exceptional prisoners—all of them well-educated technical specialists—endlessly debate dialectics and Taoist ethics, the nature of free will and happiness. "One can't give in to external circumstances, it's degrading," says a convict who has made a new life in confinement.

"A person you take *everything* from," another explains to the Minister of State Security, "is no longer in your power. He's free all over again."

Freedom is Solzhenitsyn's theme. He seems to say that freedom requires the absence of fear and deceit—qualities that have corrupted not only this sophisticated prison but the Soviet Union itself. To make his point, he moves out of the *sharashka* to show us a variety of civilians and the chain of prison command up to Stalin himself.

The portrait of Stalin is hypnotizing. We meet him muttering "True, true," as he reads a grossly flattering biography of himself. Stalin is ill, deceived by others and himself to the point of insanity. Lonely and afraid, betrayed by Tito (the British spy), he lurks in his armor-plated bedroom, drinking and reflecting that "Someone was always killing the best people and the worst were left for Stalin to finish off." With a failing memory and a nostalgia for religion, Stalin has fallen victim to that ultimate paranoia, which demands confirmation that conspiracies against him are at work.

Nothing else in the book is as good as this. There are forty-six other major characters—each short chapter in this giant novel seems to introduce another: a Marxist linguist who feels Stalin was *right* to imprison him; an intellectual who adopted the life of the common people only to reject it when he discovered that man can become human as he forges his own soul; and a peasant whose politics and religion are his family—nearly blind and sure to die in jail, he exults in his genuine freedom.

All postwar Soviet fiction is somewhat cumbersome, and *The First Circle* is no exception. Like Jean Genet, who wrote *Miracle of the Rose,* the other great contemporary prison novel, Solzhenitsyn construes his prison as if it were the entire world, but unlike Genet, he is more interested in social relationships than in spiritual malaise; his story does not drive down to the bottom of the human psyche but rather extends laterally to touch upon as much of humanity's surface as it can. The business of realistic fiction is to tell the news—and in Russia, there is still much news to be told about what life was like in Stalin's day. In this, his unfashionable novel, which stops and starts and pauses for anecdote and biographical background, Solzhenitsyn has covered an extraordinary range of human experience.

1968

When a writer has acquired a certain reputation, his publisher customarily presses a number of his minor pieces between hard covers and trots them through the bookstores. It is a harmless habit. There is, for instance, as yet no documented evidence that reading Hermann Hesse causes acne or (in cases of excess) insanity, so if a million adolescents insist on buying *Siddhartha,* why not tempt a few thousand of them by dusting off *Knulp* or even *Klingsor's Last Summer?*

So, too, the collected pieces in Aleksandr Solzhenitsyn's *Stories and Prose Poems* are minor stuff. I suspect that if it were not for the fame of the novels and the plight of this author who prefers his country to the condition we call freedom, they would not have been collected at all. I am glad to have them because to publish anything by this brave and durable man, who has been so cruelly used by his government, seems an act of obligation, but I cannot say that I enjoyed them much. Still, they will do until next year when we should have a translation of *August 1914,* the novel Solzhenitsyn considers his most important work.

The sixteen prose poems—verbal snapshots of rural churches, woods, and thunderstorms—seem no more than technical exercises, of little interest to anyone who has browsed among Thoreau's journals. The stories, which generally unwind with considerable dullness before a neat dramatic twist, lack the intensity of *One Day in the Life of Ivan Denisovich* and the scope of *The First Circle.* Solzhenitsyn's customary theme of life within an institution is either absent or muted in these pieces, so he must work without his principal metaphor of a prison or hospital that represents the whole of Communist Russian society.

But even if the short story is an inappropriate form for Solzhenitsyn's talent, these pieces still reveal many of his major concerns: the inhumanity of bureaucracy, for instance, and the retreat from urban living; the precise observation of nature and the conviction that life at its hardest is very much life worth loving. Solzhenitsyn's fascination with procedure is also evident: how the cars on troop trains are counted in wartime; how a peasant woman manages to stay alive; the problems of finding space for students and equipment in an outdated technical school. In longer fiction, I think, such a wealth of reportorial detail can be more readily assimilated; here it seems to overwhelm the narratives. There are, too, some autobiographical details in these stories: The narrator of one returns from ten years of war and Russian prison camps; the narrator of another knows he will be exiled when he leaves the hospital where his disease has been arrested.

Finally, these stories reaffirm Solzhenitsyn's resolutely moral posture. The old peasant woman for whom life has been so hard, so seemingly disastrous, is led to her death both by the greed of her relatives and her own charity. "She was that one righteous person," the narrator says, "without whom, as the saying goes, no city can stand." For Solzhenitsyn, who refused to go to Sweden to accept his Nobel Prize because he feared he would not be let back into Russia, freedom has little to do with politics or even a man's survival. "The true savor of life," he writes, "is not to be gained by big things but from little ones—things like my ability to shuffle along hesitantly on my weakened legs; my cautious breathing, to avoid stabbing pain in the chest; and a single potato, undamaged by the frost, that I fished out of my soup."

1971

Four

................The Theater of
Neurosis Presents:
"Let It All
Hang Out"

Listen. Hear those clicks? The Eastern Establishment—you know, the people who think the Far West begins on the wrong side of the Hudson River—is buckling its seat belts. Esalen is coming. You've heard rumors: The believers cry, confess, and criticize, hum "Om" at each other, take off their clothes and touch each other and, after sixteen hours or whatever of *that*, stride bravely into the dawn, new, viable, sentient human beings. The rumor I heard was that Esalen would never make it east of Wichita, but (such are the times we live in) here they are in New York: encounter groups plopping around us like H. G. Wells' rocket ships from Mars, and who can be sure that, at his next cocktail party, he won't have his flesh handled by some Esalen graduate who has been told that if flesh handling is what turns him on, why not?

Word that Esalen had infiltrated the Wichita Defense Line first reached me on a poster, mailed to my home address, announcing Esalen's East Coast Premiere at a New York hotel: a three-day orgy of lectures and brief encounters. For a huge fee, the richly curious could watch and (who knows?) perhaps get mussed up a little. Scientology was never like this, but then, Scientology lacks Esalen's sense of theater, of therapy as theater—a theater of confrontation familiar to off-Broadway fans, in which the audience participates, all atingle with a creepy little fear of psychological rape, maybe even physical danger.

At the same time, I read what may be the first encounter book, *Marathon 16*, which is set up like a play, divided into acts and scenes, featuring performers who know they are making a book, who assume stage names and, at times, personalities not their own. The book is written by the play's director, Dr. Martin Shepard, by a novelist, Marjorie Lee (who attended but did not take part in the encounter) and by two tape recorders. It is, of course, a dreadful book, one of those instant, unexamined forays into electronic journalism that, when ex-creted in print form, appeals to the vulgar curiosity in us all. Which is not to say the book is without interest or value—far from it. If read properly—that is, if the reader provides the perspective the authors and their machines cannot—the book conveys some pessimistic truths about who we are, how little we want, how desperately we want to believe in ourselves, the men and methods to which we look for help, and the alarming ease with which life comes to imitate art—and bad art at that.

Marathon therapy, Shepard says, is for healthy, curious people suffering "from the same phenomenology [*sic*]: that of incomplete awareness." Growth, adventure, risk-taking: These are what we need to remain alive. No one quarrels with that, but is it true, as encounter apologists suggest, that in the marathon experience, participants are given opportunities to live more intensely, to examine their problems and discover they are not unique, that traditional hang-ups can be discarded? Marathon therapy brings people into collision with each other in deliberately forced and embarrassing circumstances, making of each man his own and every other's analyst. The director of the group works from an agenda designed to keep everyone off-balance. He asks the participants to praise and criticize each other, to act out situations they cannot quite discuss, to confess their problems with sex and popularity and, toward the end, perhaps to take off their clothes and work each other over again. The sheer fatigue produced by such intensity in a sixteen-hour session will, as any Chinese brainwasher knows, wear most people down, leave them begging for more criticism, or moaning in ecstasy.

What is interesting in *Marathon 16* is to see how quickly ten of Shepard's friends—five men and five women who did not know each other—broke down. They approached the situation as one must in any similar encounter—whether one is handling snakes, speaking in tongues, or confessing to a meeting of AA—without irony, wit, or critical intelligence. They are drab, lonely, and unloving people who stab and caress each other with the psychological clichés they have learned from Joyce Brothers and Rose Franzblau. "An instinct," says one, "uh . . . something that goes against your daily life is. . . ." Pause, collapse. It is not exactly helpful. "What is love?" asks one man. "I don't know," the woman replies. "Then you'll never really know whether your marriage was a worthwhile one," snaps the man. If you can't define a horse, how do you know you're riding one?

None of this bilge is questioned by the doctor, who, throughout the marathon, shows little talent except for keeping cool. A girl tries—or pretends to try—to commit suicide. The doctor forbids anyone to save her—"If she jumps, it will have been her own decision." Except that *he* provoked the situation. A man is mugged in the street as the group is trying to rock a woman to heaven. Two men want to intervene, but the doctor objects: "If you are going to be here, be here."

And so it goes for sixteen hours: the group weeps, snarls, and touches itself, asks for votes on sexiness and obnoxious quotients, abuses its members for not exposing themselves sufficiently or for failing to come across as "a defined personality"—strange virtue, that!—and, toward the end of the session, when the group has undressed and the doctor has shaken one man's penis to the delight of all assembled, the group achieves a community of sorts. The novelist, who would not take part, says she would like to marry them all.

Certain values, marathon values, clearly emerge. Expose yourself—that's good. Be undefinable—that's bad. These poor people don't ask for much. "Tell me I'm a beautiful woman," says one, and they tell her; that's the rule, and so she has something and feels better, but what happens next? Out there, in the real world where civilization begins when you put something on, or hold something in, or when you put your food on a fork, instead of savoring the texture of all that gravy and mashed potato oozing between your fingers—which, if you think about it, is a sensual pleasure, a kind of natural adventure of living few of us have tried for many years. I can no more judge the merits of encounter therapy than the merits of an ABM system—whether or not they work, we seem to want them, they ease the fears of some—but as a book critic, as one quite willing to express an opinion on the evidence put before him, I wonder why a doctor would use the transcripts of this session as an argument for marathons.

He has shown us only that these people are acting out their desires in a carefully controlled environment that allows the illusion of risk and love, no more. The group disperses; the echoes remain: "I think you're a girl, and it's fine that you're a girl"; It's okay to be self-indulgent." Okay, agreed; now that the ritual-acting is finished, what are we going to *do*—out *there*? That's another problem. Robert Brustein points out that today's revolutionaries, unable to impose their revolution, stage it for the cameras; it is an act, and it dies there. The trend of the times seems to be: If you can't do it, stage it as theater; if you can't express yourself in the real world, you can always go back to the play world and do it again. When the real world fails, the play world becomes addictive. At least one member of this marathon group returned for another session. In the marathon—*that's* where freedom is.   1970

......................Even Dr. Freud
Was Stumped:
"What Does
a Woman Want?"

So there I was, waiting for the riot to begin, lying on my elbows on New Haven's Green and dozing a bit as the speakers assaulted my ears and the May air with hours of incoherent argument. I was dressed in my riot costume—corduroy pants for the proletarian look, baggy tweed jacket for the junior-faculty look, strong shoes suitable for swift withdrawals—but something was missing. An atmosphere of menace. A threat of physical danger.

Then the girls from Women's Liberation arrived. They pranced about—elated, it seemed, from some private ritual of their own—and waved a red flag on which was drawn a black fist thrust inside a womb. Cute girls, I thought drowsily, *nubile* girls with firm bodies under those dungarees and pretty faces under those crash helmets. . . . Suddenly I snapped awake. *These thoughts exploit women!* I dozed again until I felt something slap against my thigh. A copy of *Playboy*. Once upon a time, Hugh Hefner grew rich selling *Playboy* to men, but he never guessed how much richer he would grow when all the feminists began buying *Playboy* so they could denounce it at rallies and hate it in their homes. This copy, which the girls no longer needed, nestled against my pelvis and had a denounced look to it, so I dozed off again.

A shriek awoke me. All around, the girls were rising, and one stood over me, her finger in my face. *"Will you look at what this Fascist pig is reading!"*

"I think that's the end of the story," I say to my wife, "or does it need another sentence?"

"I think," says my wife, speaking without moving her teeth, "you need a transition between the sexism of that story and your admiration for Kate Millett's book."

Kate Millett's book is called *Sexual Politics,* and is in some ways admirable—a biting, bitter, and convincing argument that male supremacy, which is founded upon sex as "a caste structure ratified by nature," is untenable, degrading, and all-pervasive. Society conditions women to believe in their own inferiority. The fault, Miss Millett insists, is not in our biology but in our training. Women are repressed by "sexual politics," which, like all politics, deals with "power-structured relationships, arrangements whereby one group of persons is controlled by another." Sexual politics affects every encounter between the sexes— whether it is the persisting feudal arrangement whereby one sex offers "service" to the other in exchange for security, or the crude dehumanizing of women by such supposedly unfettered writers as Freud, D. H. Lawrence, Henry Miller, and Norman Mailer. "The image of women . . . ," Miss Millett writes, "is an image created by men and fashioned to suit their needs . . . to provide a means of control over a subordinate group." Women's enemies are the patriarchal organization of society and chivalry: Putting a woman on a pedestal, it seems, is the best way to insure her immobility.

Miss Millett was an instructor at Barnard College; her book grew out of her doctoral thesis and consists of "equal parts of literary and cultural criticism." The literary criticism—particularly her essays on Lawrence, Miller, and Mailer—is remorselessly sound,* damning these writers from their own words and worst books for the glee with which they reduce women to objects for men's pleasure. "Counterrevolutionary sexual politicians," she calls them all. Lawrence, for instance, invented "a religion, even a liturgy of male supremacy," and Miller is "a compendium of sexual neuroses." Only in the homosexual world of Jean Genet can she find what she believes to be honest writing about sex.

Miss Millett is confident and marvelously knowledgeable, spraying footnotes with both hands as she boldly tramples where scholars fear to tread. The first sexual revolution, she observes, lasted from Victorian times until about 1930, when counterrevolution set in. Freud, "the strongest counterrevolutionary force," provided the ideology: Little girls, he observed, think they are physically deficient. Freud agreed: Undress one, compare it to an undressed boy, and see for yourself. But women tried to con Freud, telling him they were socially and culturally repressed. Freud understood, and chewed his cigar: Women want what their brothers have.† Miss Millett attacks Freud with gusto. The first sexual revolution failed, Miss Millett says, because only certain forms in society were changed—not human attitudes. The second sexual revolution is only five years old. What we need from it, according to Miss Millett, is the abolition of marriage, the family patriarchal supremacy, all taboos about sex and double standards. We must reexamine our silly

---

*Not so sound, alas. Norman Mailer, in *The Prisoner of Sex*, shows how Miss Millett deliberately castrates her quotations to remove phrases that refute her point. Truth is ever the victim of even the most worthy revolutions.

†In the original version of this piece, I referred to Freud's theory of Penis Envy. *Look*, at that time trying to maintain what it called a "low profile," would not allow me to use the word penis, even in such a clinical context. The challenge, then, became to talk around the Penis Envy theory in no more than fifty words. I've let the result stand here.

ideas of masculine and feminine character traits and work toward "an assimilation by both sides of previously segregated human experience."

Perhaps, but how is it to work? No one, as Miss Millett supposes, is wholly divorced from his biology; no man can experience what motherhood, or even menstruation, means. Taboos against incest may be beneficial, and perhaps the last roots of sexual inequality can never be torn up. The Bolsheviks tried—and failed: "Everyone talked endlessly about sexual equality, but few were capable of practicing it. Nearly all were afraid of sexual independence."

Like most polemicists, Miss Millett oversimplifies, fails to ask necessary questions: What *good* results from the opposition of the sexes in society? She writes without humor, though she can occasionally muster a morose wit that ranges from contempt to sarcasm (some feminists, I am told, protest that theirs is far too serious a subject for smiling) and she writes without style, in the good gray graduate student manner, studding one chapter with two hundred and one footnotes and another with two hundred and thirty-five. This typographical concession to scholarship, however, is not altogether impressive. Although she argues from a number of disciplines, Miss Millett seems less than candid when she tells the myth of Orestes without reference to Electra (how much easier this way to make it seem a reaffirmation of patriarchy) and her assertions about biology seem nervous at best and are often simply uninformed. (The question that haunted me as I read this book was: Is she really ignorant, or is she suppressing evidence? She is clearly intelligent and, having had some exposure to the world of scholarship, is probably not uninformed; but because she considers herself a revolutionary, she is probably quite willing to distort or to suppress inconvenient evidence.) In any event, Miss Millett tosses off such phrases as "all the best scientific evidence" and "the best medical research" when she needs support for her most questionable assumptions—that there is, for instance, no basis in biology for sexual differentiation of social roles—but she cites none of this "best" evidence, though all graduate students are taught to do so, nor does she give any indication that she knows what it is.

Miss Millett's claim that *all* differences between men and women are socially imposed is demonstrably untrue; one ought to be able to affirm a common humanity without such falsifications. Anyone with an undergraduate's knowledge of anthropology is aware that women in prehistoric times were dependent upon men as they are not today, that the size of the woman's pelvis assures the long dependency of the child upon the mother, and therefore the mother was more vulnerable, less able to flee the tiger, chase the bison, or repel the hostile tribesmen from her home. No sexist shaman told the woman she had to miss the fun and the equality, tending the fire while the men whooped it up on the mammoth hunt; someone had to stay home to see that the Great Anteater, or whatever, didn't snuffle up the baby, and since catching mammoths was a matter of life or death, it only made sense that those who couldn't run as fast for as long stayed home. The conditioning was biological, not sociological. If nature had made women the physical "equal" of men by, say, giving them a small pelvis, human babies, who have large brains, would have had to be born at a much earlier stage of development, thus prolonging the period of dependency. If, on the other hand, nature had tried to get rid of the dependency problem by giving the woman a larger pelvis, the woman could hardly have moved at all.

In life, as in literature, there is generally more than one explanation for any problem. It can be argued, for instance, that since the myth of male supremacy, like the myth of the flood, has always existed in nearly all cultures, there is either something to it or we need it for some reason as yet unexplained. And yet this multiplicity of explanations is a situation all proper revolutionaries abhor: It sounds too much like the trimming of liberals, who can never get anything done. Miss Millett simply refuses to recognize the complexities of the situations she confronts. She is a preacher, not a student, and for her all phenomena have the same explanation: male chauvinism. What we need is justice, not a falsification of literature, history, and anthropology. As my wife says (between her teeth), "My pelvis may have a peculiar shape, but my brains are as good as yours." The challenge, then, is to insure that polarity be free of inequality; the adjustment is necessary and long overdue.

. . . . Our Other War: A Progress Report

You can tell how biased the news media really are by the way they cover our other war, the war against our children. Sure, the press covers our more spectacular scrimmages with the enemy who is, after all, highly visible. When our kids run shaggy and screaming into the streets to hurl bricks at law-abiding policemen, I don't blame the TV crews for trundling along behind. But what you don't see on TV is the daily drudgery of this war, the rural pacification of the kids by the silent majority of adults. Out where I live, I have heard a mother say she will not eat at the same table with her unbarbered son. I have heard upper-income commuters shout obscenities at children wearing mourning for our war in Vietnam. I have heard a father say that if he catches his daughter smoking marijuana, he will turn her over to the police himself. That is the way this war is being fought in the heartland of America. Anywhere you turn, you will hear our adult voices crack in fear, in contempt, and in hatred of our offspring, but do you hear us, do you see us, on TV? Not likely. And that, I think, is a hell of a way to cover the news of a war.

It is doubtful whether the adult backlash can take much courage from *In the Country of the Young,* an elegant old-style polemic in which John W. Aldridge fulminates over the arrogant incompetence of youth. He traces the sources of his indignation first to the postwar exhaustion and impoverished spirit of his own generation, and then to the materialism of the American character itself. We have always lacked culture, graciousness, and style, he says; we are frozen "at the utilitarian level of existence." Small wonder the children took over: "There has never been an adult society here."

Our young people, Aldridge writes, lack internal discipline; they are bored, but they can be passionate about causes. Because they are indifferent to quality and incapable of intellectual discrimination, they have no idea of what life should be *for,* no idea of how life should be lived. Collectively vociferous and militant, yet individually inarticulate and limp, they yelp about equality, which is impossible, and progress, which is illusory. They haven't been hurt enough, Aldridge suggests, so they think only in abstract terms. Unaware of human limitations, they have no interest in loveliness, in risk, in adventure, or even in civilization.

Strong stuff. It has been said that rhetoric is a factor of power rather than of understanding, and one can see sheathed in Aldridge's excellent prose the blade of literary mayhem. Enough of this soft thinking about youth, Aldridge seems to say: Cut 'em down. Like any good polemicist, Aldridge concentrates on style and brevity, on exaggeration and over-simplification. But, like the kids he criticizes, he is too abstract, too indiscriminate in his assault to be entirely effective. He grows angrier as his book grows longer; his satire sags into sarcasm. Too bad. What he says of young people is undoubtedly true of some of them, some of the time—I doubt if you can attack any part of the way we live now without being often right—but Aldridge might have let the kids be just a little right, too, about the apathy, brutality, and corruption in our society. Being right never made anyone less detestable, and you can kill with charity.

*   *   *

Killing with charity is the theme of Julius Horwitz's *The Diary of A.N.: The Story of the House on West 104th Street*. Horwitz, a former welfare caseworker, is one of the few white men left who dare to write about black men as if from a black point of view. This time, Horwitz adopts the voice and attitudes of a fifteen-year-old black girl, Λ.N., a brave, intelligent child, living with her family in a single room in a part of Harlem where welfare is the only way of life. A.N.'s world is one of carefully selected and artistically developed horror. She never knew her father; she watches her mother succumb to defeat; her twelve-year-old brother pushes drugs to support a white homosexual; her thirteen-year-old sister who shoots heroin comes down with gonorrhea; rats chew the baby's toes. "Are we a family?" A.N. asks. All around her, younger girls induce their own abortions, men rape infant boys, addicts doze in doorways, and screams pierce the cockroach-laden walls. "I can feel my body growing," A.N. writes, "I want to feel my mind growing. . . . I won't be shot down. I will escape. I will run faster than the guards who try to keep me in, whoever the guards are."

The Diary of A.N. is the peculiar offspring of the marriage of two lusts: the lust for social reform and the lust for commercial success. Obviously, Horwitz knows as much as any man about the ways welfare traps people and cripples them, reduces them to a state in which, like A.N.'s mother, they come to *like* their failure—not, as conservatives say, because they are lazy, but because they feel they deserve punishment. By imitating *The Diary of Anne Frank*, Horwitz will reach the largest possible audience, which, if it is ever going to realize how we are killing off our ghetto children, needs the kind of kick in the viscera that Horwitz is uniquely able to provide.

Unfortunately, people who read books for something other than their news or message quotient are going to be appalled by Horwitz's impersonation of an adolescent black girl. One can forgive A.N.'s selective illiteracies and her habit of describing her daily desperation in metaphorical language ("see the water going over my head"), but what of her use of ironies and perspectives accessible only to adults? Her brother, A.N. says, is a child "without a childhood." No child could *ever* think that because every child knows he has a childhood, good or bad; only an adult can equate childhood itself with what he thinks childhood should be. A.N. is full of such phony observations: The Metropolitan Museum "seems to exist to remind people of what they were once capable of doing." If you say so, A.N., but you sound to me like one more black girl exploited by a white man.

I've saved the best for last. Jim Haskins' *Diary of a Harlem Schoolteacher* is the real thing, a short, spare, honest book that will, I suspect, be read a generation hence as a classic study of one aspect of American education. Haskins is black and not yet thirty; he left a brokerage firm to teach in a ghetto school—"to become a part of a larger human experience." P.S. 92 on West 134th Street was a wreck: Classrooms had been vandalized, windows broken, dirty words scrawled in crayon on the blackboards. There was no playground (a child playing in the street was hit by a truck), little heat in winter, and supplies, when they came at all, came a year late. The custodian refused to fix the building; the librarian refused to put her books on the shelves; the music teacher refused to play for the "special" classes Haskins taught. In the street below Haskins' window, the narcotics trade and numbers racket flourished; across the street, an exhibitionist regularly exposed himself.

Haskins taught mentally retarded kids, ten-year-olds with IQ's in the sixties and seventies and emotional traumas. They couldn't read when Haskins got them, and the question is whether they will ever be able to function in America. They came to school, when they came, smelling, unwashed, unfed, and inadequately clothed. Students attacked teachers and molested younger girls, but the teachers played hooky, too, and one was caught petting a first-grade girl. One boy told Haskins' class how he saw a man cut to death; a girl told of her aunt's German shepherd dog which, because it was not fed, ate one of her aunt's legs. Haskins found one boy with a four-inch knife around his neck. "Ma says if you touch me," the boy explained, "to wait till you turn around and then stick you." "Business as usual," Haskins writes in his diary: "suspicion, hate, and fear, the hallmarks of education in the ghetto schools today."

Haskins' book is understated. He has stripped away all emotion because there is nothing he can add to the plain facts he has to report. He is an excellent writer and must be a better teacher, but will he remain a teacher in a system that seems designed to cripple children and drive teachers into other work? "In general," Haskins wrote toward the end of the year, "the school is doing much better than in previous years."

1970

. . . . The New
Journalism:
Early Phases

Fiction is flagging. The novel isn't dead, but it does seem to be spinning its wheels a bit, with its engine in neutral: a lot of familiar noise but not much progress. Much of what the novel had to offer—social reporting, exotic landscapes, and vivid characterization, all patted into place by the author's controlling hand—has been preempted by the New Journalism and by the Experience Collectors who write it.

The New Journalism has become a third force in the field of reportage. It gives the facts, certainly, but unlike the Kinsey reports it does not lay them out cold on the table, a smorgasbord from which the reader may pick and choose what suits his appetite. It is personal journalism, too, although the writer-as-artist is rarely a part of the scene. Avoiding analysis, objectivity, and self-expression, the New Journalism concentrates on the dramatic presentation of an experience.

The New Journalists are not reporters; they are Experience Collectors. John Howard Griffin dyed his skin to see what it was like to *be* a Negro in the Deep South. Truman Capote, with no protective coloration, *became* a member of a small Kansas community to investigate a single crime. George Plimpton actually tried to *be* a quarterback for the Detroit Lions. The way to get at the truth, the New Journalists believe, is to immerse oneself in the material, to become a part of the experience. When, after a few months or a few years, they scurry off to their typewriters, anxious to drop their carefully nurtured commitments and, like rat finks, eager to expose everything they have learned from milking the confidence of others, they are pregnant with the actuality, the totality, of it all. They can write a new kind of book: not just the facts, ma'am, but the "truth" of the experience—the smell, the taste, and the temperature of it, the nitty-gritty which is not only *fact,* but a projection of the facts into reasonable *invention* as well.

Forgotten conversations can be reconstructed. Thoughts too private for a character to reveal or even be aware of can be surmised. Situations can be telescoped, events isolated—everything, in short, can be shaped to fit the requirements of the book, because in the New Journalism you don't bend the book for the sake of the facts. The result is extraordinary: exciting, convincing, and above all *readable* reporting. If it reads like fiction, it is because it has been built that way: Most of the New Journalists are novelists.

Living the experience one plans to write about later can present problems. Hunter S. Thompson, author of *Hell's Angels,* defines one: "I had become so involved with the outlaw scene that I was no longer sure whether I was doing research on the Hell's Angels or being slowly absorbed by them." Another is the physical danger: Thompson lived with the Angels, "all noise and hair and bustout raping instincts," for a year. It was an edgy business. The Angels, "the rottenest motorcycle gang in the whole history of Christendom," sleazy, brutal, unwashed criminals who "look as repulsive and repugnant as possible," hate the square world but are attracted to publicity. Thompson took them into his home, bought booze for them, rode with them, talked to them endlessly, intervened on their behalf with the cops, and was finally stomped by them.

The experience left Thompson somewhat shaken and bemused, but the result is an absorbing portrait of these futile, stinking, psychopathic thugs—the only accurate picture we have. Angels call themselves the One-Percenters—"We're the one-percenters, man, the one per cent that don't fit and don't care." Ruthless conformists, they rally round their colors—sleeveless jackets encrusted with urine and emblazoned with a winged death's head—and their leader, the Maximum Angel, to ride their "chopped hogs"—stripped-down Harley Davidson 74's—from place to place, boozing, fornicating, tearing up property, chain-whipping rivals, and terrorizing the multitudes.

Thompson is at least as amused by the inaccurate and hysterical press the Angels have received as by the outlaws themselves. He analyzes the Angels as individuals and as a pack, exploring their involvement with dope, rape, homosexuality, mayhem, and racism. His conclusion is equivocal—yes and no, the Angels do and do not do all these things. *Hell's Angels* progresses by free association—subjects and stories are picked up, examined, and dropped unfinished. Thompson is alternately contemptuous and sympathetic toward his former friends, and his book is informative, lively, and funny. The Angels, victims of their own publicity, will probably like it.

John Sack's *M* is a much better book, a funny, frightening book in which the author laughs to keep from shrieking and the reader laughs to avoid weeping, a good example of the New Journalism where the line between fact and fiction has been extinguished.

M is an infantry company, trained at Fort Dix in 1966 and bloodied in Vietnam in the same year. Sack stuck with M from its advance training through its first engagement. From the jaws of the ice crusher—the Army, the government, or whatever it is that moves of its own momentum and doesn't recognize individuals—Sack has plucked individuals, ignorant and apathetic soldiers going through the motions, and their corporate entity, M.

M is people, and we get to know them very well: Demirgian, anxious to get out, baffled because he never saw the enemy; Smith, the religious man, worker of God's will; McCarthy, who wapped the officer who made him a bartender; the captain who wants to burn the villages because that will force the Vietcong to start building instead of causing troubles; the battalion commander hot for slaughter; and so on. M is also irrelevancies: the endless inspections and the talk about deodorants as the mortar shells come crumping in.

M is a nervous and mannered book which, like atonal music, has no tonic—no point of departure and no resolution. *M* is written with an affinity for Tom Wolfe's extremes of prose, with $2.50 words like "endogenously" and nonce words like "inquisiturient" that haven't been used since 1644, but *M* is triumphant: A mock epic quoting Yeats and Frost and referring to Dante, a witty, breathless book making comedy out of numbness and compassion out of horror.

1967

. . . . Norman Mailer,
Boy Reporter

1. *Mailer as Vergil:*
A Conducted Tour
Through the New Inferno

Norman Mailer has often noisily explained that he is the best writer in America. His first book, *The Naked and the Dead,* served admirably as a pad from which he might launch such a claim, and now, after twenty years, he has produced another book that offers some argument in support of it. *The Armies of the Night* is not a novel; it is a piece of reporting—an account of the Peace Movement's protest march on the Pentagon last October, and Mailer's role in that march. But it is more than this: It is a random and brilliant collection of digressive and incisive essays, of autobiographical fragments and critical speculations on the peculiar anguish and frustrations of our country and our time; and by "our time," I mean this year and last year—certainly no further back than 1965.

Mailer tells his story in the third person, and, for the first time, writes of himself with humor as well as with candor. Surprisingly, a mellow Mailer emerges, "a comic hero . . . a figure of monumental disproportions," an aging rebel, a prince of Bourbon who is often drunk, but off drugs now and wary of them, old enough to have a daughter in college. Papa Mailer is, in fact, forty-four. He shuns publicity and strikes attitudes. He is "semi-distinguished, semi-notorious," mixing Marxism with nihilism, and conservatism with large dollops of existentialism. "Taken at his very worst," Mailer writes, "he was at least still worthy of being a character in a novel by Balzac, win one day, lose the next, and do it with boom! and baroque in the style." Poking through this permissive charm and witty deprecation is a more familiar, mischievous Mailer: a vain and snobbish roughneck boxing shadows from some Jewish ghetto in his mind, victim of that exquisite paranoia that feeds on the fear it finds in the praise of others.

What did Mailer accomplish on the march? At the request of friends, he flew down to Washington two days early. Stifling his misgivings about the march and his own participation in it, he gave what turned out to be an obscene and drunken speech on the first evening (he shared a stage with Robert Lowell, Dwight Macdonald, and others). On the second day, he attended a rally at which draft cards were collected on the steps of the Department of Justice, and gave another, more sedate, address. The next day, the day of the march to the Pentagon across the river in Virginia, Mailer, Lowell, and Macdonald resolved that they should be arrested as early as possible so that they might be released in time to fly back for parties held that evening in New York. Of the three, only Mailer was arrested; held longer than he anticipated, he missed his party and most of the melee between marchers and the military. Since Mailer's participation in his own story ends before his book does, the final quarter of his account is given over to background material concerning the history of the march and a narrative of events that took place while our hero was in jail.

Because *Armies* is the most important book we have to date about an important part of the American experience, it is a pity, but perhaps it is not surprising, that many who have sampled parts of it in magazines have recoiled in outrage and confusion. Why, they ask, should he have included so much that is boorish and inconsequential? Mailer's own performance was inept when it was not gross; why then should this inglorious crusader, who had so little to do with the march, talk so much about himself? And what does he mean by claiming that this report, which is at times almost embarrassing in its candid revelations, is a novel?

There is cunning in his crudity. Mailer can, I think, quite properly claim that for all its detail and digression, there is nothing inconsequential in the book, though admittedly much that is boorish. But even the boorish bits—like the scene in which Mailer drunkenly urinates on the floor of a darkened men's room—have their comic effect, and even their grim relevance, foreshadowing as they do the actions of the demonstrators and the boorishness of the government's response.

As for talking so much about himself, Mailer is, after all, trying to lure you into reading a good-sized book about peaceniks skirmishing at the Pentagon. If his self-centeredness bores you, you may throw the book away, but would you have picked it up had he not figured in it? More important, Mailer is trying to extract from the disorder of the event a distillation of importance to us all. Whatever was vulgar and unsuccessful about the endeavor can, in retrospect, be made just and important; thus does the bond of the creative imagination weld discrete particles of experience together—and change their character. Furthermore, we are unlikely to muster much empathy for what Mailer calls "the middle-class cancer-pushers and drug-gutted flower children" who took part in the enterprise if Mailer himself, a contemporary, choleric Vergil, were not there to take us by the hand, to lead us across the Styx of our unease and our misunderstanding, and then to walk with us, interpreting the significance of these strange signs and dark figures obscurely jostling each other through circles of a new Inferno.

In spite of Mailer's moralizing and crafty organization, in spite of his skill at characterization and his monumental prose, *Armies* is clearly not a novel. It belongs, instead, to the genre of New Journalism: that peculiarly committed kind of reporting that a handful of novelists have undertaken, thereby creating, almost by accident, the only original prose form of our decade.

More than most New Journalists, however, Mailer stresses the message he finds in his experience. He has something trenchant to say about everybody and everything, analyzing the inner nature of sex, parties, and liberal intellectuals, of policemen, obscenity, and small American towns. He is good at defining militant Negroes—"Black Power groups looking somehow blacker in skin than they looked in the old coffee-and-cream days of liberal integration." You can't get sharper than that.

From his own insignificant participation in an event whose significance cannot yet be known, Mailer has written a significant book. By writing what he calls the history of his interior, he has come across an astonishing quantity of comedy—a true comedy of the shortcomings that are a part of the anguish not only of Norman Mailer but of his country, too. Better than anyone, he has caught our recent sense of frustration, futility, and despair, of idealism gone hairy, of man's best thoughts rendered useless because there is no one out there still willing to listen. Against such apathy, men can mount only a symbolic attack, a march against the symbol of their rage; against such silence, men can only mouth magic incantations and obscenities, poor shadows of the potency they once possessed. The point is, these protesters had no power; finally, they could do no more than leave their bodies to be beaten in the mindless, needless, bloody response the government offered by way of rebuttal to their demands.

I have mentioned Mailer's prose. It is by far the best he has ever written, strong in line and marvelous in metaphor, a prose that will, I have no doubt, be studied in schools of future years by students who will have no other knowledge of our war and the anguish of our days. Governments have reason to fear writers of Mailer's skill; small wonder the Soviet Union locks them away.

1968

2. Mailer as Walt Whitman: I Sing the Body Electronic

Peter, born sign of Cancer, was a Crab and therefore a critic. From his perspective of one year, the sixties looked worse than ever. Norman Mailer, born sign of Aquarius, explained why: The decade had begun with Mailer stabbing his wife and had ended with Mailer running for mayor of New York. In between, it had been more of the same: black riots in the ghettos and police riots everywhere else, the browning of the environment and the greening of students and the grass they smoked, an assortment of assassinations, and an unending war so stupid, so evil, no President would declare it.

Was there any straw to clutch at? Could Sister Ann, at the window, perceive a cloud of dust, a bold knight come galloping to rescue us from the Bluebeard in ourselves? She could indeed: In 1961, President Kennedy had set the nation on a course for the moon. The theme of the technological decade to come was: By getting up from and off of here, we can figure out how to fix things up down here. Perhaps. A friend of Cancer, who milked truth from computers at Yale, said he looked forward to the day when computers would take over book criticism, thus eliminating such passions and errors as the Crab was heir to. By late 1970, Yale offered even grander programs. A professor, a medical doctor, speaking without sedation or restraint by rubber sheets, smiled as he asked: "What sort of humans would we like, ideally, to construct?"

Human beings, he went on, "are very badly planned," meaning, Cancer assumed, that he had some alternative in mind.

Central to the national obsession for tinkering with machines, with human brains, with the lives of other nations, was the national effort to put Americans on the moon by the end of the decade. It was an ambiguous occasion, mixing metal and metaphysics, but dithering humanists, who couldn't tell a Lox valve from an Ordeal panel, knew that someone, somewhere, had paid Norman Mailer, oracle of Aquarian angst, nearly half a million dollars to make sense of it all, and now he has, in a book called *Of a Fire on the Moon.*

Mailer confronts the ambiguity directly. He is, he tells us, Aquarius—not an Age, because that has not come about, but at least a skeptic about technology. Mailer's strength as a reporter sits in his nose, in inductive, intuitive reporting, in reconstructing, as he says, "the dinosaur from the fossil bone." Mailer smells out the truth. "We cherish the sense of smell," he writes, "because it gives us our relation to time. We know how old something is by its odor; its youth, its becoming and its decay are subtly compounded to tell us at once—if we dare to contemplate mortality—how much time has been appropriated by such a life."

This passage is central to Mailer's examination because, as he tells us, there are no smells coming from NASA, from the men who are "subtly proud of their ability to serve interchangeably for one another" to "suggest any philosophical meandering." The men in Houston seem devoted to technology, not to emotion. Bravery has become irrelevant because, if you think as NASA does, knowledge eliminates fear. "It was in the complacent assumption," Mailer writes, "that the universe was no majestic mansion of architectronics out there between evil and nobility, or strife on a darkling plain, but rather an ultimately benign field of investigation which left Aquarius in the worst of his temper."

This is Mailer, writing personal journalism better than anyone else. If he cannot be engaged in the event, as he was with the march on the Pentagon, he can at least be an engaged observer, reacting with envy, with pride, sometimes with scorn and sometimes with grief that the essential mystery of the event is forever sealed beneath technocratic banalities. Mailer, the journalist, has always lived in a world inhabited by more spirits than most of us encounter; sometimes, like Prospero, he seems to command them; sometimes, like Caliban, he seems the victim of the pricks and cloven tongues that hiss him into madness. For Mailer, the moon shots were "disrupting God knows what Valhalla of angels and demons, what eminences of benignity and eyries of the most refined spook essence." Still, he was not opposed to the attempt. Apollo 11 was a marvelous adventure and may even have been ordained by a God who meant us to "reveal His vision of existence *out there,* somewhere out there where His hegemony came to an end and other divine conceptions began to exist, or indeed were opposed to it."

Mailer, however, sweats for the soul of America—"plastic, that triumph of reason over nature!"—and is disturbed, affronted, that the space people cannot grasp the enormity of their ambitions. For the artist, Mailer writes, the machine—a typewriter, for instance—is functional; it is there to be used to communicate. But for the engineer, "it was the communication itself which was functional. The machine was the art." So Mailer looked distrustfully on the astronauts. Aldrin was a man of "unassailable solemnity," Armstrong was "extraordinarily remote." Collins, however, had a sense of humor: "Of the three, he was the only one you could drink with comfortably." "Are you ever worried that landing on the moon may result in all sorts of psychic disturbances for us here on earth?" Mailer asked the director at Houston. There was no coherent reply.

To believe in technology, Mailer concluded, was to disbelieve in magic; taboos that may be real and valuable have been destroyed. In defense, Mailer constructs "the psychology of machines." Machines, as everyone knows, don't really work consistently; they develop wills of their own. Can a machine express itself, Mailer asks, "free to act in contradiction to its logic and its gears"? The plethora of errors and disasters that has plagued our space program indicates that machines can and do develop personal psychologies. Of course, machines cannot be trusted. Technology, for Mailer, is the sinner in the church of physics, but even physics, the domain of beauty, law, and order, is defective. We still do not know what light *is*, or why waves, bouncing in our ears, make sound. "If the universe was a lock," Mailer writes, "its key was metaphor rather than measure." Even savage man knew that.

Mailer's book may be the best work on the subject, but as a book, it is something less than Mailer's best. As in *The Armies of the Night,* Mailer is strongest when writing of his own engagement with the event itself and the peripheral details that point toward the character of the country today. The essence of Mailer's journalism is that it flakes off on tangential orbits, running aground occasionally, or stubbing itself into absurdity. There is a glorious part at the end where Mailer speculates on his fourth failed marriage and the burial of an ancient automobile, but a great deal of this book is devoted to what Mailer has learned about technology. He explains it well. In fact, he achieves something of a litany when he approaches the dials and knobs and gauges in the command module. Like Walt Whitman, Mailer lets his words run away in his enthusiasm, his images and metaphors tumble over each other in a wild, spawning rush. Mailer has his finger on the American artery as no other writer has, but this time, on a special assignment, he had to grapple with an event that had a significance before he gave it one. It is a damaging drawback. We will remember, I suspect, *The Armies of the Night* longer than we will remember the march on the Pentagon, but we will remember the moon launch longer than Mailer's book. To write at his best, Mailer must have no competition from his subject.

1971

. . . . .The "Times" That Tries Men's Souls

One summer when my father was ill, he taught me to read from the headlines of the New York *Times*. The letters were large and black and spelled words like M-U-S-S-O-L-I-N-I, which I thought was pretty funny but, because it was 1940, my father did not. Steeling himself against the miseries of the world, he read the *Times* from back to front in those days, and I read the paper that way today, having discovered that if I linger over television listings and the shipping news, I may not have time to read about Biafra and the ABM. Still, we who were raised with the *Times* know that it is not only one of those necessities like toothpaste and orange juice that start the world turning in the morning, it is also a worthy cause: If its finances faltered, its readers would take up a collection. The paper is, God knows, more important than appealing, but if it lacks the grace to be the Chartres of journalism, it certainly has the authority to act as the St. Peter's of the press and is well worth the extended treatment it receives from one of its alumni, Gay Talese, in *The Kingdom and the Power*.

There is a nice irony to what Talese has accomplished in this study of the men who publish, edit, and write the world's most influential newspaper. As Talese observes, they are the most inquisitive men in the world, accustomed to analyzing purges and revolutions, to peeking and prying in the name of truth; but now one of their own, a former *Times*man and a man of exhausting inquisitiveness, is doing it to *them*, reporting on the men who report the news and finding in their affairs as much passion and disorder as they have found in Washington and Moscow. Talese has, in fact, made of the *Times'* newsroom what Konrad Lorenz has made of the barnyard: an acre for aggression, where men stake out a territory for mating dances and ritual warfare. Like Adolph

Ochs, the man who made the *Times* what it is today, Talese wants *all* the news, but unlike Ochs, he *prints* all the news, including that which isn't fit, the news about *Times*men drinking, sexing, and weeping, banging their fists on tables and talking to themselves, the news about their fears, rages, and frustrations, their divorces, nervous breakdowns, and intramural vendettas. The result, of course, is a book that sails just in the lee of the libel laws and is far more entertaining than what the *Times* puts out. Although the *Times* urged its staff to cooperate with Talese's inquiry, it must now wonder whether, like Lyndon Johnson displaying his stomach scar, it is not guilty of indecent exposure. At least Talese has taught the *Times* a new rule of journalism: Those who ask too many questions end up by telling too much about themselves.

I do not mean to imply that this is a frivolous or improper book. On the contrary, Talese gets away with his zesty gossip because his intimate and surprising details lend life and credibility to the men upon whom he has based his book and the institution that employs them. Talese aims high: He plans to get inside the minds of the *Times'* top men, and his book begins in 1966 with Clifton Daniel, the managing editor, waiting for a few moments before the news conference that he conducts every day at four P.M. That conference does not take place until the book is about half done, but no matter—it counts for no more than a structural device that allows Talese to move from Daniel's Southern roots and Savile Row urbanity to other events and *Times*men.

Talese's route is complex in the extreme. He seems to roll forward, backward, and laterally in a series of circles—concentric epicycles, perhaps—that would have baffled Ptolemy. Although the book deals primarily with the events of 1966 and the great power struggle between the Washington bureau and the home office of the *Times* in 1968, Talese manages, by his circular ramblings, to cover the entire history of the paper. His story starts, stops, and repeats too often: The name of a reporter or an editor dropped into the narrative stops all motion entirely as Talese pauses for one of the biographies—there must be at least a hundred of them—that he does so well. Only a handful of men, however, are treated in depth: Adolph Ochs, who rescued the paper and established its tone around the turn of the century; Arthur Hays Sulzberger and Arthur Ochs Sulzberger, two of the publishers who succeeded him; James Reston and Harrison Salisbury, star writers for the paper; and three of the top editors: Daniel, Turner Catledge, and Abe Rosenthal.

Like a coroner, Talese lays his subjects out naked and scrapes at their insides, and, like a coroner, he seems better able to diagnose their frailties than their strengths—Catledge's Southern accent, for instance, getting "thicker with each drink," Daniel looking down Margaret

Truman's dress and "being impressed by what he saw." I can almost hear the eyebrows popping up all over the *Times'* newsroom. "Freedman played poker," Talese writes, "his expression being no different from what it was when he was not playing poker. He drank on rare occasions, and when he did, he never seemed to enjoy it."

Not exactly dull writing, but it is the kind of writing that, with increasing frequency, characterizes the best serious journalism in this country. The New Journalism, which Talese helped to develop, is irreverent. It refuses to arrange cold facts in straight lines but seeks to re-create the event, and because more space is needed to show something happening than to describe it, the New Journalism (and certainly this mammoth book) tends to run on too long. Skeptical of "objective" reporting, the New Journalism looks at appearances as well as reality, at what men *think* is true as well as what *is* true, thereby rescuing from the garbage pile some excellent approaches to the truth that had been discarded years before by more pious reporters. Most important, perhaps, the New Journalism recognizes that interpretation is inseparable from fact and that, one way or another, the journalist himself is a part of the action he describes. Irony is the prevailing tone of the New Journalism, but in Talese's book there is a good deal of sentiment as well, and the irony does not quite conceal a sense of awe, of almost religious mystery, that Talese still holds for the paper that once employed him. Like many New Journalists, Talese may find too much significance in trivial details, too much intensity, even conspiracy, floating about the *Times*. Perhaps life there is as nervous as he says it is, with everyone glancing over his shoulder, but if it is, the *Times* must be an exhausting place to be, with little time available to get the day's work done.

And yet, it is a combination of all these qualities—Talese's excesses as well as his skill in baring executive desperation and rancor—that explains why his book is so fascinating and why, months before its publication, it had become *the* book to read. Rumor has it that by early May, people who work in the book business—people who rarely read books and never *buy* them—had filed six hundred and seventy requests for free copies of Talese's ten-dollar volume.

The Kingdom and the Power is a good book, the best I have ever seen about a newspaper, but it is also an important book because it deals very frankly and in great detail with power and responsibility—how they are obtained and how they are exercised. In the long run (if not in the short), power and responsibility are more interesting than either sex or money, and I do not think we can ever have too many books about them. Talese shows what happens to men of exceptional ability and fathomless ambition when they get caught up in the kind of executive cruncher that only an organization as influential as the *Times* provides. He shows, too, what has not often been shown: the depths of despair and humiliation that, more often than not, beset the most spectacularly successful careers. Careless readers may see only the humor, the scandal, and the inside dope that Talese provides, but there is also something of a chill, a warning that may prompt more than one office Machiavelli to settle for early retirement and the joys of growing lima beans.

Finally, the book seems to me important because we should study, as part of the reevaluation that our society so urgently requires, our most prestigious and influential institutions—institutions that are not normally open to public or journalistic scrutiny. What we need is a similar book about the Department of Defense. Is anyone brave enough to take it on?

1969

. . . . Skimming
over America

Braking to take the corner at 35, I pause to read the signs before accelerating in the homestretch: gray hair at the sideburns, a slackening of sinew in the gut, and, as the hard drivers zoom past me in the outside lanes, the awareness that Bill Moyers is already the league champion. When my division was tuning up twenty-seven years ago, we hadn't heard of the East Texas Kid, then nine years old and (doubtless) chairman of his local school board. Now at thirty-six having sowed his wild oats as deputy director of the Peace Corps, Special Assistant to President Johnson, shaper of social legislation, and publisher of an important newspaper, Moyers is trustee of this and director of that. You might expect him to relax, to hobble around a golf course, and write cranky letters to the editor, but no: Having written about Americans and helped to govern them, Moyers set off last summer on a 13,000-mile jaunt to discover "what the country is about [and] who the people are." The result is a book called *Listening to America: A Traveler Rediscovers His Country.*

Moyers went from Hartford to Seattle, from Los Angeles to South Texas, and then to Washington, D.C., inspecting half a dozen crises but more often swilling endless cups of coffee as he listened to people talk: "I don't care for the media." "The colored folks have been actin' up. Eleanor Roosevelt started that." "It's the outside influence that has disrupted us." John Steinbeck, who made a less formal journey a decade earlier, had traveled incognito because "when people have heard of you, favorably or not, they change." But Moyers appears to have used his connections to get into places and meet people he might not otherwise have seen. He watched people try to change society through the system: bossism *vs.* the new politics in a Hartford convention; blacks *vs.* whites in a court hearing on integrating schools—and he watched change come about convulsively outside the system; police *vs.* Chicanos in Texas; whites *vs.* blacks in guerrilla warfare in Kansas.

Scenes such as these are the best parts of the book, and Moyers, who has most of a good reporter's best instincts, plays them out at considerable length, giving the reader the sense of watching America release its tensions. More often, however, he is just listening. He lacks the time to stay with people for very long, so he must chivy them along with Big Questions—"I asked him what Antioch had meant to him"—to which he receives some stiff replies, because "when people have heard of you, they change" and because people, given a few minutes with a famous man, tend to say what they think they believe or wish they believed. The only way to get past that is to stay with the people for weeks or months, watching the discrepancy between what they say and how they act—and Moyers didn't have time for that, although some people gave him instant examples: "What I don't understand is they call me a racist," one man said. "I do a lot of business with niggers."

Moyers talked to many kinds of people: a commander of an American Legion post, an ex-drug addict, a priest ("Agnew makes it respectable to hate"), an immigrant Italian laborer, truck drivers attempting to defy the Teamsters union, a forester who worries about Genesis (are we superior to the salmon only because we have greater firepower?), a father whose daughter had walked out on him, a son who had renounced his father, a black pastor preaching nonviolence just before he was burned out of his home. Not surprisingly, many of them say the same things. "I think we ought to face the fact that the Communists are behind this trouble in the country." "I worked *hard* and the rewards came. Isn't that what America offers?"

At best, he finds fear and anguish in the land; at worst, bitterness and hate. Americans, Moyers concludes, "want the war to stop, they do not want to lose their children, and they want to be proud of their country." For all their doubts, however, they maintain an encouraging optimism and honesty which "make it possible to travel the country in troubled times without losing heart."

Perhaps so, but Moyers has only skimmed the surface, showing us

America exactly as TV journalism shows it to us. His book, written against a deadline, seems to have been assembled in airplanes between cities. It is worthy reporting of its kind, but book journalism offers opportunities for thematic organization that can itself be a commentary on its subject. Moyers' survey has no beginning or end. Unlike Steinbeck, he does not allow his own personality or opinions to play against those of the people he meets; unlike De Tocqueville, Moyers has no original aphorisms or reflections to make on our national character. Moyers' interest is in making things happen; he would be unlikely to write what De Tocqueville wrote: "the problem of human existence preoccupies me ceaselessly, and ceaselessly appalls me." The best reporting contains a kind of metaphysical shudder.

1971

. . . . The American Way of Mayhem

Violence is the language of the mute. Hieronymus Bosch understood: He might have painted violence as a scaly creature, all hands and feet and broken weapons, bouncing up and down, his eyes bulging in an impotent scream, but with no mouth at all. Law, however, is traditionally the language of reason and justice. Like all language, it is insufficient, but, like all, it can change and grow according to what men require of it. Law is the first articulation of civilization; it is the language that rebukes and guards against the dumb brutality of violence. For this reason, we are appalled and angered when we find the practice of law increasing the violence already at large in the land.

And yet this happens more frequently than we suppose. Several recent books testify to it. Of them, John Hersey's *The Algiers Motel Incident* is the roughest, the angriest, the most impetuous, the most sensational, and, probably, the most ill-advised.

On the third night of the riots that ravaged Detroit last July, three Negro men were shot to death in a motel. It was a bad night in general; the police were exhausted, and, as the Detroit papers had it, Negro snipers had turned the city into a battleground. The Detroit Police Department argued that the Negroes had been shooting from the motel and were killed in a fight with the police.

Testimony from survivors of "the motel incident," as elicited in two trials and in Hersey's tape-recorded interviews with those concerned, points to a more sinister story: "The killings at the Algiers," Hersey writes, "were not the executions of snipers . . . but . . . murders embellished by racist abuse, indiscriminate vengeance, sexual jealousy, voyeurism, wanton blood-letting, and sadistic physical and mental tortures characterized by the tormentors as 'a game.' "

The story Hersey tells—and it is a long time before he tells it in coherent form—is that the police, looking for a gun, found instead two white women with the Negroes. In a state of mounting frenzy, they lined the motel occupants up in a corridor, beat them, and dragged them off to be killed. One man died early, literally castrated by the shots he had absorbed; his brother, back from our slaughterhouse in Asia, looked at the body and said, "They don't kill them in Vietnam like that!"

Another was killed after he had apologized to a policeman because his skull had broken the stock of the officer's gun. It is not clear when the third man was shot, but the girls had their clothes ripped off, and the other men, after being told to pray because "We're going to kill all you black niggers off one at a time," were eventually sent home. The police did not report the incident. Two officers later confessed to the killings, but up to now, there have been no convictions, though there may be further trials.

Hersey relates the incident and its aftermath of legal bumbling and harassment of witnesses to make the reader understand how the black man in America thinks about the law. Every citizen, Hersey insists, must "be able to perceive law and order as benefits to himself." Clearly, most American Negroes do not: They believe the law to be what it is in fact for them—an instrument of oppression. One Negro involved in the incident summed up this attitude when he defined justice as "a way of keeping a person from getting more than he's got."

Confronted with such inflammatory material, a critic's first instinct is to criticize America and not the book. Because Hersey's cause is just, it seems churlish to suggest that his book is inadequate—but it is. In fact, with criminal proceedings still pending against some of the characters in this book, it may even be improper. There is a tone of moral arrogance to Hersey's private prosecution of those he believes guilty. He is usually, but not always, careful of what he says, relying on Ironic Juxtaposition rather than on outright accusation to make his message clear. But it *is* clear, and it may affect the trials of the men involved. Hersey apparently feels the cause of greater justice is better served by publicizing the atrocity.

Hersey's examination of the sources and effects of prejudice takes the form of a kaleidoscopic slide show—an event in which the photographer feels no obligation to present his slides in order or to winnow out the duplicates, but insists on interjecting views of himself against the scenery, waving self-consciously at the camera. We see Hersey angry, Hersey refusing money for his book, Hersey lecturing on journalism. Mostly, we see Hersey so intent on accuracy that he will repeat virtually identical testimony. Doggedly, he establishes every detail, no matter how dull or dubiously relevant, no matter how many times he must switch narration to complete a tiny story. And everything is presented in brief snatches of testimony (each with its own little headline) culled from a vast cast of characters and court records. The intent behind these incessant breaks is to underline the drama and irony of the narrative, but, in fact, the story succumbs to convulsive spastic twitches. As in those endless Andy Warhol films that use the same technique of artless recitation, the audience becomes less involved than mesmerized by the performance.

Two characters are allowed sufficient uninterrupted time to tell their stories. One is the mother of one of the murdered men, crying for vengeance and weeping for her decent, dim-witted, persecuted son; the other is one of the policemen involved in the incident, a man who clearly loved his job "trolling for whores" with the vice squad. Perhaps Hersey means to imply that if we can learn to look carefully at such people, and indeed at ourselves, we will find the vulnerability and callousness that have produced countless similar incidents and will surely produce many more. Perhaps, but then, Hersey is both cautious and arty. His book cries out—for justice and for proper editing.

1969

. . . . Culinary Metaphysics

Robert Farrar Capon's *The Supper of the Lamb* is something like a great book and carries many classifications before it. Capon is an Episcopal priest and "an Anglican, or moderately high-church, cook." His book, therefore, is an exhortation to Christian metaphysics, but because Capon, like Rabelais, Herbert, and Hopkins before him, is a writer-priest who knows what *this* life is all about, it is also a cookbook. More than that, it is a celebration of all creation, an ingenious metaphor and an extended essay on the astonishing oddness and superfluity of the world. It is a baroque book that evokes the ghosts of Browne and Burton. It is also a witty and persuasive critique of the materialism with which we satisfy our spirits and the mediocrity that we allow to please our senses.

Now that you know what the book *is,* I can safely turn to details. Capon's concern is to tell us how to prepare a single large leg of lamb for eight people four times. He will no more hurry the instruction than he expects you to hurry the preparation. Let the professionals meet their deadlines; this is a book for the amateur, the lover who is not bored by the world. And since "a silent lover is one who does not know his job," Capon puts his heels up on his stove, sips from a glass of cooking sherry and digresses at length about what he does not like—electric knives and stoves, Teflon, diets, prepared foods, and efficiency—and what he does like—food, wine, playfulness, humor, leisure, sanity, substance, fasting, and the joy to be discovered in small things.

"The world looks as if it had been left in the custody of a pack of trolls," he writes. "Indeed, the whole distinction between art and trash, between food and garbage, depends on the presence or absence of the loving eye." The loving eye is ours—if we can learn to appreciate what we see—and God's (Capon makes his transitions very smoothly), since the world exists only because "God likes it; therefore, it stays." With God in the world, we cannot fall into the mean-spirited heresy of making things in the world over to our own use. "The world exists," Capon writes, "not for what it means, but for what it is. . . . Man's real work is to look at the things of the world and to love them for what they are."

So it is with onions, as well as with people. "I must teach you first how to deal with onions," Capon says, presumably because onions, though marvelous in themselves, are easier to cope with than are people. Capon will show you that an hour spent in the company of onions is an hour profitably spent—one must enjoy not only the results of cooking but the process of cooking, too—and he will show you also how proper consideration of an onion fixes the location of heaven. He throws in an essay on knives, another on stocks and gravies, and a hymn to water as it is transmuted by the seasons into wine. Other chapters cope with pastries, entertaining in the grand manner, physical and spiritual heartburn. And, at the close, there is a royal rasher of recipes.

"We are free," Capon writes, "nothing is needful, everything is for joy." Think for a moment. If you are honest, you will probably disagree with all three statements, short and inoffensive as they are. Hence the need for a book like this. It contains an uncommon quantity of wisdom, and not an ounce of foolishness. Capon would insist that if you buy any of his ideas, you must buy them all—from the onion to the Christian cosmology, all are inseparably linked. Many readers will not be able to agree, but I hope they will pick what they can from this remarkable volume. *The Supper of the Lamb* is the kind of book we need to set our priorities in order when, inevitably, they fall awry.

1969

......................Art & Action:
Books to Read While
Waiting for the Revolution

Summertime, and the windows are open. Sap and students rise in the spring, but in June the temperature escalates and so do angry voices—voices in the streets shouting "Pig" and "Burn," and voices in books demanding "an end to racist exploitation at home and imperialist genocide abroad." Perhaps the first casualty of any revolution is not truth but language. It is easier to take sides in a scrap than to remember the humanitarian concern that provoked the battle, easier to zap people with monosyllables and Marx's tattered rhetoric than to persuade them with argument. It's more fun, too: Let the honky warmonger bug his eyes in fury; he'll never understand anything anyway.

To see language used to suppress thought or to coarsen feeling, to see language used to make us less than human, is a frightening if familiar experience. An irony of our time is that we see language misused in this way to support just causes. Many of today's revolutionaries, insensitive and ignorant of history, seem determined to narrow the base of their support. Those who, like Rap Brown and Julius Lester, have bled a lot no longer want to talk to us—"Too long a sacrifice," Yeats wrote, "can make a stone of the heart"—and we who read their books often find it hard to keep our liberal goodwill in working order. Some lines from Brecht can help:

> *We who prepared the ground for friendliness*
> *Could not be friendly ourselves. But you,*
> *When things have come so far that man helps*
> *His fellow man—make allowances for us.*

Because noisy and cruel books, venom and violence spewing across their pages, always receive more notice than is their due, I thought it worthwhile to look at two equally radical but very measured books which, because they are cool, quiet, and precise in their appreciation of language and history, may very well go ignored.

John Berger's *Art and Revolution* is ostensibly a critical study of the work of a Russian sculptor, Ernst Neizvestny. Casual readers should not be put off quite yet. Berger, aware that few people know of or care about Neizvestny's work, uses it as a base from which he strikes out to explore fundamental definitions of art and first principles of courage, integrity, and man's role in society. Like most critics, Berger intends his criticism to be provocative whether or not Neizvestny is a good artist. In this he succeeds. The fascination of his book lies not in Neizvestny's work but in the triangular tension Berger discovers in the life of the artist, the medium in which he works and the history of Russian art from medieval times to the present, which both shapes and impedes what Neizvestny tries to do.

Neizvestny was born in 1926. He is, says Berger, "a notorious, officially condemned, decadent and 'unpatriotic' sculptor." His work is not particularly modern; it looks like sculpture done in Europe after World War I. There is a hint of Henry Moore in it but none of Moore's tranquillity; its vigor and anguish are closer to Rodin's work—had Rodin punched holes in his figures' intestines. Neizvestny's work is unknown outside Russia because it may not be exported; moreover, Neizvestny must obtain his materials and cast his figures illegally. The Russian government is scared of him because he is *not* a rebel, because he conceives of his work as public monuments and offers his vision as an alternative to the government's view of art.

Neizvestny's situation leads Berger to a careful analysis of realism and naturalism in art. Realism is an attempt to portray a representative example of the totality of an experience, but naturalism is unselective, concerned only with the credibility of the immediate experience. The serious artist, Berger explains, runs into trouble when the state tries to fossilize art, sacrificing the complexity good art requires for poster art, short-term propaganda designed to serve the regime. What Russia has done, Berger says, is to make its idea of art-as-propaganda a permanent doctrine, thus cutting off any possibility of future development in Soviet art.

Berger works backward and sideways, examining the prophetic quality of Russian art, the public quality of sculpture and the intimate relation of sculpture to the space it occupies. Because Neizvestny nearly died of a wound in the war, he has acquired a fine eye for measuring our distance from death. Most of us, Berger observes, look at death from the prospect of living and thereby become aware of how precarious life is. Neizvestny reverses the process: Having come from death, he is aware of the tenacity of life. His theme of human endurance lends importance to his work.

Although Berger flirts with Hegelian and Marxist terms, his essay is, until the end, free of critical cant and clichés. In the last few pages, he calls for the revolution that will bring equality to all men and advises those who cannot help bring it about to commit suicide. Ah, well. It is astonishing that writers who can think as precisely and use words as exactly as Berger can become flatulent when confronting the misery of the masses. Its final pages excepted, *Art and Revolution* is a concise and brilliant book; I found myself trying to memorize whole paragraphs.

In *The Urban Guerrilla,* Martin Oppenheimer takes a cool, antiseptic look at what might happen if Berger's revolution came to America—say by the end of this summer. Oppenheimer is a sociologist and obsessed by the jargon of his trade, but, somehow, the jargon works to his advantage: Chaos is reduced to neat and precisely measurable laws of probability. I'm for that (Down, chaos! See how easily I can squeeze you into my computer!), even if it means that a riot, which I once thought was broken heads, blood, snipers, and burning buildings, becomes "proto-political behavior" and "a primitive form of political action."

Oppenheimer is primarily concerned with the plight of the Negro in America today. He foresees three programs our government might follow: 1. repression, which leads to a police state and a race war; 2. integrationist reform, which simply perpetuates the present stagnation; 3. Black Power, which, even if it results in black separatism, is no better than neo-colonialism because Negroes on this continent, no matter how they are organized, are inseparably linked to white society. The alternative, as Oppenheimer sees it, is revolution, and a "revolutionary situation potentially exists" in our society.

But, says Oppenheimer, a revolution will not work. Our society is too healthy to support one. To prove his point, he lumbers patiently through a whole catalogue of antisocial action, defining the difference between peasant uprisings and rural banditry, and then examines the mass revolts of modern history—from the Paris Commune to the Warsaw risings in World War II—all of which failed, with disastrous results for the rebels. He is skeptical, too, of the way modern revolutions tend to betray their purposes. Nearly all are begun by an elite corps and end with repressive bureaucracies. "The kind of people," Oppenheimer remarks, "who become active in insurrections and survive it tend not to be the kind of people who will create a positive, humanistic order."

Finally, he looks at the conditions necessary to sustain a revolt and finds none present in our society. Few radical critics of the way we live now have either the honesty or objectivity to say that we need a revolt, but cannot have one. Oppenheimer presents three "scenarios" of what might happen if revolts were attempted. Negroes rising in a ghetto would be massacred within forty-eight hours. A gradual buildup of terrorism and sabotage, however, might end with the disruption of the government and an appeal to a strong man: Left-wing risings often end in right-wing repression. Oppenheimer himself has hopes for a nonviolent revolution, led by the alumni of the SDS, which will stage small-scale "creative dislocations": strikes and slowdowns, tax and draft refusal. It seems hardly credible, and Oppenheimer apologizes for it.

Would-be revolutionaries can find much practical information in *The Urban Guerrilla*. It appears to be the first book about the actual specifics of guerrilla warfare in an urban setting, which, of course, is where the war will come, if it ever does. Oppenheimer is not sure it will, and his book is therefore more optimistic than most. In any event, it will not come for a decade. Perhaps that is as much optimism as we can ask for.

1969

·················· Distemper from the Docks

Men fear thinking as students fear final examinations, and as that natural fear in students is increased by tales of failure, so does men's fear grow by the failure of thought. Certainly the contemplation of ideas, as an intellectual exercise and passage to other worlds, is good and virtuous; but the fear of thought, an inhibitor of action, is weak. Yet in many thoughtful books there is sometimes a mixture of slovenliness and pigheadedness.

Does that rhetoric seem familiar? If you can detect a whiff of Bacon lingering about the prose, it is because it is difficult to write about Eric Hoffer without falling into a cheap imitation of his aphoristic style, a style he developed from reading Bacon and his contemporary John Florio, translator of Montaigne.

Hoffer is, of course, the thinking man's longshoreman. He spends three days a week laboring on the docks, another day as a professor at Berkeley, and, presumably, the rest of his time reading, thinking, and writing the kind of concise and orderly essays which appear in this book, the third volume he has published since his phenomenally successful *The True Believer.*

The Temper of Our Times contains six essays on Mr. Hoffer's objections to the quality of life in America today. His principle theme is lack of maturity: "Up to now in this country we are warned not to waste our time but we are brought up to waste our lives. . . . It takes leisure to mature. People in a hurry can neither grow nor decay; they are preserved in a state of perpetual puerility." Frenetic activity and lack of leisure rob man of his humanity as well as his maturity; what disturbs Hoffer most is man's apparent willingness to settle for being something less than a man.

Everything contributes to this falling off: "Power is always charged with the impulse to eliminate human nature"; so are nationalism, machines, mass movements, government, intellectuals, nature, and change. In his essays Hoffer examines many subjects—our inability to cope with automation; the fraudulent failure of the Negro revolution; the need to establish a class of permanent students as a part of the American way of life; the antagonism between man and nature; the elements of juvenile primitivism, if not juvenile delinquency, in much of our thinking and our institutions; and the catastrophic effect of those he calls intellectuals in the governments of nations.

A stoic, a pessimist, a conservative to the bone, Hoffer is a sparkling writer and a dangerous thinker. The rhythms of his prose invite an acquiescence in his prejudices; everything he says is impressive at first glance and half of it remains impressive upon examination. But there is a glib and facile slickness in his compulsion to generalization: "Man became what he is not with the aid, but in spite, of nature." Such a pronouncement is typical of the Hofferian Half-Truth: Darwin and Freud put nature back in man; now is Hoffer trying to gut it out again? Or is he saying that we are only human insofar as we have raised reason above biology?

"That which corrodes the soul of the Negro is his monstrous inner agreement with the prevailing prejudice against him." Now there *is* a statement—fascinating, challenging; it seems to fit if you squint at it through the dust of certain evidence, but is it *really* true? Hoffer doesn't try to prove the point, or any of his points; neither does he consider the objections to his theses; nor does he always define his terms. Hoffer's purpose, we must remember, is not to persuade by argument but to stun by aphorism; that way all the messy compromises that thinking involves can be avoided. Thinking is really what bothers Hoffer; there is a distinctly anti-intellectual stench to these pages. Hoffer seriously believes that intellectuals seek to dehumanize mankind—a belief that could be sniffed at seriously only if Hoffer had condescended to define what he means by "intellectual."

What passes for argument in Hoffer's essays relies upon a shaky transition from an unprovable (or at least unproven) assumption to an often witty conclusion and an admirable, if perhaps untenable, generalization. Example: "The technology developed during the late Neolithic Age," he writes, "lasted almost unchanged down to the industrial revolution. A greater gulf lies between us and Washington than lay between him and the Egyptian farmers who labored for Cheops." The trouble with this is that it is garbage, offered in total contradiction of common sense. One can see the poor point poking through—technology has developed more in the period between Washington and us than in that between Washington and Cheops—but it is vitiated by imprecise language that implies more than perhaps was meant. What, for instance, does "almost unchanged" mean? The printing press, the compass, and the telescope—technological inventions which profoundly changed man's life and thought—intervened between our Neolithic ancestors and George Washington. Has Hoffer forgotten them? Or does he discount them? We have no way of knowing, only the suspicion that he is so fond of the sweeping statement that he doesn't stop to think. Moreover, Hoffer seems to imply that technology creates a more insuperable gulf than do culture and language. Of *course* we are closer to Washington than Washington was to Cheops. Washington spoke English, for one thing, enjoyed the same arguments, food, and music that I do, and was a democrat. I'd be glad to have my daughter marry Washington, but not Cheops' farmer.

Hoffer's arguments are shoddy and his famous prose slipshod. And yet he likes good prose, likes it for the right reasons. He writes of Florio's Montaigne: "The sentences have hooks in them which stick in the mind; they make platitudes sound as if they were new." This is what Hoffer has striven for in his own prose, and he almost gets there. He deserves better than his place with Zane Grey in Eisenhower's pantheon of favorite authors; I would not dislike him so much if he were not taken so seriously by those who should know better. Hoffer may try to imitate Montaigne's style, but, lacking Montaigne's mind, he will always fail.

1967

. . . ."In a Free Society,
You Have to
Take Some Risks."*

A few years ago, the police in my exurban town decided to set up a corps of civilian informers who would be encouraged to look suspiciously on their neighbors' activities and report whatever irregularities they observed to the police. Democratic institutions would be preserved, of course, by assuring informers that their identities would be kept secret, even from those they had accused, and by welcoming, without inquiry into qualification or motive, all volunteers.

It was a popular move around here, I can tell you. Scores of citizens dusted off old Junior G-Man badges and polished up old grudges. Our local paper stopped whining about bleeding hearts and idle teen-agers, to whine instead about the minority of malcontents who objected to the plan. The paper also printed a letter from one of our town's rich old men, who said that if he had to choose between preserving his freedoms against attacks by government and preserving his mailbox against attacks by vandals, he would choose his mailbox every time.

Eventually, the plan was defeated, but the story has a point, a point that rests with that old man and the millions of Americans like him who prize their mailboxes more highly than their freedom—or, to be precise, the *other* guy's freedom, which most people think is somehow separable from their own. Perhaps eighteenth-century ideas of freedom and democracy are no longer relevant in the overcrowded country we live in today, but it is nonetheless disturbing to watch those ideas, which once we cherished, fall before the meretricious arguments of ambitious lawyers, who use our fears to further their own careers in politics.

In *Justice: The Crisis of Law, Order and Freedom in America,* a study of the men who run the Department of Justice—and by extension, a study of Americans' attitudes toward crime in this past decade—Richard Harris shows us these lawyers at work, calmly, diligently hacking away at the rights of every American. Harris, who has written at length over the years about our government's relation to justice, believes that our

*The quotation that serves for my title comes from North Carolina's Senator Sam Ervin. This review, written in February, 1970, was set in final proof by *Look,* which was then in a hassle with the Department of Justice. It was never published. "We had to make room for an advertisement," I was told at first, and later I was told the truth.

present crisis has come about because in order to fulfill a political promise—to fire Ramsey Clark, then the Attorney General, and to reverse the rising crime rate in America—Nixon has politicized the Department of Justice. The men Nixon brought to the Department, from Attorney General John Mitchell down through the assistants he selected, are, says Harris, singularly ill-equipped and disinclined to cope with the issues before them. What they are doing now, far from solving the problem of crime in America, aggravates the conditions that produce the crime.

For example, Harris says that Mitchell's attempts to slow integration in the South—a scandalous case of sacrificing justice for political ends—will drive more Negroes to Northern ghettos, where much of the nation's crime is bred. Similarly, the politicalization of the Department has cost many experienced men their jobs, thus reducing the Department's efficiency, and has made it difficult for the Department to attract young, idealistic lawyers. Instead of trying to upgrade the skills and standards of police forces everywhere, Harris says, the Department now gives them money directly with which to buy new armaments, which will undoubtedly be used. The irony, as Ramsey Clark has observed, is that the suburbanites—those who suffer least from crime—"would deprive those who suffer most"—the ghetto dwellers—"of the very programs that would attack the underlying causes of crime."

One must expect such ironies when justice is made a game that politicians play. The ironies, Harris feels, begin with Nixon's attack on Clark himself. According to those who watched his performance, Clark was the most aggressive crime buster ever to serve as Attorney General. Even Nixon liked Clark and admired his efficiency—but the way to get elected was to denounce Clark and to fool the voters into thinking that crime in America was somehow Clark's fault and that he, Nixon, could do something about it. Harris' portrait of Ramsey Clark is that of a capable, humane, self-effacing man with a scrupulous regard for the Constitution and the integrity of his Department.

By contrast, says Harris, John Mitchell was unfamiliar with the governing process, disdainful of social theory, ignorant of the history of the problems confronting the country, out of touch with the young, the poor, and the black, and unconcerned with the threat his actions posed to the Constitution. One of Mitchell's first official acts was to violate the First Amendment: He announced that "activists" would be denied permits to do whatever it was he thought they had in mind. The men Mitchell brought with him were worse: The man to be put in charge of the Department's Civil Rights Division, for instance, clung to his membership in all-white fraternal order. Mitchell and his men, as Harris shows them to us, are not stupid, not malevolent, but they are intemperate in their language, insensitive to the desperation of many Americans, indifferent to justice when it appears to thwart what they take to be their political mission. They are cold, narrow men, unspeakably ambitious, determined to suppress dissent and use the awesome power they can easily amass to force order, if not law, upon the people. Harris is appalled. Is the rule of law inviolable or, under Nixon and Mitchell, is it now negotiable in political terms?

Harris is one of our most skillful and knowledgeable reporters. His account of Justice's attitudes and operations is entirely persuasive and is of course confirmed by events that have occurred since his book was written. He begins his argument slowly, in a minor key of calm and detailed inquiry, and builds through impeccable transitions in time and focus, gradually shedding his tone of cool and reasonable discourse until, at the end, when the atrocities are laid out cold for the reader, Harris' voice achieves an iron ring of anger. I have not read a grimmer book about our government in years and urge all those who are not yet alarmed by our country's planned progression toward an abridgment of freedom and justice to read it without delay.

1970

. . . . Two More American Tragedies

. . . Report me and my cause aright
To the unsatisfied. (Hamlet, V: 2)

At the end of the play, you remember, with bodies strewn thigh-deep across the stage and a new administration banging at the castle gate, Hamlet broods about his reputation. The latest poll, pinned to his tunic pocket, shows Danish opinion divided: 47 percent for Claudius, 43 percent for Hamlet, 2 percent for Fortinbras, and 8 percent undecided. The average Dane, Hamlet knows, will forgive his prince's sanity gap, but a quantity of corpses requires delicate explaining. Hamlet appoints Horatio, loyal if a bit thick-headed, palace historian, and dies. Too bad he forgot Osric, special consultant to the king and a secret scribbler as well. Osric has seen everything, and Osric plans to get his book on the market first.

So now, with the corpse of the last administration still warm to the touch, we have the first insider's report: Eric F. Goldman's *The Tragedy of Lyndon Johnson*. It is important that we have such books. Whether or not a President understands the people, the people must have every opportunity to understand the President and the terrible demands that the office makes upon him. Goldman's book is in part a history of the first half of the Johnson Administration and in part a memoir of Goldman's frustrations in his role as Johnson's tame intellectual. Flawed as his book most certainly is, it is nonetheless valuable for its group portrait of the President and his aides, men who worked under incredible strain. Astonishingly, because Goldman failed to accomplish what he had hoped and quit in a barrage of recrimination, it is a sympathetic portrait.

Goldman, a professor of history at Princeton, came to Washington in December, 1963. The President asked him to form a task force of "the best minds" in the country to suggest goals and programs for the new administration and—in a typically Johnsonian move—to keep the task force *secret*. Goldman stayed on as speech writer and a special consultant, the liaison between the White House and the people with whom Johnson felt least at ease: intellectuals and "Metroamericans," a term Goldman coins to describe those influential Americans—liberal, educated, affluent, and pragmatic—who live in the cities and suburbs of the nation. Goldman hoped he could help Johnson "achieve a genuine relationship with the part of America that was also able and also cared," but, as the world knows, he couldn't. Johnson's distrust of intellectuals verged on paranoia: He dealt with the "sonsofbitches"—Johnson's word for writers and professors—"as if he were negotiating with an alien force." Any critic of Johnson's war in Vietnam was open to attack: "Liberal critics!" he once shouted. "It's the Russians who are behind the whole thing."

Nowhere else does the President look so shabby. Goldman presents him as a well-intentioned, able manager of vast energy, a man with a "broad streak of simple patriotism, often sentimental in his thinking and evangelical in tone." Convictions were not included in the syllabus of Johnson's political education, but he eventually acquired some and, through "political osteopathy," did something about them. Goldman's descriptions of Johnson's conversion to the cause of civil rights and Johnson's handling of Governor Wallace during the march from Selma show the President at his best. Johnson pursued "some dogged version of the credo that America means a better shake for the ordinary man," and he had faith in education. "He had," Goldman writes, "the belief of the superficially educated man in the magic of education and a feeling that if he could only find the right formula, he would loose an unending stream of 'ideas.' " Finally, Goldman feels that Johnson was a "strong man overwhelmed by forces, from within and without. . . . An extraordinarily gifted President who was the wrong man under the wrong circumstances."

Goldman's book is full of good anecdotes and perceptive sketches of Johnson's aides, his wife, and his unfortunate Vice President. His prose has a cutting edge that is used only rarely to settle old scores. His greatest strength is his ability to link any event—the passage of a major bill or a defect in the Presidential personality—to some current of American character or history. And yet his book is strongest when it deals with events in which Goldman took part and weakest when it tries to be history. Goldman describes the Johnson legislation very well indeed, and the 1964 campaign rather dully. All of this is available elsewhere. What is lacking in Goldman's book—and what any work of history needs—is an appreciation of the mood of the country. Goldman, enjoying "the exhilarating feeling of being part of the command post of the nation," misses the depth of bitterness, the anguish, and sick numbness felt by so many who were not part of the action in the capital and who realized, for perhaps the first time, how powerless citizens in a democracy could be.

The intellectuals—most articulate of the disaffected—alienated Johnson and made a shambles of Goldman's White House Festival of the Arts. Now Goldman lets out a shriek of rage—not against the President but against his own kind. Rational argument succumbs to rhetorical artifice as he insists that only a minority of intellectuals oppose the Vietnam War and do so for base reasons—because they want to conform or to grope their way up some slippery academic ladder. What right, Goldman asks, have *intellectuals* to be heard on something as complex as foreign policy? It is a sorry business, unworthy of a historian. Intellectuals, believing they have an obligation to speak out in a democracy, wanted, for the most part, only to say something as simple as "Stop the killing abroad. Stop the corrosion at home. This is not what America is all about." People in power, wrapped up in the complexity of detail, tend to forget how simple the essence of things can be; they forget, too, the extent to which their own complex, professional knowledge can mislead them. Goldman, the historian, should have remembered.

The second American tragedy takes place at the opposite end of the nation's political scale. Two days before he disappeared, Eldridge Cleaver told Robert Scheer of *Ramparts* magazine that the cops would kill him if he were returned to prison. As of this writing, Cleaver is still fugiting from justice. But, like Christ, Zapata, and James Dean, Cleaver has not *really* left us. People are bugging the FBI with reports that he is alive and well in such improbable places as Ithaca and Elk River, Idaho. According to the underground press, nine people were arrested by mid-December: seven "on suspicion of being Eldridge Cleaver," one for "impersonating a revolutionary hero," and one for wearing a "very convincing" rubber face mask made to look like Cleaver.

Last year, Cleaver, the most eloquent of today's radical black leaders, published *Soul on Ice,* a spiritual autobiography written from prison to show how someone of mature years can discover how he can yet become a man. Cleaver might have become one of our best writers had he not thought it more important to become involved with the Black Panthers, preaching "a guerrilla resistance movement that will amount to a second Civil War." I think Cleaver is wrong, but I cannot blame him; if what has happened to him had happened to me, I'd be running around with guns and slogans, too. Cleaver, who rather likes the white man and has a gift of irony, invites me (and others) to join him anyway. I don't join him because the blacks' cause is not worth sacrificing everything else our society has achieved, but I'm still a bit embarrassed by my refusal.

Now, Scheer has pasted together a collection of Cleaver's articles and speeches in a book called *Eldridge Cleaver.* It is not a good book, though there is good stuff in it. Mostly, it is a polemic, a call to arms and violence: "Total liberty for black people or total destruction for America." There is a modicum of interest here—in seeing where intelligent, radical black men stand today, and what Cleaver said when he found that good writing was not enough—and at least the book makes us hope Cleaver may live to write better books, and that America must someday admit that political prisoners and political refugees are a fact of its political life.

1969

. . . . Up Against the Wall, Please, So You Can Hear Me Better

Much has been said about the responsibilities of power, but nothing, I think, as succinctly wise as Goethe's axiom that power should act, not talk. A certain spastic convulsion of the mouth seems to be the occupational disease of our modern revolutionaries—certainly it would be easier to like Fidel Castro or Rap Brown if they could keep their tongues behind their teeth. For a while, you remember, the monumental silence of Che Guevara enchanted us all, but this picture of the model revolutionary, quietly cultivating his neighbor's garden, could not survive the posthumous publication of his speeches and letters. In death, Che proved as banal as the rest. New recruits to the ranks of revolution might do well to imitate Mao, who seems to understand that the time to talk your mouth off is when you have no power; once you have got the machine guns pointing at your audience, you shut up, wave gently at the multitudes, and write obscure poetry that your literary critics will be afraid to admit they do not understand.

These, and some rather darker thoughts, are the results of reading two accounts of the student revolution that nearly destroyed Columbia University last spring. One of them, *Crisis at Columbia,* is simply the text of the report of the Cox Commission, that being the fact-finding committee established by the Columbia faculty to look into the causes and history of the revolt. Such official reports have lately become an important staple in the American reading diet, but this is a good one, sound and concise, intelligent and more readable than most, though a moralistic tone ("These were plainly dishonorable acts") is too often attached to the narrative of events.

Much more detailed and much more exciting is *Up Against the Ivy Wall: A History of the Columbia Crisis* by Jerry L. Avorn, Robert Friedman, and other members of the staff of the *Columbia Daily Spectator.* We must not be paternalistic about the authors' youth: This is, by any standard, a remarkable work of journalism and, I am convinced, essential reading for anyone who has not given up hope that he may yet understand what it is that young people are trying to tell him. One reason the book is so good is that its authors had both the space and the inclination to explore, if not the character, then the behavioral reflexes of the two antagonists. These two men, Mark Rudd and Grayson Kirk, emerge larger than life, as if between them lay the entire generation gap, a gulf that divides the neurotic violence of youthful idealism from the blind insensitivity of an educator whose university had become a whited sepulcher.

Rudd is a victim of the mouth-over-muscle syndrome I mentioned earlier. He and his SDS storm troopers excelled at seizing university buildings, refusing to debate university officials, and hurling obscenities at the police. A combination of silence and violence might have proved more terrifying, as SDS learned from Columbia's black militants, who were even more morose and menacing than SDS. Rudd's flaw, however, was his weakness for the podium and bullhorn, for publishing letters and leaflets from behind the barricades. The violence, now, is gone, but much of Rudd's verbiage remains. Removed from the atmosphere of Armageddon, it seems strange: Good arguments collapsed before Rudd's ignorance, good sentences damaged by crumbling syntax, youth's moral indignation weakened by hysteria. There is also the memory of these revolutionaries, the first in history to spend the better part of their time hollering for amnesty from the power structure they intended to destroy. It was hardly an edifying spectacle for the hordes of spectators who might have been radicalized if only Rudd and his friends had had more of a taste for martyrdom.

There is a danger that we may not take these students and their revolution seriously. Yet we must take them seriously—first, because they will not let us alone if we do not; second, because they are right in what they criticize; and third, because if we are still alert, we may yet cure our ills without the revolution that the Ruddites call for.

Unattractive revolutionaries could be curbed more easily if only those against whom they revolt were not more unattractive still. For all his own ineptitude, Rudd knew his opponent. "Grayson," he wrote to the president of the university, "I doubt you will understand any of this." Grayson Kirk, a sixty-four-year-old man with jowls, a three-piece suit, and a talent for fund-raising, didn't. Kirk thought SDS was a bunch of "nihilists" who had no business criticizing Columbia's support of the Vietnamese War or the university's eviction of black people from their homes in Morningside Park. As a devout supporter of remote and totalitarian discipline, Kirk had no use for SDS's appeals for due process in matters of student punishment. Even when Rudd told Kirk exactly what SDS stood for, Kirk wouldn't listen; but then, he hadn't been listening for years. Like Louis XVI, who wrote *"Rien"* in his diary the day the Bastille fell, Kirk refused to act on a report he had commissioned two years earlier on student participation in university policy. Kirk, said one professor, "hasn't spoken to anyone under thirty since he was under thirty." Very likely, Rudd knew that Kirk would respond to aggression exactly as Rudd intended him to do, thus hastening the "confrontation," the physical clash which showed uncommitted students and faculty that the administration's authority was based not on moral right but on its ability to suppress dissent. The cops busted the students, the university succumbed to a strike, and, by the end of the summer, Kirk had gone. Nothing of the sort had happened in an American university before.

The editors of the college newspaper knew more about what happened than anyone else. They had an *entrée* into conferences that were barred to other members of the press—particularly those meetings of the liberal faculty group that tried to mediate the revolt. These editors have put together the full story of the crisis with such loving care and meticulous attention to detail that they have managed to re-create the intense drama of the experience, proving, rather than telling us, just how dangerous it was. They have also come up with some marvelous vignettes:

• Students milling aimlessly on the campus as a professor of politics mutters, "They have absolutely no strategy, absolutely no strategy."

• Rudd telling his followers, when they occupied an administration building, that he was not prepared to make a stand or to risk his life.

• A city policeman calling for reinforcements saying, "I'm at Fordham University."

• A varsity wrestler, one of the politically conservative athletes who posed a threat of violence, saying, "If this is a barbaric society, it is the survival of the fittest, and we are the fittest."

• Postgraduate architecture students taking pride in designing what they believed to be impregnable barricades.

Up Against the Ivy Wall is critical of Rudd and his followers to the extent that they misunderstood what was actually happening. Otherwise, it is a judiciously partisan book, fairly describing the activities of the senior faculty, but unabashedly favoring the students' point of view. Never, I'm afraid, will we get Grayson Kirk's side of the story, but if there is any criticism to be made of this account, it might be that not enough attention is paid to the junior faculty, those peculiarly vulnerable liberals who wrestled with their consciences and the pressures to turn radical activist during those dangerous days.

My wife was one of those. She stood against Low Library in the faculty cordon designed to keep the warring factions apart and safe from violence. She sympathized with the revolutionaries' grievances, but not their attitudes. She was troubled by their mendacity and their paranoia, and amused by the masculine supremacy of this revolution in which Barnard girls reported that they were expected to make sandwiches. But she was most disturbed by the revolutionaries' cold-blooded willingness to manipulate people—often their allies—emotionally, deliberately exploiting issues that had troubled many decent people simply to gain supporters for SDS's cause. Like most fanatics, they treated people not as if they were individuals but as if they were psychic counters to be pushed around in some revolutionary game.

So the revolution lost one adherent. But the story is far from finished, which is all the more reason why all of us should read this early chapter.

1968

. . . . An Imitation of Excess

Bad thinking, as Orwell once reminded us, makes bad language. That was a quarter of a century ago and Orwell was seething over what people did back then: They bombed villages, machine-gunned cattle, set fire to huts and called it "pacification." It seems that the deterioration of language is inescapably linked both to violence and to the disintegration of thought. Political speech, Orwell wrote, is "largely the defense of the indefensible," and political language consists of "euphemism, question-begging and sheer cloudy vagueness." These grim deductions, more than the vagaries of the Nixon Administration, are the real subject of Philip Roth's *Our Gang,* perhaps the funniest and most complex exercise in sustained political satire since *Animal Farm.*

The spark that ignites Roth's holocaust flies from President Nixon's pronouncement that "from personal and religious beliefs I consider abortions an unacceptable form of population control." A popular view for centuries: Dean Swift proposed that the Irish eat their babies to "prevent those voluntary abortions . . . alas, too frequent among us." Even if, as some suggest, Swift was only funning, Trick E. Dixon, the hero of *Our Gang,* is serious. If Lieutenant Calley could not see that a woman he shot was pregnant, Tricky says, then Calley "could *not* be said to have engaged in an unacceptable form of population control, and it would be possible for me to square what he did with my personal belief in the sanctity of human life."

Tricky and his gang—various flunkies, journalists, and even the Presidential prayermonger, Billy Cupcake—are concerned with Tricky's program of "Prenatal Power," of giving the vote to the embryos because, as Tricky observes, they accomplish difficult changes of structure "without waving signs for the camera and disrupting traffic." Nor are they likely to be taken in by the media. Much good it does Tricky. The Boy Scouts rise and Tricky's soldiers bravely shoot some. The blame is fixed on Curt Flood, who is trying to destroy baseball and may be hiding in Denmark, where the Pro-pornography government holds power. Tricky bombs Copenhagen, citing Danish territorial designs on America since the eleventh century.

Finally, because all good satire must show the villain still going strong at the end, Tricky is not even deterred by his own assassination; he campaigns to overthrow Satan in Hell. "I call what he has done here surrender, and let me tell you something—I think that's what the leaders in Heaven are calling it, too. Because make no mistake about it—I know the other side, I have met with their representatives. I know the kind of ruthless, fanatical people they are." No reason to think Tricky won't win.

The voice is unmistakable—"now, winding down the trial system will of course be a great boon to the dignity of our judges, who will no longer be forced to demean themselves by dealing with the most undesirable elements in the population." And so are the mannerisms—the sweat furtively wiped from the upper lip, the veneer of sweet reasonableness, the unconscious racism and the football metaphors, the desperate scratchings at dignity, the political cynicism he cannot recognize as such. "Nobody is going to believe that," Tricky says, "and that is why I don't even attempt to make a case for it." It sounds almost decent.

If *Mein Kampf* was not a funny book because Hitler's approach to brutality was calculated, *Our Gang* is hilarious because of Tricky's casual approach to a brutality he cannot see. Of the veterans who protest the war, he says: "Everybody knew they were just a bunch of malcontents who had lost arms and legs." Roth presses, too, for the humor revealed in a relentless literal-mindedness that feeds upon itself; as in a tautology, no assault is made on meaning, but reality is, through language, fended off. The Boy Scouts, an aide of Tricky's argues, must be killed by gas because "enough blood has been shed in our century." Finally there is the ghastly humor that comes from treating all values as disposable commodities: "Though I don't have my file with me," another aide says, "I'm sure we've used the truth some time or other in the past, too." That "too" makes the joke: All stratagems are now made equal.

The absurdity of Roth's fabricated situations conceals a legitimate target: the tendency of our governments to hold truth and decency in contempt. It is tempting to take *Our Gang* very seriously indeed, but it is, finally, a very funny book, funny in the way that Dryden, Swift, and Pope were funny. The point of such a satirical assault is that it *must* be outrageous, must be overdone, even if in the process a joke or two is trampled to death. When imitating excess, as here Roth imitates the public riot that is now our government, a style that is itself excessive becomes a kind of criticism, endowing events and attitudes with an intensity that implies not just a nastiness here below, but a primal malfunctioning of the cosmos. Even Roth's use of crudely derogatory names for his characters echoes the Great Tradition: Dryden called his rival Shadwell "Sh—— —" as in "But loads of Sh— — almost choakt the way."

Our Gang is, perhaps, more rooted in specifics than is the greatest political satire—than is, for example, *A Modest Proposal*—and therefore, if it is read a quarter century hence it will be read with footnotes climbing up the pages. But reading Roth's book today, and putting it down to read headlines of the Administration's plans to deprive a million and a half children of meals in school, is a disorienting experience. The trick is how not to confuse the joke with the reality; if, in fact, the reality is not the joke. "Language most shewes a man," Ben Jonson wrote: "speake that I may see thee."

1971

Five

. . . . A Sense of
Who and Where
You Are

Autobiographies make many readers nervous. We resent what looks like vanity in others and we ask all the wrong questions. Who *is* this fellow, anyway? If he's not famous, what can he have done that's worth the telling? If he's young, what can he have learned about life? Surely a man who writes about himself while in his middle thirties is offering the reader only half a loaf? Nonsense, of course. An autobiography is a report on a muddle of events tied to a length of time. Properly sorted out, observed from a narrow perspective and with sufficient intensity of vision, these events can be translated into something that makes sense, into something of significance.

This quest for significance in something as close to an artist as his own life is what makes autobiography such an appealing form of writing. There is a thrust at immortality in autobiography, a premature whiff of the Last Judgment when the only question is: How do you account for your life? Autobiographies by little-known writers can be reassuring: A man need not be involved in great events to write greatly about his life. Minor autobiographies prove that the possibility of greatness lies in us—in what we do with what little we have and what grace we can find in looking back on it.

Minor autobiography thrives on anguish, obsession, ecstasy, and doubt. Once it was the fashion for major autobiography to show such feeling—one thinks of Augustine and Abélard, of Cellini and Rousseau—but it is not the fashion now. Today, the memoirs of important men are often greatly tedious because the men's importance lies only in what they did or what they saw, not in what they are, or in how they write about themselves. "Attlee and I to lunch at Downing Street. The PM frowning. Could have been Tobruk, could have been the fish, which was from a tin. Rain by afternoon and so early to bed." Such stale and witless trivia fascinate newspapers and book clubs. Meanwhile, marvelous memoirs by writers no one knows founder on sales of fewer than 1,500 copies.

Laurie Lee's books are an exception. Lee is an English poet, but his reputation rests on his prose, on his recollections of childhood in *The Edge of Day,* a book that sold half-a-million copies, and now on its sequel, *As I Walked Out One Midsummer Morning.* "When I was nineteen years old, still soft at the edges, but with a confident belief in good fortune," Lee writes, he walked away from his village in Gloucester, carrying only a few clothes, a blanket, and a violin that he played for pennies when he needed food. Walking was different in the 1930's: There were few cars, few travelers, fewer questions. Lee walked south to the sea, which he had never seen, and then to London. He slept in the fields. "I was a young man," he writes, "whose time coincided with the last years of peace, and so was perhaps luckier than any generation since."

From London, he sailed to Spain. He knew neither the language nor the history of the country, and, for his pains, he was attacked his first night by Galician wolves. Still, when he awoke the next day, he knew he had made the right choice. "It was for this I had come," he says, "to wake at dawn on a hillside and look out on a world for which I had no words, to start at the beginning, speechless and without plan, in a place that still had no memories for me." Nearly prostrate from the heat and the hallucinations it inspired, Lee walked from Vigo, on Spain's northwest coast, east to Valladolid, and then south through Segovia, Madrid, and Toledo, to Cádiz. From Cádiz, he followed the coast east to a small town where, with the villagers, he waited out the winter and saw the beginning of the Spanish Civil War.

Lee's memoir covers only two years of his life, but it is the most uniquely beautiful and irresistible exercise in autobiography that I have read in years. It is written in prose that is blunt and sharp by turns, a luminous language thick with sensuality, a language honed to sharpen the tastes and smells of remembered experience, the echo of Spanish sounds and the reflection of Spanish light. It is a robust, masculine, funny book, affirming with each drink and woman the author's delight in life. It is also a story of a man growing up. Quite unobtrusively, Lee stresses his ignorance and innocence. He sees Spain as none of us can ever see it now; in an age when books, film, and television make all experience come to us slightly secondhand, we cannot be quite as virginal as Lee was, or totally surprised by what we find. Lee's writing reflects this innocence. He makes no generalizations about the country or its people, and few references to its history and literature. Nothing that he describes is anything more than itself, but what he describes he makes his own and makes it very much alive indeed.

The effect is extraordinary, but Lee is not finished with us yet. It is, as I said, a story of growing up, but if it begins in innocence and moves to a country that has not changed in two hundred years, it will end in experience and turmoil. Lee came to Spain without knowing why. He marked time in a world without barriers, a world of shared hardships and good fellowship. War comes; tranquillity is shattered; Lee returns to England but cannot stay. He comes back to join the Loyalists. It is a harder trip this time, but this time he knows why. Good stories tend to end this way: Beyond the knowledge and the strife there is a calm that comes from doing what one knows one has to do.

The village that Lee walked out from must have been much like the one Ronald Blythe describes in *Akenfield,* a sort of collective autobiography of a small Suffolk community that is only partly affected by the twentieth century. Akenfield is a town off the Roman road, where plowmen talk softly to their horses and where, when someone dies, the bees he kept will be informed so that they will not die, too. Population: 298. The people have an appreciation of beauty, but they are conservative and perfectionists: Even today they plow straight furrows because for the farmer, a man who never read a book and rarely spoke, a straight furrow "was his signature, not only on the field but on life." There is, says Blythe, an "internationalism of the planted earth," but the minister believes that "Fatalism is the real controlling force, this and the nature gods, the spirits of the trees and water and sky and plants. These beliefs seem to have no language, but they rule."

From a quiet people, Blythe has drawn a remarkable self-portrait. The people speak for themselves, telling of the old days and the old trades. "The old people think deeply," one of them says. "They are great observers. . . . They didn't move far so their eyes are trained to see the fine detail of a small place." The blacksmith tells how he stayed in business because new people buy old houses and want everything restored just as it was. The wheelwright, the thatcher, and the saddler tell their stories, but over all there is the rebellion of the farmer who is leaving the land, leaving the feudalism that exists even today. Outsiders who have come to Akenfield, attracted, perhaps, by "the land joining the sky in the huge way it does in Suffolk," stay to complain. "I find the East Anglians cold and hidden," a farmer says. "I have never experienced such coldness before. They can be barbarous and there is an innate cruelty in them." Akenfield resists outsiders. The logbook of the school shows teachers from foreign towns sinking in defeat: absenteeism, lack of discipline; in 1916, the temperature in the classrooms was 38 degrees and villagers agreed that "education interrupts work."

Blythe makes his own comments but allows the villagers to talk at length, and weaves their testimony together. The village simpleton, in a passage of pure poetry, tells of his seduction. A gardener admits that though he is only thirty-nine, he is "a Victorian . . . and that is why the world is strange to me." "The old men had art," an outsider says, "because they had damn-all else! It kept them from despairing." A gravedigger jokes about last things: The secretary of the golf club "was buried facing south so that when he rises he can see the links." Perhaps the most moving testimony comes from a bell ringer, a man who rings chimes across the length of England, "drugged by sound and arithmetic," who speaks of the concentration and coordination that ringing changes requires. Kipling would have liked him and put his speech into *Puck of Pook's Hill,* but then *Akenfield* has a feel of Kipling to it: old ways still alive in England.

1969

. . . ."What Is All This Juice and All This Joy?"

Stopping at a tavern one afternoon, my father-in-law discovered his friend, the minor poet, weeping into his whiskey. "It's terrible," the poet sobbed, as soon as undiluted drinks were brought, "my father died last night."

For a time, the two of them sat there, the one shedding tears and the other sympathetic noises, the whole situation kept just bearable by drink. Finally, with a snuffle, the poet asked: "You wouldn't have a pencil, would you?"

My father-in-law produced one, the poet produced what looked like a grocery bill, turned it over and began to scribble. As he wrote, his tears dried. He began to make noises that sounded suspiciously like "Wonderful, wonderful."

"Wonderful?" My father-in-law was appalled. "*What's* wonderful?"

"This poem about my father."

"And that," says my father-in-law, "convinced me that poets have no moral sense at all."

Plato knew that and expelled the poets from his republic. Poets, artists of every kind, are dangerous because they give us pleasure by depicting pain. It does not seem right that we should be exhilarated by Kafka's anguish, Maugham's handicap, or Butler's vindictive revenge upon his father, and, of course, we are not: It is what the writer makes of his fear and pain that counts. Through his alchemy, the artist redeems suffering, turns the lead of existence into the gold of art or, perhaps, finds the gold that was always there. "Literature," Emerson wrote, "is the effort of man to indemnify himself for the wrongs of his condition," but there is more to it than that. In some books, perhaps only in a very few, the bitterness and rage that we expect to find are both translated: The pain, clearly, *was* there, may still be there, but it has become a catalyst and not a subject. What makes these books so marvelous is that they celebrate, in the midst of impotence or holocaust, the complex joy of living.

I approached Christy Brown's *Down All the Days* feeling as I would if some dithering mother had told me her six-year-old daughter was about to entertain me by singing Bellini's "Casta diva"—given the resources of the performer, there is no way the work can be done well. I was wrong. Brown is thirty-seven, Irish, the tenth of twenty-two children born to a family in a Dublin slum. He has athetoid cerebral palsy—"a brain-damaged vegetable" he has been called—and cannot eat or drink without help, cannot walk or talk at all. He has, however, complete control of the little toe on his left foot and needs nothing else: With that toe, he typed this novel.

It *is* a novel, if only by convenience, because Brown reports on events and attitudes he has not witnessed, but the central character is a boy named Brown, a mute cripple, assumed to be simpleminded, who must be wheeled about in a cart, "grunting like a pig." Locked in "the walled garden of his thought," prisoner of his eroticism and desperation as well as his useless body, he turns his "slaughtered senses" on the over-crowded life around him, observing the rutting and fighting, the singing, sweating, profanity and vomit, the smell of spilled beer and the gurgle of a whiskey bottle upended in a widow's mouth.

In his own home, people slept three to a bed. His father, a bricklayer and a desperate man, raged at his mother, who was pregnant every year. He beat her, flailed his belt at his offspring—"Somebody has to beat the fear of God into the little buggers"—cursed his daughter, who fled to London for the comfort of the blitz, and his sons, Army deserters who served their terms in the stockade. Is this father a man to be hated? Not at all—perhaps not even to be pitied. The boy in this story, like Brown himself, "saw all this gay, hurtful life spread in generous haphazard prodigality around him like a warm sea, and he grew weak with tongueless tenderness." The father, on the night before his fatal accident, achieves a kind of Joycean apotheosis as he stumbles home tired from the pub, brooding on the breeding of women and the passing of man's desire: "Every time a man poured his seed into a woman, he poured some of his heart's blood into her as well, the sap of his muscle, bone and sinew, his animal strength, and each time, he got less and less, weaker and weaker, till there was just a shroud of skin hung upon a frame, shaking and bending in every wind like a bloody scarecrow."

What further recommendation does a novel need? The boy sits in his wagon and looks on life with hungry joy, aware of the comedy as well as the intensity of what passes around him. Brown is particularly good with dialogue—writing of widows drinking and talking with pride, hatred and nostalgia of the men who kept them pregnant—and good at sentences written to be read aloud for the pure Irishness of them: "Oh that ferrety little fairy of an auntie blackening him in her eyes at every hand's turn." Marvelous, and so is this boozy, brawling book.

Richard E. Kim's *Lost Names* is a very different kind of autobiographical writing, but it shares with Brown's book qualities that are increasingly rare in good books these days: joy in life and an acceptance of one's lot; optimism in the face of adversity; and an unspoken conviction that even under the most appalling conditions, life can proceed normally. Kim's novels, *The Martyred* and *The Innocent,* are concerned with moral ambiguity, with the nature of divine and human justice, but no such problems intrude into these seven fragments of autobiography, which Kim has written almost as if they were short stories.

In the first episode, Kim, at the age of one, is taken by his parents to the last town in Korea before the Manchurian border. His father, we learn, was a patriot who had organized a resistance movement against the Japanese occupation of Korea, spent years in jail, and is now delayed at the border by the Japanese Thought Police. At night, the family walks into Manchuria, across the frozen river. When they return to Korea in 1938, Kim is enrolled in the second grade of a Japanese-run school. On the first day, he is beaten by a sadistic teacher and forced, with his class, to bow to the rising sun, which rises above the Imperial Palace in Tokyo. Japanese is taught in the school and supposedly spoken in Korean homes; we who speak English cannot imagine what it must be like to know that no more books will be published in our language, that our language is in danger of extinction.

In the most moving of the seven stories, all Koreans are required to register for new names, Japanese names. Kim's father and his friends wear black armbands, ask forgiveness of their ancestors and future generations, and mark the date: February 11, 1940. Kim's father was prosperous, a Christian, and an important man; some of the Japanese deferred to him. He chose the Japanese name Iwamoto, meaning Rock Foundation. "On this rock, I will build my church," he tells his son. When the Japanese begin to lose the war, Kim's father is arrested again. Kim, now thirteen, is made man of the house; he must make a decision to spare some Japanese and help to lead a raid on police headquarters.

In this book, for the first time, Kim's vision of man's place in the world, of man's obligations, is as clear and as simple as his prose has always been. Perhaps, when we sort out the issues and events of our childhood, the directions seem clearer than they do in our adult undertakings. Perhaps, but I doubt it. Joy and certainty are disappearing from the tone of our age, and of our literature. We are more conscious of pain than of the possibility of redemption, through art or any other means. We should be happy, then, to receive two books an fine as these.

1970

. . . . Setting One's Life in Order

What a man writes about his own life is usually more interesting than what others write about it. It is certainly more durable: few biographies survive the generation that produced them. Not so with autobiographies. The problem here is not that of an author trying to relate a man to his age or to his art; it is the problem of an author trying to explore his own existence—relating himself, as it were, to what he has done, or what has happened to him. The author sets his life in order, perhaps for the first time, as we watch. This is the unique function of autobiography: to show us not the result but the process of form being made from chaos.

The story that Harding Lemay tells in *Inside, Looking Out* has the elements of an American classic. The fifth of thirteen Canadian-American children living in poverty on a farm, he retreated early to a world of books and movies. His father was cruel—"I began to avoid him by the time I was 12"—and his mother, once pretty, succumbed to alcoholism and insanity. "You're too good for us," she told him once. "Don't grow up to be like your father." Lemay concluded that almost any human being was too good for the lives his parents led, and at seventeen he ran away. Later, when he returned, he found his mother muttering prayers and curses from her rocker and his father corroded by bitterness. "I can't take money from you," his father said. "Of all my boys, you're the only one I've never liked." A few weeks after Lemay left, his father hanged himself.

In New York, his money stolen, Lemay took refuge in a boys' home where he read books all night in the toilet. Older women lent him books, paid for his theater tickets, and helped him into jobs. In time, he went to acting school, studying with Martha Graham in the generation of actors that produced Marlon Brando. After the war—the Army providing only the indignities and brutalities Lemay had learned at home—there were years of student acting and poverty, of loneliness and thwarted hopes. Lemay married; it didn't work. Ashamed and contemptuous of his family, Lemay had built a phony past for himself. "I became a man I detested," he writes: "arrogant, touchy, promiscuous, unloving, and unlovable." Unable to look for jobs, he spent his days cataloguing the casts of forgotten films. He knew now that he was a mediocre actor—and that he hated acting. But he was still running from life. He had fled his family and now he fled his wife as well.

Remarriage and better jobs in the book industry helped Lemay recover, but there was one great hurdle left to overcome. Lemay took a job with Alfred Knopf, most distinguished of all American book publishers. In what will be the most-talked-about section of his book, Lemay provides a devastating portrait of Knopf and his wife at the end of their careers when they were "victimized by the inflated vanities" that flattery breeds. Knopf, as Lemay shows him, insulted his editors in public and tried to wean their authors from them; he boasted that he was a gentleman but appalled outsiders by his rudeness. Nevertheless, Knopf liked Lemay, promoted and abused him until Lemay decided that Knopf was "a man whose esteem was not worth the humiliations he exacted as its price." Once again, Lemay quit—but this time he did not run. He quit to write plays—which have not yet been produced—because he finds that more rewarding than success in publishing. This time he quit because quitting was the courageous thing to do.

Not a man to attract a biographer's attention, but that is the joy of a personal memoir: It does not matter who the author is or what success he has achieved—what matters is the book he fashions from the rough materials of his life. I think that Lemay's recollections of his family and his service in the court of the Knopfs are themselves worth the book, but the whole is better than that. It is a very tough, unsparing self-evaluation, an honest book that shows how a man not used to honesty can work toward it. It shows how difficult it can be to learn to accept what one is—and to build on that. It is, very simply, an account of how a man forced himself to become as full a man as he could be.

1971

.... *Mon Dieu,* We Frenchmen Are Romantic!

Now, see, after I get my wrists free from the rings on the wall, bend back the bar in the dungeon window and dive into the sea, I'll steal a small boat and sail to an island where the chief's daughter will fall in love with me, and I'll probably have her younger sister, too (that being the life-style, you know, among the savages), and everybody will sort of bow down to me until I get tired of that, after about twenty years, and return to hunt the man who sent me so unjustly to jail, only he doesn't recognize me (chuckle, chuckle): *You're in my clutches now!*

Snore. Sleep usually set in at that point—after a hard day's learning in the eighth grade and an evening, finished by flashlight, with *Les Misérables* or *The Count of Monte Cristo.* How I loved those books then, 1,200 pages each of tiny type, and how glad I am I don't have to read them now. These nights, before the snore intrudes, I stand on the center court at Wimbledon—"Prescott's service is slower now that he has a cast around his elbow," Jack Kramer whispers to the television fans—but *zap!* Rod Laver never saw it coming. You will say: Age has moderated this man's ambition. Perhaps, but I expect reruns of the dungeons and chieftain's daughters now that I have read *Papillon,* which is, one way or the other, the best escape-from-prison story of all time. Henri Charrière, whose story it is, makes Jean Valjean and Edmond Dantes look like delegates from the Ladies' Auxiliary, inspecting the local jug.

Papillon sold a million copies in France in less than a year, which makes it, some say, the greatest best seller in French history. Already, two books have been published denouncing Charrière's story—they, too, have become best sellers—and though they insist that *Papillon* is fiction, not fact, the fuss must seem like small change to Charrière, who has survived worse ordeals and who looks like Jean Gabin, gazing with distrust at the reader from the back of his book, his nose swelled by wine and his shirt cut low to show the butterfly tattoo that gave him his underworld name.

This is Papillon's story, as he tells it: He was a safecracker, a gentleman crook in Montmartre, who, in 1931, was convicted of murdering a pimp. The charge was unjust, Papillon insists; the government would never have arrived at a conviction except for the perjured testimony of a stoolie who bought his own freedom for the price of Papillon's, and the stupidity of the dozen "cheesehead" jurors who couldn't care less. Papillon was sentenced to life at hard labor in the penal colony in French Guiana, an extensive interlocking system of prison camps known to outsiders by the name of one of them: Devils Island. Every year, 80 percent of those sent there from France died—from leprosy, yellow fever, dysentery, and malaria. Papillon, unlike most of the convicts, was determined to live—he wanted freedom and revenge, dreamed of tearing out the tongue of the prosecutor who had had him convicted and of blowing up police headquarters in Paris. Like many of his fellow convicts, he secreted in his large intestine a metal container stuffed with banknotes. Whatever else happened to Papillon in the next thirteen years, he was never poor.

He arrived in French Guiana in 1933. Within thirty-seven days, he escaped with two companions in a rotten boat. They hid in the brush and then paddled to an island leper colony. There, they bought a better boat for their escape by sea to Colombia—where they were jailed again. Again, Papillon escaped, to live half a year with the Indians, getting two women pregnant and collecting pearls. Tired of this idyllic life, he left— to be caught and jailed again in a dungeon where the tides swept in with rats as big as cats, with crabs and centipedes. Returned to the French colony, he was sentenced to solitary confinement on an island known as "the devourer of men." For two years, he paced his dark stone cell—five steps and turn—never speaking to a soul. Eight-inch centipedes fell from the ceiling, but Papillon learned to let them march over his naked body: Their sting could burn a man for six hours and leave him with a fever for twelve. Upon his release, Papillon plotted other escapes—by dynamite, bribery, and sleeping potions, by assaulting guards in chapel and by secretly building a raft that he buried, piece by piece, in a grave. Nothing worked. Papillon, with one blow of his knife, killed a fellow con who informed on him. He was sent back to solitary for eight years, a term no man had ever survived.

Released early, he gained the confidence not only of his fellow prisoners, whom he always led, but of the wardens and their wives. In time, he and a companion escaped from Devils Island—the first men to do so—by flinging themselves from a cliff into a wave, clinging to rafts of coconuts. Papillon's companion died slowly in the quicksands of the South American coast, but our hero, after a spell in a Venezuelan jail, finally was freed—thirteen years after his conviction.

What happens to Charrière is interesting enough, but the way he tells his story makes it engrossing. Never content with reciting the facts, he involves us in each dilemma as it develops: How shall we judge this cell, or find this warden's weakness? Papillon survived where others died because he was strong, personable, and inventive—and because he had a sense of moral outrage.

Charrière re-creates each incident in detail, which has enraged his critics. "You think I went into that hell with a typewriter?" Charrière snarled when the truth of some minor and major episodes was questioned. The truth does not matter, some people will say, just as they say Leroy Anderson's "Sleigh Ride" is as good as Bach's "Hunting Cantata" if you think it is. Nonsense. Art—and telling one's own story well is an art—involves not only the artist's inventive skill, it involves his honesty. Much of what is disputed in Charrière's story—whether he was guilty, for instance—is probably irrelevant, but some of what is not disputed seems most unlikely. When he drank from the bowl at the lepers' colony, did he really find a leper's finger at the bottom? No one will ever know; no witness survives.

I have developed my own yardstick for measuring literary situations where proof of the truth is impossible. It is a faulty device but the best I can offer. Revelations about life—particularly about life in adversity—that confound our expectations are likely to be honest. Incidents that seem to round out our expectations of what a story *should* include may be true, but they are suspect. *Papillon* is rich in the latter. It is a grand story, if an embroidered one, a story not only of how it was, but of how it should have been.

1970

. . . . Ill at Ease in America

Fame never made anyone happy for long—not Dean Rusk,* not Timothy Leary†—which is why famous people are so interesting. The very famous are different from you and me: They are better known. But there is

*Former government employee.
†Former chemical engineer.

something more: They are marked men. Even as we hold out our autograph books, we can feel the chill of mutability. We know that a just (*i.e.,* vengeful) universe will redress the balance at an amusing tilt. In time. Just wait. Thank you, Miss Parker; thank you, Mr. Barrow.* We close our autograph books and step back, out of range of the machine guns.

Fame being what it is, feelings of loss, of irony and melancholy pervade *Exiles,* Michael J. Arlen's book about his parents and himself. He did not know his father in the twenties, when his father was a celebrity, an Armenian who had made his home and fortune in England. The elder Michael Arlen, born Dikran Kouyoumdjian, was the friend of such pukka-writers as Maugham, Fitzgerald, and Hemingway, was himself the highest paid short-story writer on either side of the Atlantic and author of *The Green Hat.* A play? Novel? Movie? All three? No one under forty knows, which perhaps confirms something about the adhesive qualities of fame.

By the time the son came to know his father, Arlen had been rejected by England, could no longer write, had no money. "He really wasn't doing a damned thing except having lunch with people," the son writes, but he kept his style, his charm, his stickpin and silk tie. In earlier years, his son reports, Arlen "did okay, better than just okay. . . . He could buy a long damn canary-yellow Rolls-Royce. And speedboats and good clothes." His astrakhan coat, for example: "Mr. Arlen," a reporter asked, "what do you think of yourself as an artist?" "*Per ardua ad astrakhan,*" Arlen replied. "And," the son writes, "he could afford to marry my mother," who had a title of sorts, and lots of exotic European nobles for ancestors, and some property the Greek government kept confiscating, and a taste for moving around from London to Cannes and spas in Austria. She, too, had style, but, as their son implies, style was not enough to keep two beautiful people, two of the first "modern" people, happy in a residential hotel in Manhattan when all but style had gone.

They were, he writes, "in a kind of exile, and sought to find a home, a country, in one another, and very nearly did." As you might expect, the son, too, found an exile of his own, moving among schools in England, Canada, and America, a normally bungling, normally erotic youth, ill at ease with the lacquered lives his parents so determinedly maintained.

Exiles is half memoir, half autobiography, a book about tension, failure, and bitterness, written with sympathy, wit, and love. Finally, without making any great statements or proclamations, it is a book about resolutions: how one comes, or fails to come, to terms with life,

*Free-lance financier, d. 1934.

with success and failure, even though there are no answers, perhaps no lessons to be learned. Arlen's recollections are highly selective, but I am convinced that his book is absolutely true, that its tone of irony, of self-deprecation and isolation, has been honestly arrived at, and that without seeking to justify his parents, Arlen has at last come to a workable relationship with them, which is very hard to do; perhaps most people never manage it. Arlen's prose is itself a wondrous tool: Nervous, mannered, at times studiously informal, at times deliberately banal, it breaks most of the rules by reviving no-no words like "nice" and "really," phrases like "I guess" and "things like that." An English teacher would climb the wall, flailing his red pencil. Arlen's prose combines diffidence and sureness of touch; there is a tentative, exploratory quality to it, as if he were just making up his mind about matters as he wrote. He isn't, of course, but I like the effect. And *Exiles* is a rare book that I very much admire.

Ambivalent thoughts after reading Jerry Rubin's book, Do It!: It is not a good book; it could not have been. Rubin, like many Yippies, is a dropout, a child of the television age, who communicates by noise and spectacle. Because he cannot express himself well in words, his book is composed of slogans better suited to scrawling on placards than on pages. Rubin has no commitment whatever to honesty, and only a partial commitment to seriousness, so there is no telling where the truth lies in this lighthearted, occasionally entertaining account of his baptism in the Berkeley Free Speech Movement, of his running for mayor of Berkeley, of his appearance before the House Un-American Activities Committee, and of his part in the battle of the Pentagon and the riot in the city he calls "Czechago." The Yippies, of course, are dedicated to spooking the white middle class. "The Marxist acid-head," Rubin drones, apparently defining himself, "the psychedelic Bolshevik . . . a street-fighting freek . . . so ugly that middle-class society is frightened by how he looks." Well, maybe, but the spookable middle class in, say, Cicero, Illinois, is not about to read *Do It!*, a book more easily written than read, that amounts to no more than the unspeakable yammering at the unspookable.

Is it wasted effort? Yippie-watching is like kettle-watching: The nagging question is whether so much energy can someday be harnessed in the service of man. Now that the Katzenjammer Kids have dropped their cherubic smirks, what can they do for the world? I think the answer is clear. By appearing before the House Un-American Activities Committee, first in the costume of a revolutionary soldier, and then as Santa Claus, Rubin revealed his genius. In spite of his coining puns like "subpoenas envy," Rubin's talent lies not with words, and certainly not with books; it lies in making a very necessary exhibition that the rest of us dare not make. "The role of the revolutionary," Rubin writes in his sharpest moment, "is to create theater which creates a revolutionary frame of reference. The power to define is the power to control." The Yippies, creating "theater," put their bodies on the line when we will not do so, but when there is a need for someone to do so, if only because many things in our society need redefining now. As always, much of the essential fighting of our time, of any time, is done by those with whom we cannot easily sympathize—by freaks, by nuts. They go to jail. We stay safe, perhaps learning something about the way we consent to be governed today.

We must give them this much, and this much more: Rubin and Abbie Hoffman, who wrote a rather worse book, are genuine revolutionaries injecting elements of what Harvey Cox calls festivity and fantasy into our linear solemnities. We can be serious, the Yippies seem to say, without being solemn. We want to change the *quality* of American life. What is harder to swallow is the brutal prattle: the joy in burning anything, in simple destruction, without recognizing that pain hurts. So far, Yippies have hit only the easy targets: churches, colleges, conventions—institutions that are really in no position to strike back. Rubin, perhaps, is the most articulate of the Yippies, but he is not as good at persuading, or arguing, or even thinking, as he is at self-congratulation. *Do It!* is worth reading but not worth taking seriously.

1970

. . . . Meretricious Books

Every now and then we see in a magazine an article by an author who feels compelled to explain why he wrote a particular book. Mark Harris now reverses this procedure: He has written an entire book, *Mark, the Glove Boy,* to explain how he wrote a banal article for *Life* magazine on the Nixon-Brown 1962 California gubernatorial campaign. From which we deduce the following rule: The amount of space an author requires to justify his mediocrity increases in geometric proportion to his egotism.

Harris' egotism begins on the front of the jacket where he apologizes for having conceived of a fantasy in which he assassinates Nixon, a joke which, in view of recent events, turned to ashes in its author's mouth.

"On this Saturday afternoon in November," Harris writes in his portentous prose, "God clearly weeps: yesterday President Kennedy was murdered in Dallas. To tell you the shameless truth of myself . . ." And here we have the Harris juxtaposition: No matter what the event, we are never far from "the shameless truth" of Mr. Harris.

He seems to have had two purposes in writing this book. First, he feels today that he was not sufficiently unfair to Richard Nixon in his *Life* article; this book will redress the oversight. Mark Harris the campaign reporter is very much the smiler with the knife: His book contains springs, traps, foul blows, and even an imaginary concealed pistol with which, as he shouts *Sic Semper Tyrannus!* he shoots Nixon. No one could ever claim this was a balanced or even a reasonable picture of the campaign, but there is in it the element of skillful political assassination. For all his self-confessed hysteria, Harris can put his finger on why Nixon repelled too many people. He sums up Nixon's political mind, "which knew so little about itself, or, knowing, failed to understand." Nixon, he says, performed so badly he may have wanted to lose; he was a man of low intellect, he lacked self-awareness and "a vision of the end." What Harris means by this perplexing phrase (nuclear catastrophe? the awarding of seats in heaven to the elect?) he never says, nor does he tell us whether Governor Brown had such a vision.

This criticism, for the most part, remains in the realm of fair commentary. But Harris has a far more important reason for writing this book. For every page spent on Nixon, he must spend ten entirely upon himself. Critics of the French Romantic movement often speak of *le moi,* the author's preoccupation with himself. Harris, who cites his achievements as a teacher and political seer in the jacket copy where he proclaims himself the "hero" of his book, takes himself very seriously as a writer and has a refreshingly high regard of his own work. Infatuated by the potential of *le moi,* he uses this account of a journalistic assignment as a vehicle for providing *les plus belles pages* from his autobiography. The subtitle of this book might better have been, "Or, How I Grew in Wisdom, Virtue, Ability and Influence With Occasional Unfavorable References to the Outside World."

After Harris elucidates his various virtues, the book's title, reminiscent of Horatio Alger, suddenly becomes clear. The purpose of this book is not *really* to write about Nixon and the California campaign. It is Mark Harris' own success story, set into the most vulgar framework possible: how Mark, the Glove Boy (he had worked as a delivery boy for a glove manufacturer), and Nixon (Dick, the Grocery Boy) both worked their way from humble origins to world renown. Dick Nixon, however, settled for personal success as the ultimate dream whereas Mark Harris struggled to achieve the public vision, the cosmopolitan sophistication, the basic humanitarianism lacking in this heavy-bearded candidate for the governor's mansion.

The egotism, the vanity, the insufferable arrogance of these bald comparisons and self-serving assertions will shake the most hardened reader of political claptrap. Why did Mark Harris, not at all a bad novelist, feel he had to do it? What does he gain by telling us how much wiser, better, and more virtuous than Mr. Nixon Mr. Harris is? Anyone as determined on character assassination as Harris is should remember the basic rule of the game: Whatever vilifications you pile on your victim, you must refrain from extolling your own virtues. This book, with its hero and its villain so clearly labeled, can find no room to discuss Governor Brown who also took part in this epic confrontation of the forces of light and darkness at California's polls. *Mark, the Glove Boy* is a tasteless, unconvincing and pernicious book.

1964

We who have served some years in New York's literary world profess an interest in a catholic variety of subjects. Baseball ranks high among them. So do martinis, poker, and the inroads that homosexuality has made into our profession. We can be prodded to talk about books, but we would rather talk about money and, failing that, we talk about ourselves. "Who's in? Who's out?" asks a senior member of the Editors' Lunch Club as he sits down to eat. "Who's hired? Who's fired?" We meet again next Thursday and when we do it is certain that nearly all of us will have read—and will discuss interminably—Norman Podhoretz's autobiography, *Making It*.

Farrar, Straus, as we all have heard, paid a fortune, something like $25,000, for this book by—who? Norman Podhoretz. Podhoretz! Yes, the man who wrote a few reviews for *The New Yorker* before that magazine let him know that he wasn't needed anymore, the man who then wrote some incredibly sloppy book reviews for Huntington Hartford's *Show* magazine, reviews so bad that at least one reviewer got his start as a regular critic by showing his boss just what was wrong with what Podhoretz was doing in *Show*. *Show* collapsed, of course, but Podhoretz endured, as editor of *Commentary*, which is undoubtedly an excellent thing to be. One of the reasons why Podhoretz wrote this book is to convince us that being editor of *Commentary* is perhaps even more of an excellent thing than it really is. Another reason is that Podhoretz wants to show us, who are still wiggling our toes in the wetlands of intellectual endeavor, how he attained the high pinnacle, how a bright boy from a Brownsville slum could acquire "the habit of writing A-plus papers," could acquire scholarships to Columbia and Cambridge, could publish in such diverse and sophisticated magazines that he became (as he tells us) "held in almost priestly regard. . . . I basked in smiles of love and bathed in admiring eyes." This is not a joke. These are Podhoretz's actual words. As it happens, Farrar, Straus decided to say to hell with their $25,000 or whatever it was; when they saw the book they declined it. Farrar, Straus has perhaps our best or second-best literary list of authors and has to watch out for pollution; just a little seepage in the basement will, after all, undermine the foundations. I presume they did not decline it before they read Norman Podhoretz telling us how he cracked the most exclusive literary club in America, and how he now presides there as a minor guru.

Lest you suspect that there is an unseemly measure of vanity in Podhoretz's overflowing cup, Podhoretz hastens to assure you that there is. Lest you suspect that Podhoretz's tone is a bit shrill for a man at the peak of his career, that such apologetics are usually reserved for the punch-drunk boxer trying to convince you that he once KO'd Braddock, Podhoretz replies that our age is unable to talk bluntly about success. "Ambition," he writes, "seems to be replacing erotic lust as the prime dirty little secret of the well-educated American soul."

He is wrong, of course. I don't mean that Podhoretz is wrong when he tells us he cares more for situation than sex; if he tells us that, I have to believe it. He is wrong because he misunderstands the lusts of men in general. Men (and not only Americans, as he claims) have always been consumed by ambition, and when, like Podhoretz, they have made something of their lives, they often write about their struggle to success. It is true that they rarely write with as much naked vanity as Podhoretz extrudes; that they have not done so means either that they were not so obsessed with their importance or that, remaining ambitious men, they prudently decided that their own best interests might best feed on tact and discretion. What jars the reader of *Making It* is not Podhoretz's protestations of vanity but the complexity of his vanity. Podhoretz does not, from the evidence offered in this book, recognize half of his infatuation with himself; I infer this from the contrast between the blunt way he tackles the vanity he admits to and the other, more standard insinuations of vanity that he does not seem inclined to discuss.

The result is a fascinating and an infuriating book. Anyone involved in the book industry will find it fascinating simply because the avaricious, aggressive world that Podhoretz describes in such clinical detail touches upon the world we know, but we are not of it. The book should prove fascinating, too, to any reader interested in watching an ego grapple with itself, seemingly content to excrete from the conflict a portrait of an unsympathetic man. Finally, it is fascinating because some of it is excellent: Podhoretz's descriptions of the agony of writing, the nature of the writer's ambition, and the problem of writers' blocks are actually quite good indeed.

But in the end, and for several reasons, *Making It* emerges as an appalling book. Virtually none of Podhoretz's proclaimed critical skills is in evidence in these pages. He can write for many paragraphs about critics he admires in terms of trite superlatives ("the most influential art critic in America . . . one of the best essayists in the English language") without attempting to suggest *why* these critics are good, without suggesting why these favored commentators, by virtue of language, insight, or perspective, are important. One feels, reading this book, that Podhoretz doesn't quite know why he admires the men he singles out for praise. He seems to lack a critical vocabulary. It is appalling, too, to see how dearly he clutches his college grades, as if they could be of importance to him now; appalling to see how he can characterize his contemporaries only by whether they made their reputations faster or slower than he. Finally, it is appalling to see how everything for him rests upon reputation: "Authority in writing," he says, "need not be accompanied by consummate skill or any other virtue of craft or mind," which is perhaps true, but Podhoretz is willing to settle for it. He can quote other critics' claims that the business of the critic is the search for truth, but he does not agree: When speaking for himself, and his guard appears to be down, arrogance emerges as a more important critical skill than truth. That is, if you're going to make it like Norman Podhoretz.

Podhoretz made it because he is a born joiner. He has been, by his own admission, willing to subscribe to the prejudices and attitudes of the few critics he admires—and that, of course, is what no independent-minded critic can possibly afford to do. This is the book's last appalling secret: not that men secretly lust for success but that, right from the beginning in Brooklyn, Podhoretz, who lusted for success, felt comfortable with the gang. After Brooklyn with its street gang toughs there was Columbia, with Lionel Trilling, and Cambridge, with F. R. Leavis. Back home there was the best "family" of all: the *Partisan Review* crowd—the Cosa Nostra of American literary endeavor—murderous, self-elected, exclusive, alienated, they scratched and bit among themselves. They were, they announced, the only intelligent people in America: No one could be recognized as an intellectual without their imprimatur. Podhoretz nodded and genuflected, hoping (oh, please!) to get invited to their parties. He accepted their foolishness and their brute insensitivity (whatever it takes to get elected), along with their undeniable intellect.

Making It is a book about the price you pay to get ahead. Podhoretz's career would indicate that the price you pay to get ahead in the book world—that is, if like Podhoretz you must belong to the Establishment—is the obligation to buy, if not others' ideas, at least the rigid attitudes that shape them. What Podhoretz lacks is humor and perspective, the intellectual sensitivity to be repelled by the clannishness and uniformity that acceptance by the "family" imposes. In the crunch, he lacks the moral courage to take a stand apart, to say to hell with you and your ranking system, your predictability and your reputation-rubbing.

Dost thou think, because thou art virtuous, there shall be no more cakes and ale? Apparently, he doth.

1968

..................Narcissism and Negotiation: An Interview

I stopped before the reception desk at the MPO screening room in Manhattan. The pretty young girl looked up. "What is your product?"

A weighty pause, and then the only answer I could think of: "Jules Feiffer."

"Of course," the girl said and pushed the Feiffer button on her phone. A few minutes later the man himself walked in, clutching a copy of The Olympia Reader. *Feiffer is thirty-six and wears dark-rimmed glasses. His face is a perfect oval; he is already nearly bald. His rather harmless features appear to be clustered in a group at the center of his head.*

I had come to the studio that day to talk to Feiffer and to see a preview of his second film (his first had won an Academy Award). "The Feiffer Film," as it is called, begins with a countdown and an atomic blast. It is composed of real-life enactments of some of Feiffer's more famous cartoons and will be shown both to college audiences and to the newly created Montreal Film Festival. The film, of course, is only half Feiffer: The flawless dialogue is still there, but the flawless drawing, refined to the point of superlative crudity, is missing. And that's a lot to miss, as Feiffer recognizes—"I don't really believe that you can successfully translate one thing that's complete in one form to another without missing the form that it was taken from"—but he likes the film anyway. In any event, he is concerned with the quality of cinema: "We need a war every now and then, if only to improve the quality of photo journalism."

Later in a private room at a restaurant, Feiffer talked until the waiters began to scratch and yawn:

*   *   *

About God: God is one of the basic motifs in this country. The only thing we believe about God is how He appears in print and whether He's used as an expletive.

About Sick Humor: I'm afraid I was responsible for this whole god-damned term sick humor, because it was the original title of my strip. Others used it, meaning: *He's* sick, *they're* sick, but not *we're* sick, and my feeling, my meaning of the term from the very beginning, was the people I did are healthy members of a sick society, normal people, not sicker in the society's terms than anybody else: This is what is happening. I dropped the term when it became abused.

In the beginning it was not so much being sick as it was updating . . . until Mort Sahl, who really began it (and Nichols and May, and Lenny Bruce and what I was doing in the *Voice*), there really had been very little done on urban humor as it existed for our particular generation, as opposed to what Bob Hope was doing. Humor had become stereotyped comments on a sort of life that really didn't exist anymore: Domineering mothers-in-law, dumb cops, lazy Negroes, and bumbling husbands.

About Camp: One of the reasons there is such a thing as camp is that now with social comment, with humor, with the kind of general anti-establishment criticism going around, there can be a nostalgic reappraisal and appreciation of things that many people once rejected as cornball or baloney, because at one time it was dangerous. It stifled comment, you know, to say that Jack Benny was good and Mort Sahl was bad. Now that that battle has been won, you can say yes, Jack Benny *was* good, for this reason and that reason. Camp began first of all as a homosexual, a derisive, term: the outside world looking mockingly at what they think of as the inside world. It would be like Negroes looking at a bunch of whites. Camp is not just nostalgia, though it ended up in nostalgia, a lot of things that happened in our youth look better now than they did then simply because now we see it as even worse.

About Analysis: This is a country that basically hates analysis and so has to immediately grab on to a label which destroys analysis. Rather than talk about Lyndon Johnson's *policies,* we talk about his *image.* Rather than talk about what might have created an atmosphere in which such a thing as camp could take place, we talk about what camp is. We're so fascinated about talking about the label, we don't discuss what *made* us talk about the label. We're infatuated with an analytic pose without finding anything out. We have what I can only call trickle-down psychosis, with barely literate kids using words like "compulsion" even though they don't know what it means. It's the language of our time.

About Language: Language is used as a barrier to keep the audience away, to keep it from getting any closer. The beats use a lack of communication to keep people away rather than to keep them near. What's fascinating is how the Negroes will create a tongue in order to keep the whites out. The whites will pick up the tongue. The Negroes will have to create a new tongue. The white hippies will come along, pick up that tongue, and everybody is off creating new languages in order to keep the bourgeoisie away.

Nobody's really interested in communicating. I mean no boy is really interested in finding out what a girl is about. He's interested in one thing. No girl is interested in discovering the real person underneath his fake person; she's interested in either having some fulfillment in sex or being made to feel like a beautiful person. Since both of them are going in opposite directions because they're interested in opposite things, they have to find a set of rules that allow them to sit at the same table or lie in the same bed.

The rules are called conversation. "Did you like that movie?" What rules really are is a form of negotiation. People don't really talk, they negotiate. I'm not saying this is bad or wrong and let's all be honest and say come to bed; I suspect the reason we're paying attention to it today is simply because the status of the sexes in society is changing and so negotiations change.

About Children: You should not think in terms of parent and child, but of labor and management. It's strictly a class relationship between the haves and the have-nots . . . Most of the grownups I know have never been children. They were born at age fifty and don't know what it was like to be eleven or twelve. I remember being told, "You're crying over this? When you get older, you'll discover there are more important problems." Maybe there were more important problems, but those were the only problems I had.

About Huey, one of the characters he has created: I know how I got Huey. I was at a Village party, sort of Up-Village, Twenty-fourth Street, and there was this murderous-looking hulk of a guy in a darkly lighted room who looked just like Brando. This was the year when everyone looked like Brando; they were all unemployed actors. He had tiny wisps, modern dancers, hanging from each side of his neck and he was walking along with two girls loving him completely and he could do anything.

And his roommate was a Bernard type, a totally ineffectual guy, who said, "Girls come to him at nine in the morning and he takes them to bed and they leave him money, he needs money, and they go away. How do you get to be this guy?"

About His Drawing: I have a name for my style. I call it Bad Drawing. At its best it's an editorial style of drawing, a novelistic style of drawing, simply because the drawing exists in order to explain something about the characters saying certain words. It's important to me that the look in the man's eyes is right, and the set of his mouth and the way he holds his hands. The thing that bothers me most about my work or any work is when something is put in that's not needed.

About the Battle of the Sexes: It's a misnomer. I don't think there is a battle between the sexes. A better word is negotiation. I think the only battle that ever exists is between somebody and himself. It's a battle of narcissism, a battle of self-image.

Negotiation means that both parties are continually trying to seduce the other party out of his stand. Not trying to win over, not trying to kill, not trying to destroy, but trying to get their own way by wheedling. It's an act of narcissism rather than an act of war. The key is narcissism. They're all thinking about themselves. And what I'm doing in my cartoons is what I smell around me. Here and there my sense of smell may be out of date or mistaken, but I have to operate with what I see.

About Black Humor: Black humor doesn't exist. It's a nonsense term designed for commercial purposes to make what was once called sick humor newly salable.

About Man Against Organization: It's a battle against impersonalization. I once had a short correspondence with Blue Cross over a difference in a bill. I said, Look, I've been paying Blue Cross fees for fifteen years now, I have not made a single claim, I think I am entitled to an answer from a human being, a personal letter. I got a form letter back. The box was checked, you know, "Your answer is, A, B, C or D." There's nobody out there. I have a cartoon coming out in a couple of weeks about a company called Consolidated Pollution, or ConPol as they call it, which is interested in giving the *positive* side of the air pollution story.

About the Art of Satire: There are a lot of people called satirists who are by my definition buffoons, lampoonists, or clever sketch artists, but by no means satirists. For me the idea of satire is that which tries to get to the root of a situation and expose it with a degree of humor or a degree of exaggeration, and says something nasty about the nature of society. At its best, it's an analytic tool which is a weapon for its own cause. The only way to attack society properly or efficiently is to be aware that one is a member of it and is no more free of its compulsions or temptations than anybody else whom he may be making fun of.

Satire must state the conditions as they exist in sharp terms. Humor may be the coating of the pill, but the pill has to be there before you can swallow it. And it has to be in a form that's swallowable before anybody will pay any attention to it. I think humor, when it *over*coats the pill, is making a mistake. Toward the end that it identifies the pill, it's doing its job.

I had an argument with Marya Mannes, who talked about satire really being love and the reason we criticize is out of love. I took sharp exception to this. I said it becomes too self-congratulatory to say we're only doing this because we love everybody. I said that hate is terribly important. I said it begins out of a love that is thoroughly frustrated and becomes hate, exists as hate because it was not given a chance. It says, "Goddamn it, you told me this and you told me that and then you did just the opposite, but you're still going around talking that way, and every example you show is something else. I love the examples you gave me, but I hate the way you carry them out, and so I both love and hate you." All we see is the face of the betrayer. There has to be a love-hate relationship because you don't attack things you don't have an interest in.

Hate should not be a bad word. Hate is very important in coming to terms with who we are, because if we outlaw hate we outlaw serious thinking about those things that make us persons. Only when you can take every part of you and investigate it, and say, yes, this is the hateful part, I can accept that, this is the way I am, here's the part that wants to kill, the part that wants to cheat, the part that wants to betray, all this in one package and that package happens to be me, only then can you proceed somewhere.

The very nature of satire is against building. Satire is there to point out specific defects, with an eye to indirectly point out a direction that hopefully people will follow.

1965

················Being with It

Fifty-nine pages are hardly enough to separate the covers of a book, and yet Rachel MacKenzie's *Risk* requires more of a reader's time and his emotion than others many times its length. Miss MacKenzie describes, in as few words as possible and without a trace of self-pity, her ordeal with surgery to heal an aneurysm of the left ventricle of her heart. There was a good chance she would not survive the operation, which required many doctors, or the agonizing days that followed. "I love being alive," she told her doctor, and as X rays were taken and catheters prepared to thread through blood vessels into her heart, she said, "I mind waiting." In her story such fragments stand for much that is not said.

It is a story of pain and anticipation, a story of the awesome skill of a few doctors and the petty cruelties of others. Finally, it is a story of courage: not only the courage to confront suffering and the likelihood of death, but the courage to remain an active participant in a human adventure that has, to a large extent, been dehumanized by the magic of technology. In its extremest forms, medicine tempts us to passivity, tempts us to relinquish our personalities, which seem only to impede the proper servicing of our guts by men who understand our greatest crises better than we ever can. The triumph of Miss MacKenzie's experience appears to be the extent to which she resisted becoming an object; she was, she insisted, part of the team that was to attempt a miracle.

1971

··············New Notes
from the Underground

Books written from prison by men condemned to death share a passionate concern for the proper conduct of life. However, most of the men who wrote these books—Boethius, More, and André Chenier, for example—were prepared for the abridgment of their freedom and their lives by their education and careers, by years of constant challenge from authority. They accepted the garrot and the scaffold with a sense of achievement, convinced that the experience of prison, even of execution, was accidental to their lives. In recent years, however, we have seen a different breed of prison writer: men whose lives were shaped by prison, who developed in reaction to the humiliation and desperation of confinement. Such a man is the author of *Soledad Brother: The Prison Letters of George Jackson.*

Jackson is twenty-nine, a black man raised in a Chicago ghetto. He went to jail at fifteen; at eighteen, he was sentenced to a term of one year to life for stealing $70 from a gas station. To get parole, Jackson says, he would have to knuckle under, but that is not for him: "All my life I've done exactly what I wanted to do, which explains why I had to be jailed." A black man leaves jail, he says, when he becomes compliant, when the guards "see that thing in his eyes . . . resignation, defeat—it must be stamped clearly across the face." And when that black man leaves, he leaves his manhood behind, a price too high for Jackson: "If I leave here alive, I'll leave nothing behind. They'll never count me among the broken men." Now Jackson faces an automatic death sentence if he is found guilty of killing a prison guard.*

Jackson's letters do not make a book in any ordinary sense and must not be read as such. They were not meant to be read by any but their recipients: Jackson's parents, whom he cajoled, abused, and forgave for not preparing him for the world he found; his younger brother, who was recently killed while kidnapping a judge from his California courtroom; his lawyer; and Angela Davis, a black Communist teacher who was implicated in the courthouse killings. He has been failed by life, he says, and by his family, by those who he felt might have helped him.

Probably nothing so artless has been published by a black American—or anything as close to the bone. All the black polemics and autobiographies I can think of, including Eldridge Cleaver's letters from prison, were carefully shaped for publication, but these letters are the raw stuff, ragged and bleeding, or proudly refusing to bleed. None of our usual suppositions can be brought to bear on this book that Jackson never meant to write. Few white men can imagine what it is to feel to alienated, or what it is to have their perspectives entirely formed by the experience of prison. Erratic as they are, and occasionally self-consciously literary ("I have felt the sting of the knout and I live in the shadow of the ovens"), Jackson's letters show us something of the process

---

*Jackson, of course, was killed in 1971, in what appears to have been an attempted prison break.

of becoming a man under such circumstances, and of becoming black.

What is most striking is Jackson's disciplined determination. Carefully, he tries to strip away his "slavishness," to annihilate the white man that lurks in the heart of every American black man. His ego, emotion, and sentiment—"the shallow unnecessary things"—must go, too. "The harder it gets the better I like it," he writes; "I need control." He reads Fanon and Mao; his syntax stiffens in the Marxist mold. He thwarts the sex urge with one thousand push-ups every day, denounces God, and analyzes Whitey: "The evil that lurks in their hearts; I see the *insane* passion inherent in their characters." Occasionally, he offers little lectures on history: The Chinese, he says, feel an "ethnic solidarity" with their "brothers" in Africa, and no one has spoken Latin for fifteen hundred years. At times, he is cautiously optimistic: "I know that I am the original man and will soon inherit this earth." To his brother, he wrote a description of himself, the former slave now reborn as black: "You're supposed to be representing me, meaning that you are to be strong, intellectual, watchful, serious, unapproachable."

Throughout most of the letters Jackson is nervous, anxious to persuade. Only in recent months, as events have closed in on him, has he achieved the glacial serenity of acceptance that Jean Genet admires in convicts, an inversion of values that seems to break down the barrier between violence and violence as metaphor. "They hate us, don't they?" Jackson wrote Angela Davis. "I like it that way, that is the way it is supposed to be." And then he wrote: "We die altogether too easy. . . . My credo is to seize the pig by the tusks and ride him till his neck breaks." Inevitably, one thinks of Bartolomeo Vanzetti, whose life was not shaped in prison, though he said it was given meaning there. The slave has the right and duty to rise against his master, Vanzetti wrote, but the right to violence begins only where liberty ends. Ultimately, violence must be renounced: "The more I live," Vanzetti wrote, "the more I suffer, the more I learn, the more I am inclined to forgive, to be generous. . . . Violence as such does not resolve the problems of life."

Jackson's letters have, unfortunately, been edited for publication. The syntax had been prettied up to suit a Vassar sophomore's standards, eliminating the rhythmic rhetoric of the spoken word, the tendency to eject words in clusters, that comes naturally to Jackson and to all who, in history, have written the literature of protest. "Like I said" becomes "As I said," which is just stupid editing, no great harm done, but "black," when applied to men, carries a small *b* in this book, when Jackson always wrote it with a capital. Conversely, "Negro," which Jackson wrote with a small *n*, carries a big one in the book. This is insensitive editing because the difference mattered to the author. And what possible good comes from taking an interesting arrangement of clauses like "You are in-

volved, I hope," and reshaping them as "I hope you are involved"—
which sounds like a letter from the United Fund?

Minor editing of this sort, whittling or emasculating George Jackson's
style, occurs throughout the book. Still, we could probably live with it
and assume that the editor was ignorant of how revolutionaries have
traditionally written, even assume that his boss has ordered him to
conform all prose that passes through his hands to the *Girl Scout's
Manual of Usage*—except that the editing gets worse. Why should he
have censored what George Jackson wrote? Prison censorship of letters is
bad enough. Even so, Jackson's comments in his correspondence on
magazines like *Ramparts* and on the hypocrisy of the New Left, have
been excised from the manuscript of this book, a copy of which I worked
from to prepare this review. Why should the editor have struck out such
fascinating clues to Jackson's personality as his statement "I never knew
that I could be capable of such utter disregard for so many people"? And
why cut out such a passage as this: "And, too, the symbol of the male in
America (Anglo-America) is and has always been the gun. The male
child is taught from the womb to aggress. Aggression is built into all the
games, the cartoons, the movies and books he reads later on in life.
Having a penis means nothing if one cannot fight, shoot, lie, drive and
count out the *next male*." Incredible, just incredible—and yet similar
passages are routinely lined out in the manuscript.

Well, George Jackson will survive this indignity, as he has survived so
many others. The anguish comes through anyhow, as do the bitterness
and banality, the sloppiness and eloquence. "Strength comes from
knowledge," Jackson wrote after denouncing God, "knowing who you
are, where you want to go, what you want, knowing and accepting that
you are alone on this spinning, tumbling world."

1970

. . . . The Black Experience: Life vs. Rhetoric*

For nearly four years it has been fashionable for white critics ambling
between Jerusalem and Jericho to draw back their cloaks and cross to the
other side of the road whenever they spy a black book moaning by the
wayside. "Better let one of its own kind take care of it," the white critics

*A review of *Gemini*, by Nikki Giovanni; *Notes of a Processed Brother*, by Donald Reeves;
and *South to a Very Old Place*, by Albert Murray.

explain, "I don't understand that sort," and—particularly if the book is an autobiographical or polemical tract that seems unrelated to the white experience of America—they add: "It can't be moaning at me."

Admittedly, some of these books have been rather scary, mixing racism and mangled Marxism as they do, and some black writers have said "Right on" to the white critics' default, but the default has been a grave mistake. First, the most interesting black writing today comes from books like Malcolm X's *Autobiography,* from George Jackson's prison letters and from Eldridge Cleaver's *Soul on Ice.* Second, if we agree with Bacon that "it is by discourse that men associate," then it is foolish, perhaps even paternalistic, for a critic to disqualify himself from appraising any man's attempt to use words to construct new myths and arguments.

I believe that in much contemporary black writing language has broken down to the extent that it ceases to order and investigate truth and is used, deliberately, to screen readers—black or white—from reality. "Black people," Albert Murray writes, ". . . may misrepresent themselves, whether through incompetence or by design." "The usual revolutionary dialogue," Donald Reeves, now nineteen, calls it; "the soothing, masterly oratory that we substitute for the reality of our situation." And this is the crux of the matter: the adoption of rhetorical postures that isolate the black experience from life.

How does this come about? For one thing, in many black books today the writer seems to be talking to more than one audience. Nikki Giovanni, for instance, is a twenty-eight-year-old poet who mixes her engaging autobiographical essays with dubious exhortations to a kind of black revolution that will never happen here. The former are written with wit and the compressed rhythms that she brings to her poetry, but in the latter the truth of concrete experience yields to the rhetoric of abstract argument. Expressions of hope become assertions of fact: the revolution, as she writes elsewhere, "will go on," when in fact it has not begun and never will; if we have a revolution in this country, it will be of a different kind.

Next, there is an insistence on the part of many black writers that their art cannot be separated from their revolutionary message. "Once you write for your people, others will judge that your quality is failing," Miss Giovanni complains and indeed it does, falling into the worse kind of racism and inaccuracy. How are we to cope with her suggestion that "it is questionable whether the honkie has a mind"? Or with her poem, a dancing, teasing, skillful poem that says "Can you stab-a-jew/Can you kill huh? nigger . . . Can you piss on a blond head/Can you cut it off?" White liberals will say she doesn't mean it, but *she* thinks she does, though I doubt she really believes that the white man's Bible says "Do unto others as they have done unto you." It's the old Humpty Dumpty trick: The meaning doesn't matter, but only who's to be master, that's all. "In the end," Miss Giovanni says, "it's always a power struggle."

In most black militant writing a kind of programmed rhetoric creeps in: part Jew-baiting, part denial of the white man's humanity—"the white man is no hueman" Miss Giovanni writes—part misappropriation of the ideas of Frantz Fanon and Che Guevara. Any discipline requires its own language, but it should be clear—as it is not clear to black militants—that a diversity of perspective is necessary to avoid error. Black militant books puff with rhetoric that was never intended to apply to the American experience. "The big thing with them nowadays is to sound revolutionary," Albert Murray writes. "They are responding to what they read instead of what they know . . . they haven't really read very much."

No, but they've all read the same books and they accept the "house nigger" concept from Malcolm X, though the concept is discredited; the colonial theory from Fanon, though Fanon would not have applied it to America; the revolution from Guevara, though Guevara said it couldn't happen here. The black militants grab what suits them from their prophets without reckoning the contradictions. Their attitude toward authority is ambivalent: Don Reeves condemns high school principals as irresponsible despots but accepts without question Malcolm X's peculiar interpretations of history. Like many angry blacks, he writes well of his own struggle and badly of history at large, ascribing to intentional repression much human inertia and incompetence. We see this in most revolutionary writing: a calcification of human process into rhetorical attitudes, denying what Yeats called the "complexities of mire or blood." A pity: Br'er Rabbit, at least, would not have needed Fanon to tell him what the briar patch was like.

Still, Reeves is young and incredibly able. He came from a Brooklyn slum to take over the student government of an elite Manhattan high school and then the student council for all New York's high schools. He plotted the overthrow of the Board of Education and drew up a students' bill of rights which, though it may be economically naïve, is otherwise enlightened. Reeves was knocked down, of course. Sleeping with a white girl didn't help him with his black constituency; official intransigence and the fragmentation of his support destroyed him just as he was arguing his case on television and in the papers.

Arrogant, energetic, and quick-thinking, Reeves makes his efforts seem worthwhile even though he is a little excited by himself, even in retrospect. "Uncle Tom," he yelled as he grabbed the mike at a meeting—"I felt it was my duty to attend and disrupt these meetings," he explains—"Kitchen Spic; and these Jews who have exploited your communities for centuries." He "kicked over their tables, got the community people to come up on stage"—and yet, he's likable, if not a man to be messed with. Always he doubted himself: "I felt uneasy over the speed at which I had been able to take over the meeting," he writes. "People could be led too easily, and I felt this was dangerous to their own security."

The same kind of honesty redeems much of the absurdity, the quick dips to vulgar polemics, of Nikki Giovanni's book. "The truth is," she writes, "that there is this shell all around you, and the more you say, 'All right, you can come in' to someone, the more he questions the right of the shell to exist. And if you fall for that and take it away, he looks at your nakedness and calls you a whore. It's an awful thing when all you wanted was to laugh and run and touch and make love and really not give a damn." This is quite different from Miss Giovanni's other lesson—that she has learned to compete with whites in the pursuit of power and racism. The Code of Hammurabi: an eye for an eye—but the trouble is that we will soon run out of eyes and have a blind society. "If I saw a sick old white lady on her way to a convalescence home I'd kick her in the ass," Miss Giovanni writes, "and rob her of the twenty cents her dollar is worth." A compassionate society is not an easy one; it is neither so just nor so entertaining as Miss Giovanni might like, but for all her affectlessness and talk of violence, Miss Giovanni does not come on as evil as she wants to be. "People keep calling me a hater," she says, "and really I'm a lover." I think she is.

We come finally to Albert Murray, who is fifty-five and skeptical of "writers who are most insistently blacker than thou" and skeptical of statistics about integration in the South because, as he says, he just wants "to see how it feels. I'm operating on my literary radar." Murray returned to the South on an assignment from a magazine to talk to liberal whites and to get a feel of "downhome." He rather liked what he found: Integration is going better than some whites give it credit for. Murray accepts none of the black militant clichés, knows that revolutions come from the top of society, not the bottom—has, in fact, written a brave book, talking, as he does, of Duke Ellington and Count Basie (rather than Aretha and Dionne) and describing himself as "a writer whose nonfiction represents an effort to play literary vamps and intellectual riffs equivalent to the musical ones Duke Ellington feeds his orchestra from his piano."

Murray is very much the together man with a sharp ear for speech patterns. Like all travelers, he wastes a lot of time on inconsequential mutterings from famous people, but his narrative comes alive when he talks to unnamed Negroes in Mobile: What motherwit and perspicacity then emerge! These blacks are entirely opposed to the efforts of their revolutionary brothers and very funny about them, too: "the white man only too glad if they rather learn about Africa instead of how to run the world," one says, and another, defending Lyndon Johnson's war policy because he put blacks in high office, says "that's exactly what we need, some mean old crackers on our side, for a change."

Such pragmatism is worth more than all the processed political clichés of would-be revolutionary activists. For what is finally depressing about polemical rhetoric is not that it bears no reality to a particular situation or to life at large, but that it inhibits thought; not that it is an untrustworthy tool, but too simple a tool for the occasion, and it is therefore a simple device to transmit to others, who then themselves stop thinking. It is particularly sad to see a student pick it up. "Blacks are superior to whites," wrote one college student recently, "because blacks are descended from kings and queens and whites from the lumpkin proletariat." When the teacher objected, the student gave her "the look"—not an "Off the honky teacher" look, but a dull look, a look that said, "From her, what else would you expect?" And this is the sad part: Where learning should thrive, the language wilts; the result of such rhetoric may yet be silence.

1972

.... After the Curtain

Three seasons ago, as you can hardly fail to remember, Richard Burton played Hamlet on Broadway. He pranced on and over the iambics, snarled like a chain saw, honked like a taxi, and declaimed, "O, what a rogue and peasant slave am I!" with such musical timing that you could, as if at a piano recital, beat the rhythm on your knees. There were other actors on stage, too: You may remember Hume Cronyn as Polonius, and Alfred Drake as Claudius, but do you remember William Redfield?

Redfield got star billing playing Guildenstern—no mean feat. One of those meticulous craftsmen who hover near the top of their profession, he offers no competition to such electric players as Burton, Olivier, Scofield, and Gielgud. But then those who scale the glassy pinnacles of any profession can seldom do what Redfield does here. There is an invariable ratio that applies to all show biz books: The importance of the book decreases in geometric proportion to the fame of the author. An unimportant actor who is devoted to his art often can, when the curtain comes down, discourse upon it with detachment and wit.

Redfield's *Letters from an Actor* is simply one of the best books ever written about the theater, made all the better for having been written from the inside while something important was going on. This account of the Gielgud-Burton *Hamlet,* from its casting and rehearsals through its out-of-town engagements and New York opening, takes the form of letters Redfield wrote to a literary agent. Written late at night and later revised, these letters are acerb and affectionate, a rare combination of intimacy, insight, and good gossip. It is astonishing how much of permanent value can be said about the way an actor thinks and lives in connection with such a dubious production.

Whatever the result, the *concept* of the production was intriguing. It would be played in rehearsal clothes, Gielgud said, because one is always rehearsing *Hamlet* and because rehearsals often provoke a freshness and rhythm lacking in formal productions. "This 'Hamlet,' " wrote Redfield, "is intended to be a highly modern, fast-moving crowd-pleasing production and will likely be one of the most successful Shakespearean productions of all time."

Indeed it was. While Gielgud dithered, Burton made it so. Burton and Gielgud, Redfield felt, represented spontaneity and discipline, "the thrilling bad boy and the watchful don." Gielgud underrehearsed and underdirected the production. "A fine thoroughbred refusing his jump," Gielgud seemed to have no concept of the play; he "vaporized his responsibilities with a puff of humor." Redfield and the others bit their nails, but not Burton, all energy and courage, "the classically trained actor who had become Pop Art."

Comments on the production, however, are only a small part of what Redfield offers. His anecdotes about Olivier and Ralph Richardson are hilarious. His quarrel with Gielgud's assistant and his attempted seduction of the actress who played Ophelia are darkly funny. There are odd scraps of information—Iago has the longest role in Shakespeare's plays and Claudius the fifth longest!—and many thoughtful observations on the actor's art:

"Acting is an art defiant of logic. It comes from the soul and it is a slippery business. There are rules and they should be observed, but the rules alone will never make great acting."

"The actor must have the soul of a fairy and the hide of a walrus."

"Being a movie star has nothing at all to do with being an actor."

"Show me a working actor and I will show you a man with a cement stomach."

Written with grace and urbanity, with wit and sparkling turns of phrase, *Letters from an Actor* should be remembered long after the Gielgud-Burton *Hamlet* has been forgotten. If there is any justice, that is. But there isn't.

1967

⋯⋯⋯⋯⋯⋯⋯⋯⋯⋯⋯Hemingway: The Whole Truth and Nothing But

"We have good fun," Hemingway wrote when he was fifty-six, "and that is more than most people have." It is a characteristic affidavit, a compound sentence made of simple words and complex emotions. Happiness, for Hemingway, was not a by-product of living; it was a species of big game. You had to talk about it a lot and realize most people weren't good enough to get it, but there were seasons when, if you hunted it aggressively and were skillful and lucky enough, you could bag some of it, enough to show your friends before another season came and you had to turn your gun upon yourself.

It was this combination of bravado and vulnerability, I think, that proved so attractive to my generation when we were in our teens. We knew, of course, that geniuses are not like you and me (they have more talent), but if we could not *be* Hemingway, we could be the kind of men Hemingway would take as friends, Robins to his Batman. We rejected the criticisms of our teachers and our parents, but a grunt of disapproval from Hemingway would have shattered our self-esteem. Fortunately, not many of us met him. Of all the writers in American history, only two have achieved the status of culture heroes—Hemingway and Scott Fitzgerald. From Berkeley to Harvard, we were taught to admire the work of T. S. Eliot and Henry James, but I never knew anyone who wanted to *be* Eliot or James. Disastrous though their endings were, the writers who appealed to us seemed to have achieved the good life while accomplishing good work. Fitzgerald and Hemingway had "good fun."

Nobody could write a boring book about Hemingway. The variety and intensity of what he wrote and what he did, the tension between his successes and his failures, the impact of his style on the last two generations, assure the interest of his life. Now, after seven years, Carlos

Baker has finally been delivered of his great labor, *Ernest Hemingway: A Life Story,* the authorized biography. Such a mammoth book will probably remain the definitive biography as well, if only because nobody could conceivably add anything worth knowing to the mass of detail and documentation that Baker has assembled.

Carefully and convincingly, he sorts the myth from the fact (a particularly difficult job with Hemingway, who lied about his prowess from infancy) and identifies the people who served as models for the famous characters in his fiction. Baker's aims are completeness and objectivity— laudable aims for a scholar, but limiting for a biographer. Baker's art is that of the retrieval system: He sweeps away all concern for shape, for controlled digressions, for point of view and style, to present—first, foremost, and forever—facts. This is a book built to last. We will, in time, change our opinion of Hemingway, the man and his work, but Baker has foreseen that problem, too; he protects himself against the fickle shifts of reputation's breezes by avoiding any kind of evaluation— of the man or of his work. Baker's immortality may lie in the footnotes of the work of future scholars, but it is to his credit that the book of facts he has made is, though innocent of art, entirely fascinating.

The portrait takes shape quickly. "Fraid a nothing," said Infant Ernest, and, when he was five, he lied to his grandfather that he had stopped a runaway horse. His parents, helped by the rigors of summers in northern Michigan, taught him courage and endurance, the joys of hunting and fishing. Writing for newspapers taught him the virtue of simple, declarative sentences, which would, in time, lead him to sum up the art of writing: "All you have to do is write one true sentence. Write the truest sentence that you know." Hemingway's sentences, Baker writes, were "declarative, straightforward, and forceful as a right to the jaw." He "dealt, almost singlehanded, a permanent blow against the affected, the nambypamby, the pretentious, and the false."

By the time Hemingway was twenty-seven, the mold was set. In the war in Italy, he learned fear, was badly wounded, considered suicide, and saw the birth of the myth that was to overtake the man. Within a few years, he had been married and divorced, had become a father and, after desperate years in Paris, gained recognition as a writer. He followed the *corridas* in Spain, boxed and skied, argued with the important writers of his time. What was still to come—more marriages, wars, fights, and increasing fame—were variations on these well-established themes.

Baker's finished portrait is beautifully balanced and admirably complete. It is, perhaps, a bit conservative, surprisingly tasteful: Baker must know more about the friction preceding Hemingway's divorces than he reveals, and he is disinclined to follow Hemingway's sexual adventures. Hemingway "boasted that he had bedded every woman he had ever wanted and some that he hadn't," but Baker accentuates Hemingway's shyness, speculating that he probably did not have an affair with the woman who became Brett Ashley, and that in *The Sun Also Rises,* Hemingway projected his own inhibitions into Jake Barnes' emasculating war wound. (This, by the way, is exactly the kind of critical speculation that infuriated Hemingway.) With similar decorum, Baker dresses in as much decency as he can muster the madness that overcame Hemingway at the end. Nevertheless, the whole man is here, with his boyish charm and black rages; his modesty and his boastfulness; his self-pity and his charisma that made other men yield to him; his superstition and his anti-Semitism; his bullying, competitive drive to dominate his friends; his generosity and unexpected cruelty; his "life-long preference for the uncommon common man"; his fondness for dirty tricks and his susceptibility to accidents and illness; his bitterness when his masculinity was queried. *"Mens morbida in corpore sano,"* a critic said. "The pendulum in his nervous system," Baker writes, "swung periodically through the full arc from megalomania to melancholy."

The further in time one gets from one's subject, the easier it becomes to write a biography that is itself a work of art. Writers close to their subjects usually renounce the luxury of art, at least until the facts are in. Baker's job was to collect the facts; the extent of his achievement can be seen in the one hundred and six double-column, single-spaced pages of notes and acknowledgments that follow the text. Baker's quest for completeness has its deflationary aspects—I would rather not have known *why* the leopard was found frozen on Mt. Kilimanjaro (he was chasing a goat)—but it leads to an indispensable base of fact from which other more artful books can be written. Nor can Baker's kind of book approach the immediacy and conviction of a memoir like A. E. Hotchner's *Papa Hemingway.* A memoir may be limited to a small perspective, but the impact of extended scenes and uninterrupted conversations with the protagonist carries a truth that is as real as Baker's broad, external view. Baker is contemptuous of Hotchner's credulity, yet the lies that Hemingway told about himself, hoping they would become part of the record, are essential to an understanding of the man.

In reviewing a book as excellent and as substantial as this one, it may seem unfair to quarrel with minor points; nevertheless, Baker does make some irritating errors of judgment. He relegates too many fascinating details to notes grouped at the back of the book where few will ever read them. He introduces famous people by familiar nicknames inappropriate to formal biography: "Dos" Passos, for example, and "Dotty" Parker, "Archie" MacLeish. He fails to solve the problem of how to write about something already better described by Hemingway: hunting scenes in Michigan, for instance, skiing scenes in Austria, or the terrifying spectacle of Christians fleeing the armies of Ataturk. Baker does the best he can with his own words, but his book would have been sharper if he had quoted Hemingway's descriptions of these events. More serious, however, is Baker's incessant paraphrasing of Hemingway's letters. Letters are an essential part of a biography like this; unfortunately, there is an embargo on the publication of Hemingway's correspondence, a prohibition that apparently extends even to this authorized biography. Baker does not alert the reader to his problem—why, I cannot guess— but leaves him to flounder in reams of indirect, unquoted discourse, making him wonder just exactly what it was that Hemingway did say. This confusion is a pity, but it is the only major fault of an otherwise extraordinary book.

1969

Six

.....................Aggressive
Anthropology:
Lo, the Poor Indian!

Suddenly, anthropology is *in*. Why not? We may be a nation of baby-burners and mother-muggers, but the fault may not be ours. We may club children, shoot statesmen, and run riot in the streets, but we're *sensitive* about it. We're the self-conscious generation. We talk a lot about how beastly and unspeakable we are, so why not read about our beastly and unspeaking progenitors? It makes it all seem so natural. Of all the world's fauna, the new anthropologists tell us, only ants, rats, and men make war on their own kind. Now that's very comforting; it makes our American way of life seem inevitable, so let's hear it for LBJ before he fades from office.

But there's a better reason for anthropology's recent popularity. Anthropology has gone aggressive: Torn from the grip of scholars by playwrights and polemicists, it is now being written by a sock-it-to-'em school that knows it's not how right you are that counts but how you write it wrong. Naked apes? Territorial imperatives? This is the jargon of publicists, not scientists. Like the Vermont farmer, anthropologists have learned that if you want a donkey to do something, you must first slam a hammer between his eyes—to get his attention. You understand, reader, who the donkey is in this equation: To get our attention, anthropologists sacrifice tomorrow's distinction for today's fame. And, as always, the Book-of-the-Month Club, with its pail and shovel, follows not far behind.

Take, for instance, Peter Farb's new book, which has a title so ungainly that, once it is spelled out, a review seems unnecessary: *Man's Rise to Civilization as Shown by the Indians of North America, from Primeval Times to the Coming of the Industrial State.* It is a fascinating and worrisome enterprise: a book so slick and well-written that it holds our hushed attention, so well-documented and informative on a subject most Americans know little of that it commands our guilty respect, yet so opinionated and sloppy in its argument that it looks as vulnerable as a puppy rolling on its back.

Farb's intention is to present not only a lively and detailed study of the variety and complexity of North American Indian cultures but a theory of cultural evolution as well. The Indians, because they developed their cultures almost entirely apart from the influence of the Old World, form a "living laboratory" in which we may learn much about the tribes, now lost to history, from which we ourselves have come. A study of the Iroquois, Farb insists, tells us much about how the ancient Hebrews organized as tribes; in like manner, there is great similarity between the Aztec and Assyrian states.

"Environment does not determine man's culture," he writes, "it merely sets the outer limits and at the same time offers opportunities." Neither does a society change through conscious choice; rather, it makes unconscious adaptations that often result in profound change. The catalyst is usually a new technology: The Cheyenne Indians, for instance, were an agricultural society until, in the eighteenth century, they acquired Spanish horses—these horses proved the tool the Cheyennes needed to hunt the bison that had hitherto run unmolested past their villages.

Farb discusses the Indians in order of the increasing complexity of their societies. He begins with the Diggers—the Shoshone, organized simply on the basis of the family and living much as men did a million years ago—and proves that they are not, as they were once thought to be, as primitive as the apes. The difference between man and the apes, Farb says, is that an ape's social life is ruled by anatomy and physiology, but man's is ruled by culture. Culture, to an anthropologist, "is all the things and ideas ever devised by humans working and living together. It is what it takes to be human."

From the Diggers, Farb moves upward in social complexity through the Eskimos and other primitive bands to tribal societies like the Zuni and Iroquois, then to the chiefdoms of the Northwest Coast and the Natchez sun worshippers, and finally to the Aztecs, whose state achieved a European splendor. In conclusion, Farb describes both the beginning and the end of the Indians' story: Their migration to North America thirty thousand years ago, following big game between the glaciers on the land bridge now covered by the Bering Straits; and the failure of the Indian to cope with the white man's murderous onslaught.

So far, all is safe and sober, but perhaps not very salesworthy. Farb has the answer to that: Two other elements—one legitimate and the other highly questionable—provide the yeast that will raise both his sales and the temperatures of his fellow anthropologists. Farb is, first of all, a master of dramatic detail. His story is stuffed with Iroquois torture, Aztec sacrifice, peyote dreams, self-mutilation in search of visions, and the atrocities of aborigine puberty rites. It is also crammed with pithy aphorisms designed to shake up whatever little we thought we knew of Indian culture:

- "The more primitive a society, the more leisured its way of life."
- "All primitive peoples are extremely anxiety-ridden."
- "Pure selfishness has given the Eskimo a reputation for generosity and earned him the good opinion of missionaries and of all others who hunger and thirst after proof of the innate goodness of man."
- "Witchcraft is aggression for which society has not provided channels."

It's hard not to love a book that contains this kind of grit, but after a while it is apparent that Farb is entranced with his own outrageous assertions. It may be that our Memorial Day makes us kin to the Zuni, with their cult of the dead, but Farb merely insists that this is so; he does not prove it. Even more annoying is Farb's tendency to simplify. If half a dozen explanations of a phenomenon have been advanced, Farb picks one as exclusively true and discards the rest. The truth is generally more complex than that. For example:

- Incest, he says, is frowned upon because it prevents alliances that can be gained by marrying out of the family. Fair enough, but perhaps other forces are at work: Sexual jealousy can destroy a family unit; civilization may progress by men learning to renounce their parents; and surely there is joy and vitality in a *variety* of love.
- Every language loses 19 percent of its words every thousand years. This sounds swell, but a written language can freeze a great part of its vocabulary; because it can also reintroduce words that have slipped from common usage, it would seem likely to lose words more slowly than a preliterate language.
- The pain of puberty rites is simply an *aide-mémoire*: The initiate receives the clan's accumulated knowledge with such pain that he will never forget it. OK, but what about the idea of *earning* knowledge, or the older generation's pleasure in making young people hurt a bit before granting them equality?
- If the great men of history had not been born, others would have done their work. Farb attempts to prove it by showing how scientists arrive independently at the same discoveries—but this proves nothing. The Great Man theory of history was never meant to apply to scientists. Europe would not be what it is today without Napoleon—no other man would have marched on Moscow. And although Athens produced many

corrupt men, no one but Alcibiades could have launched the fatal expedition against Sicily.

Farb progresses thematically. He plunges into the middle of his story and drops the beginning near the end. He may bludgeon his readers into submission as often as he persuades them by argument, but his book is marvelously readable—and it is certainly what is making the scene today: aggressive anthropology.

1968

.......................How to Make
a Good Indian

Not too long ago, we knew who the bad guys were and how to handle them: "There is not a bit of doubt that killing women and children has a very dampening effect on the ardor of the Indian," a historian wrote in 1886. "Scalping and mutilation also strike terror to the Indian heart." The historian was J. P. Dunn, Jr., who wrote *Massacres of the Mountains,* a history of the Indian wars in the West, ten years after Custer died at Little Big Horn and four years before Custer's regiment slaughtered three hundred disarmed Indians at Wounded Knee. Dunn's observations are contained in his defense of the Sand Creek Massacre of 1864, in which a Colorado regiment, especially raised to kill Indians, decimated six hundred peaceful, sleeping Cheyennes. The attack, Dunn wrote, was justified "under all the rules of civilized warfare" because the Cheyennes, even the four hundred women and children, were "hostiles," and "there was no truce with them." As for reports that the Cheyennes had immediately hoisted an American flag, and a white flag of surrender, too, that was no cause "for stopping troops in the midst of a charge, and especially in the surprise of an enemy's camp." The object of the white man's policy, Dunn often tells us, was ever "one of benefit and kindness to the red man."

Dunn's book, which has been recently reissued, pipes the brave tunes of Manifest Destiny, self-assured songs that are not often heard today, except perhaps in the Army's reports on our war against the Vietnamese, or in police reports on our war against the Black Panthers. In fact, there is something very odd about the way we have written about our wars with the Indians. Although there is no lack of good books about Indians and their civilizations, there is almost nothing about Indians in the books we write about American history as a whole, either for ourselves or for our children. In the 1,050 pages of *The Wars of America,* Robert Leckie gives only four to our wars with the Indians in the West. Samuel Eliot Morison, in his mammoth *Oxford History of the American People,* refers only briefly to Indians, ignoring the characters of both the Indian civilizations and their extraordinary leaders. And yet these are excellent books. Many Americans will learn all they will ever know about Indians from movies and from just such books as these.

Our general historians have failed us, insofar as Indians are concerned, in three regards. They have failed to see that our historical relation to the American Indian has been far more important to the shaping of our nation and our character than, say, our wars with Mexico and in the Philippines. They have failed even to ask who the Indian was and what we might have learned from him, particularly from his attitude toward the American land. "To the Indians," writes Dee Brown in *Bury My Heart at Wounded Knee,* "it seemed that these Europeans hated everything in nature—the living forests and their birds and beasts, the grassy glades, the water, the soil, and the air itself." Now it seems that if we are to survive, we must come back to what Chief Joseph knew: "The earth," he said, "was created by the assistance of the sun, and it should be left as it was. . . . I never said the land was mine to do with it as I chose." Finally, the historians have failed to find a proper way to write about the Indian. They still play modest variations of the Manifest Destiny theme, an octave lower this time, but nonetheless recognizable: "How tragic that it had to be." . . . "Inevitable historical process." . . . "The government"—as one book for teen-agers says—"made promises it could not keep," which implies that the government is not really to be blamed. People tend to write about Indians in the passive voice: Things were done to them, as if there were no efficient cause.

Brown's book has a subtitle: "An Indian History of the American West." It is not that. Brown is not an Indian, and his book deals only with the climactic wars from 1860 to 1890. Nor is it, like recent books by Peter Farb and Alvin Josephy, a study of Indian cultures, but rather a political history, a military history. It is also an appalling and a noble book. "Americans who have always looked westward when reading about this period," Brown writes, "should read this book looking eastward." Fair enough. His book makes no pretense to objectivity. Drawing heavily on the Indians' own narratives of raids and wars, he paints a wartless, even romantic portrait of his subjects, but that makes his book no less an excellent primer to red (Indian, that is) thinking.

I wish I could say that the stories Brown has to tell are well known; they are not. General Carleton's determination to push the Navahos to a barren reservation, for instance, and Kit Carson's scorched-earth warfare that forced them there. Or Little Crow's painful decision to lead the Santee Sioux in an obviously ill-fated war against the whites in

Minnesota which resulted in a trial in which three hundred and three Sioux were convicted and, later, in America's greatest mass execution. Then there was the Sand Creek Massacre in which Colonel Chivington, a former minister, announced, "I have come to kill Indians, and believe it is right and honorable to use any means under God's heaven to kill Indians." That day, white soldiers "cut out the private parts of females and stretched them over the saddlebows and wore them over their hats." After the battle, Black Kettle, chief of the Cheyennes, said: "We are different nations, but it seems as if we were but one people, whites and all."

And so it went: the Fetterman Massacre outside Fort Phil Kearny in 1866, when the Sioux, Cheyennes, and Arapahos served notice that they would not accept the white man's intrusions in the Powder River country; Custer's raid at Washita in which one hundred and three Cheyennes were killed, of whom only eleven were warriors; the betrayal and massacre of the Apaches; the extermination of the Modocs; the pursuit of Chief Joseph; the war for the Black Hills; the exile and murder of Sitting Bull; and, as the carnival announcers say, more, much more.

Looking eastward, Brown gives us the Battle of Little Big Horn without any reference to Custer's insubordination, egotism, or political ambition. All through his book, Brown underplays his effects, leaving us to make summations and conclusions, particularly of the pattern of Indian errors. Indians assumed that the white man's promises would be kept; that friendliness would be returned; that there was room enough in America for all; that the white man could be beaten, or at least delayed; that flags of truce and provisions of treaties would be honored; and that someone—the Great Father in Washington or his agents—would understand what land meant to the Indian. The Indians assumed all this, and they were wrong, every one of them, on every count.

"No one who fights with the white people," said one Indian chief, "ever becomes rich, or remains two days in one place, but is always fleeing and starving." "Let me be a free man," Chief Joseph told the government in Washington, "free to stop, free to work, free to trade where I choose, free to choose my own teachers, free to follow the religion of my fathers, free to think and talk and act for myself." As Brown observes, no one listened. That was not the kind of America the leaders in Washington had in mind. "I feel that my country has gotten a bad name," Sitting Bull said, "and I want it to have a good name; it used to have a good name; and I sit sometimes and wonder who it is that has given it a bad name." And when Cadette, the Navaho chief, finally surrendered, he said: "Do with us as may seem good to you, but do not forget we are men and braves." Forget? Hell, it was easy to forget. Whoever thought they were men?

1971

.......................Opening
the Earth

An important aspect of the New Barbarism, or of any barbarism, is its loutish pragmatism. Example: A college freshman reports that a man peered at a book she was reading, and then at her. "What did King Arthur ever do for *you*?" he asked. She should not have been surprised. Barbarians are simple folk, perplexed by the multiplicity of man's ideas and aspirations. What *use* is it? they ask, as if nothing is important unless it is usable. Nor do barbarians like to be jostled in their certainties. Because they would be happier if there were not so much to think and worry about, they strive to reduce the area of man's concern. Another man might groan that he will never have the time to learn what he wants to know about quasars and Milton, about history and archaeology, but the barbarian doesn't even see the problem: Such study isn't *relevant*, he says.

It has always been so. Terence's claim that nothing human was alien to him has never won much applause in the barrooms and classrooms where barbarians gather to grunt and suppress ideas. Barbarism doesn't change; what I call the New Barbarism is only Old Barbarism made audible. In good times, there is little news from the barbarian front; the snuffling self-righteousness and barking paranoia continue as always, but nobody *listens*. In bad times, however, when there is a war, or economic instability, a proliferation of ideas and information becomes intolerable to those who have always distrusted them. This crucial combination of optimum communication and pessimum stability—what Germany experienced in 1933 and what we, in a different way, are experiencing now—provokes a perverse kind of Populism. Then the barbarians blow their battle horns: The right flank attacks the purveyors of information, blaming them for society's instability; the left flank occupies the classrooms, blaming scholars and teachers for their irrelevance. Behind the barbaric yawping is a rather plaintive cry: Life's too complicated. There is just too much to know.

Unfortunately, people who should know better start to nod and blame themselves. Even worse, those who write "irrelevant" books begin to apologize for them. "What will it all have mattered?" Geoffrey Bibby asks at the end of *Looking for Dilmun*. Fifteen years of Bibby's life have led to this book, one of the most exciting ever written about archaeology, but Bibby pauses, wondering if he can find a reason for moving so much sand. And so the barbarians have reached us all: Everyone, it seems, must justify extending man's knowledge and understanding beyond the realm of instant practicality.

Bibby is an English archaeologist, working for a Danish museum. Since 1954, he has led teams of Danes on digs in the oil-rich sheikhdoms on the Arabian side of the Persian Gulf. He began with a single colleague, cutting into the grave mounds of Bahrain, an island that contains "the largest prehistoric cemetery in the world." Within a few years, he directed several teams working along the coast from Kuwait to Oman, uncovering cities, temples, and palaces dating back to the third millennium B.C. More important, Bibby found what he was looking for: an ancient civilization undreamed of a century ago and, until this book, unheard of by all but a few scholars.

The civilizations of Egypt and Mesopotamia were referred to in the Bible, but Dilmun, which may have been as great and flourished for two thousand years, has been forgotten for two thousand years. Word of its existence first came in the mid-nineteenth century, when scholars deciphered the Mesopotamian cuneiform. Part of the great Babylonian epic *Gilgamesh* is laid in Dilmun; Bibby believes he has found the place in Bahrain where the legendary events took place. More important, Dilmun served as a trading center between Sumer and the Indus. Its merchants roamed the known world, bringing luxuries from India and copper from the lost kingdom of Makan (Bibby thinks he may have found Makan, too) to Ur and Babylon.

On an island off Kuwait, Bibby discovered a Greek Temple—"as Greek as the Parthenon"—and then an entire Greek town, with a kiln and molds for statues resembling the Venus de Milo, the Winged Victory, and a portrait of Alexander the Great. In Bahrain, which appears to be the capital of Dilmun, he found seven cities stacked upon each other, one dating from 2800 B.C. and, by finding the city wall and customshouse, was able to piece together a picture of how the people of Dilmun lived. Most interesting of all, perhaps, was his discovery in Arabia of seven-thousand-year-old relics of the Ubaid culture, the first agricultural settlers who moved into the region that became Sumer. This discovery raises important questions. The nearest Ubaid site was 400 miles to the north. It had been previously thought that civilization came to Arabia from the east—but did it come from the north? Or did the Ubaid people come from Arabia, when it was a green and pleasant land, and move north?

Bibby leaves many questions unanswered. He and his team lack the money to continue. Someday, of course, he will go back, but in the meantime, we have this wonderful narrative account of his expeditions in search of Dilmun. Bibby is a good writer, aware of the drama inherent in any search for hidden treasure, and of his obligation to explain unobtrusively and in laymen's terms as much of the techniques and lore of archaeology as are pertinent to his story. Best of all, he can make the ignorant reader, who may have doubts about poking into the sand for broken bits of pottery, share his excitement in the quest. "Now," he exclaims, "the Greek town lay before me." There is no doubt that he sees it just as the followers of Alexander left it. Few men make for themselves the opportunity to discover whole civilizations; the wonder is that Bibby, who literally opens the earth in search of man's history, can for a moment ask, "What will it all have mattered?"

1970

· · · · · · · · · · · · · · · · · · · The Search for
an Accurate Past

Like all countries, America tries to tidy up its past. It isn't hard to do. Historians are roughhanded lads, and if they can't do the job with a broom, they will do it with shovel and ax. Bury that moldering Indian that died—oh, years ago!—he looks less like a man than ever, and who wants to smell him now? Chop down the slave quarters at Monticello and Mount Vernon. We don't need them now, they make bad public relations, and—who knows?—maybe someday they never will have been. Besides, such embarrassing reminders of our recent past interfere with our American myths. You remember the myths. We grew up with them, and believed them:

- We support liberty at home and abroad.
- Only misguided or malicious nations think that what we want is not best for the world.
- Our government tells us the truth and represents our interests.
- We can solve our problems.
- We want to solve our problems.
- We are the *good* guys.

Myths are not necessarily false, and there is some truth yet to these. Recently, however, we have had to ask ourselves questions about them, and that is why many of us who grew up with them, and believed them, fidget and curse so much.

Many of us feel today that we have been sold something of a bill of goods about our country and its past. Our recent doubts, mistakes, and tragedies remind us of our need to sort out the facts, to look again at who we are and what we have done. We know now that there has been a credibility gap in our history books—that too much has been forgotten, suppressed, or glossed over—and we have begun to react against those architects of error, the theoretical historians. These are the villains: the armchair generalists, the anthropologists of time who offer patterns to explain the behavior of man, who formalize and fossilize such facts as suit them into theory—and call the theory truth.

Theory injures facts. It also makes them usable, but, for the moment, we seem to want to get as close to the facts of history as possible, hoping, as the Freudians believe, that if we can get all the facts, and get them straight, if we can look squarely at what happened to us and not just glance sideways at what we want to see, we may be able to heal the wounds in our national psyche. The facts we find may seem fragmented, confusing, even contradictory, but if we look at them long enough, we may make sense of our history.

So, in the last few years, an attempt has been made to let the past speak to us directly. Our new interest in hearing voices from generations gone has launched a modest rush to republish primary documents from American history. We should not be deceived: The man who selects the documents, who decides what from the past is of interest to us now, may reveal as much personal bias, or as much conformity to fashions in history, as any Whig or Marxist can muster in his interpretation.

The most ambitious undertaking in this area is the *Encyclopaedia Britannica*'s *The Annals of America,* an eighteen-volume set containing 2,200 essays, articles, speeches, poems, and manifestos from every era of our past. There is bias here, of course. *Britannica*'s editors find more that is worthy of their notice as they approach the present, which I regret, and they have a marked penchant for the arts, which I applaud. The selections have been chosen with exceptional taste and intelligence. Unfortunately, the editors believe that everything that has been done or dreamed of in America can be reduced to "25 Great Issues," which are discussed in two additional volumes called the "Conspectus," a pedant's term, which, I suppose, means "the together look." These added volumes are useless baggage, but perhaps they appeal to school and college librarians of less than adequate cranial capacity. And since the set is priced at $164.50, libraries appear to be its intended destination. This is a pity. I have been looking through it for two months now and find it full of unexpected riches and delights.

*   *   *

Today's fashion for documentary history is matched only by today's fashion for black history. Both are combined in Arna Bontemps' *Great Slave Narratives,* an anthology of three memoirs that are so remarkable—for their passion, for their information, and for their readability—that I urge everyone who cares for the neglected history of his country to read them without delay.

Two are quite brief, telling of their authors' escapes from slavery. In "Running a Thousand Miles for Freedom," William Craft tells how he and his wife escaped from Georgia on a train. Craft's wife was nearly white. She bandaged her face and her right arm to disguise her sex and conceal her illiteracy. Craft posed as the slave of this young "gentleman," and, as he looks back on the event, he obviously relishes the humor of their dangerous masquerade.

James W. C. Pennington's "The Fugitive Blacksmith" is also an exciting chase story, but its particular interest is its author's observations on slavery. White people, he says, were always telling slaves: "Oh, you must not be impatient, you must not create undue excitement. You are not so badly off"—the same kind of talk you can hear, word for word, anywhere in America today. After he escaped, after he had been awarded a degree from Heidelberg while he was still legally a slave, Pennington looked darkly at his "free" condition: "I was a slave in another and a more serious sense," he wrote. "All my serious impressions of mind had been with reference to the slavery from which I had escaped. Slavery had been my theme of thought day and night. . . . It cost me two years' hard labor, after I fled, to unshackle my mind; it was three years before I had purged my language of slavery's idioms; it was four years before I had thrown off the crouching aspect of slavery." Never, he said, would he recover from his loss of education.

The jewel of the anthology, however, is a full-length memoir: "The Life of Olaudah Equiano, or Gustavus Vassa, the African, Written by Himself." First published in 1789, Vassa's tale is unique because it is the only slave narrative that relates what life was like in Africa before the slavers came. Vassa came from the kingdom of Benin, which was by no means a primitive society. As he remembers it, it was a utopia where the maidens were chaste and everyone was employed; where the citizens were bright, beautiful, affable, industrious, and just.

Vassa was kidnapped at the age of eleven and sold from hand to hand. Eventually, he reached the sea and the white man; he had heard of neither before. When he saw the slave ship, he was convinced he would be "eaten by those white men with horrible looks, red faces, and long hair. . . . I had never seen among any people such instances of brutal cruelty." He was taken to Barbados and then to Virginia before he could speak English. He went to England where he saw snow, which he thought was salt falling from the sky; he wanted to learn what books had to tell him, so he held them to his ear. He fought for the English in their galleons against French ships, and then returned, still a slave, to the Caribbean, where he watched white sailors rape black women while they were still on the slave boats. He saw slaves mutilated, flogged, hanged, chained, muzzled, and burned. Starting with a few pennies, Vassa bought and sold fruit until he could buy his freedom for 40 pounds, only to find that there was still no justice for free black men, and that if shipwrecks, thirst, or icebergs didn't kill him, the white man surely would.

Vassa's story is that of a black Robinson Crusoe, the story of a shrewd and able man who is temporarily down but is certainly not defeated. His is an extraordinary tale because he traveled so widely and took part in so much of the violent action of his times. Like Craft and Pennington, Vassa found his haven in Christianity, and it is possible that solicitous clergymen had a hand in the preparation of all three memoirs. Unlike many of today's militant blacks, these writers see Christianity not as the white man's opium but as a faith founded by a man who was definitely not a white American. In other respects as well, these books reveal a remarkable sophistication, a cosmopolitan cast of thinking. "Does not slavery itself depress the mind?" Vassa asks, "and extinguish all its fire and every noble sentiment?" Yes, for most slaves, but not for the likes of these.

1969

. . . . After Ulysses

There is something of Ulysses in every man: an urge to travel toward adventure, perhaps toward self-discovery. Most of us suppress the temptation because idleness in Ithaca has much to recommend it. It is, after all, easier to endure an aged wife than chase a cute young nymph; simpler to thaw a frozen egg roll than hunt the stag and boar; safer to believe an electronic oracle speaking in tongues of Huntley-Brinkley than follow some restless call to war and a wine-dark sea.

And so, in the new great age of exploration, we doze before our television, a pretzel drooping from our fingers, until—"Wake up, Harry!

He's coming out!"—we snort to consciousness. There he is: beneath the
fishbowl and the asbestos, Mr. Small Town America, a man much like
ourselves (had we not gotten out of shape). He bounces up and down and,
like any American in a foreign country, snaps pictures and grabs
souvenirs. He leaves his litter by our flag, which is not left to dangle
limply, but is propped in a state of permanent erection. Our hearts
flutter faster through the cholesterol: Old Glory and a plastic sack of
urine, preserved together for eternity!

Ulysses, I suppose, would have scattered beer cans, had he had them,
across the blue Aegean, but I kept thinking, as I read Alan Moorehead's
Darwin and the Beagle, of how much the art of exploration has changed
in the past century. From Ulysses' day to Darwin's, exploration was a
leisurely exercise for the rich, the idle, the lonely and eccentric. Erratic
men, escaping from themselves or the entanglements of domesticity,
stumbled on discoveries not programmed in their voyages. There is, in
most great discoveries, a fortuitous element, but today, we leave nothing
to chance. Everyone from NASA to Thor Heyerdahl knows the limits of
what he intends to prove before his raft hits water.

In 1831, when he was twenty-two, Charles Darwin signed on the
Beagle as an unpaid naturalist. He was not at all the kind of man you
want with you in a capsule heading for the moon. Darwin had dropped
out of medical school, ducked a career in the clergy, and was seasick as
soon as the *Beagle* left port. Even so Robert FitzRoy, the *Beagle*'s
captain, was glad to have him. FitzRoy, with his twenty-two
chronometers, planned to establish a more accurate fixing of longitude
and map uncharted parts of the South American coast. FitzRoy was a
Tory aristocrat and a man of fixed values. He "believed every word in the
Bible absolutely" and suggested that Darwin, as he messed around with
butterflies and fossils, might look for evidence to substantiate the account of Creation found in *Genesis*. Darwin, the clergyman *manqué,*
agreed. But as the boat beat around the tip of South America, and as
Darwin stuffed birds, mounted insects, discovered new specimens, and
dug skeletons of giant sloths from the clay of Patagonia, some doubts
intruded. Creation, Darwin decided, did not take place in a few days but
was a continuous process that had been going on a long while. The
Andes, clearly, were young as mountains go, and in the Galapagos where
he wrestled with tortoise and iguana, Darwin found that the fish, the
shells, the insects, and the plants were all unique, peculiarly adapted to
the conditions of the various islands. There was, he discovered, a menace
in beauty. No living creature is safe; the weak impersonate the strong.
The moth pretends to be a scorpion, and the beetle blushes like a
poisonous fruit. When he realized that he had found different forms of
the same species, Darwin knew that he would never make a clergyman.
On this trip, he began to develop his theories of the origin of species and

the evolution of life on earth that he would not, for a long time, dare to release in the world.

For years, Alan Moorehead has specialized in narratives of great explorations; no man alive writes them better. But in *Darwin and the Beagle*, he falls a little off his mark. He does succeed in his most important task: presenting a vision of a cruel but timeless and innocent world. His prose is as supple and direct as ever. This time, however, Moorehead does not appear to have followed the explorer's path himself. He used to do so, and there was, in his accounts, a sense of personal discovery. This book, written in collaboration with his wife, seems to have been dredged up from some film presentation of the story. For the first time, Moorehead has allowed his text to be balanced by an equal quantity of pictures. Too bad. The pictures, from contemporary sources and many reproduced in color, add to the book and to its price, but Moorehead, knowing they would be there, seems content to let them convey the color that once he wrote into his narratives. Moorehead also seems to have experienced some difficulty in taking notes for this book. Many of the quotations he draws from Darwin's writings are not presented accurately and each time Moorehead diverges from what Darwin really wrote, he weakens Darwin's prose. Even so, the book is a good one, looking before and after into Darwin's life, but it is overshadowed by one of the great classics of exploration literature: Darwin's own account of his trip in *The Voyage of the Beagle*.

1969

· · · · · · · · · · · · · · · · How Shall We Save
Us from Ourselves?

It had been a rough night. Outside, dawn birds complained about the approaching sunrise. Inside, I nursed two friends who had decided that, for kicks, they would escalate from marijuana to hashish, and, to maximize the effects, bake the stuff into the most *dee-lish-us* chocolate-chip cookies. I didn't have much to do except find the remaining cookie before the baby or the dog did, bring my friends thirty-six glasses of water, and pat them occasionally on the shoulder as they bounced, weeping and giggling, across the furniture and halfway up the wall.

There was a doctor there, the kind you call in for such cases, who hadn't practiced medicine in years. To pass the small hours, we talked about the doctor's research: In time, he assured me, we would breed hostility out of man. It could be done by surgery—I imagined a genetically castrated race of men bearing flowers to and fro—or it could be done by chemicals, yes, by drugs! I looked nervously at my friends, who were scratching at the upholstery and laughing gently. What if man needs to be aggressive? I asked. Nonsense, the doctor said, man must exterminate his own aggression or he will kill off everything that lives on earth. That is possible, of course, but many naturalists are convinced that we can no more safely get rid of our hostility than we can get rid of alligators, or wilderness, or swamps. We simply don't know what these things are good for. We haven't even found the right questions to ask.

Konrad Lorenz believes that man needs to be aggressive: Love and friendship are by-products of hostility. In *The Dawn Warriors,* Robert Bigelow, a New Zealand zoologist, extends the Lorenz theory further and by doing so claims to solve "the greatest of all mysteries: the evolution of the human brain." Man, says Bigelow, is the most savage animal of all; paradoxically, he is also the most cooperative. Man's ability to make war and his ability to cooperate are inextricable: Each ability is strengthened by the other, which explains why man's brain has, in the last couple of million years, trebled in size.

Central to Bigelow's flamboyant theory are several assumptions rejected by the majority of anthropologists. Man has been at war, says Bigelow, since he was an Australopithecine, one to three million years ago. Most anthropologists argue that man is innately peaceful, that warfare began in the cities of Sumer a few thousand years ago. The evidence for prehistoric warfare, however, is strong. Recently, we discovered a walled city at Jericho dating from 6800 B.C. Are we to believe the inhabitants built the wall for exercise? And why, if man is peaceful, did our Neanderthal cousins vanish when our ancestor, Cro-Magnon man, arrived? Men with the smallest brains, Bigelow argues, were killed off quickly, even though they had little to fear from animals. Other men must have killed them. Thus, warfare is as old as we are. Man survives as his genes and brain improve, as the victor sows his seed among the vanquished women, as man develops the intelligence to cooperate with others for more efficient warfare, for more efficient defense. Our alliances, like our brains, grow because both cooperation and survival require increasingly elaborate communication and social organization. Perhaps, says Bigelow, the hydrogen bomb, the ultimate example of cooperation-for-conflict, may persuade us of the necessity of cooperation-for-survival.

I was convinced by Bigelow's theory until I read his evidence. It is an attractive theory, and I wanted to believe it. "This sense of the kinship of all forms of life," Shaw wrote, "is all that is needed to make Evolution not only a conceivable theory but an inspiring one." If Lorenz and

Bigelow are right, a troubling uniqueness is removed from history: Moses' difficulties holding his tribe together until it was strong enough to slaughter the Canaanites can be compared to the problems of the Iroquois, or to the motives that impelled the men who sacked the cities of Mycenaean Greece. If peace and war are complementary conditions of mankind, if man's smile is cousin to his bite, then age-old distinctions between good and evil may not be as sharp as once was thought. Bigelow's theory is optimistic. If he is wrong, if man has not always warred against his brother, then we are a degenerate species indeed.

Still, Bigelow's argument is as shoddy as it is intriguing. There is no evidence that he has done any work in anthropology. His assertions are based upon reading other scholars' books, and, too often, he cites encyclopedias and newsmagazines as sources to support his facts. By foraging through history, he collects tantalizing scraps of proof, but because much of what he gathers seems dubious or irrelevant, no pattern of proof emerges. Without the pattern, there can be no conviction.

Half the fun of reading popular anthropology is to see how scholars, coping with the same phenomena, arrive at contradictory conclusions. They have no laboratory in which to conduct precise experiments. We must take what they offer, then, with considerable skepticism. Don't let anyone cure your hostility. You may have use for it yet.

As everyone knows, Dr. Benjamin Spock and four others were brought to trial last year for conspiracy "to commit offenses against the United States," meaning that they had, from time to time, spoken out against the Vietnam War, signed petitions, collected draft cards from disaffected youths, and generally acted as if their freedom of speech were in some way protected, and as if they could not be prosecuted for acting according to their consciences or for their political opinions. Rash assumptions, these. At about that time, Lewis Hershey was slapped down by the government. Hershey, aging director of the draft, is a man so removed from reality that he insists young men should be made to conform to what Hershey thinks is good for the country by using their fear of military service as a club with which to beat them into submission. Our government doesn't disagree with this, but it was angry that Hershey let his views leak to the public. To cover his embarrassment—"a graceful way out for General Hershey," a lawyer said—the government indicted Spock and the men he didn't know, or had barely met, for conspiracy. Jessica Mitford, an English lady who has become one of our sharpest social critics, tells the whole sick, funny, alarming story in *The Trial of Doctor Spock*.

Conspiracy is, legally, a vague term that relieves the prosecution of proving any wrongdoing on the part of the defendants. To do something may not be a crime, but to agree to do it, and then not do it, *is* a crime.

On this charge, Spock and the others were brought to a federal court in Boston where the jurors were screened by the FBI and dismissed if they were black or carried a book or if they were women and had, perhaps, read Spock's book. The trial took four weeks; the jurors dozed; the judge, who was eighty-five years old, made jokes, cut off objections, and often aided the prosecution in its faltering attacks. A guilty verdict was returned for four of the five defendants: "Guilty as charged by the judge," one juror told Miss Mitford. The trial, as Miss Mitford reports it, was a travesty of anything resembling justice, an anthology of bigotry, indifference, and judicial error. When the case was upset in a federal court of appeals last July, one could only wonder why, at the lowest level, the law so anxiously plays the role of lunatic. Why can't the Bar Association create harmless advisory committees to which judges over seventy can be relegated? Why is so little justice, so little intelligence and humanity, applied to a case before it is appealed? Why do we have political trials at all?

Miss Mitford writes her book in the best tradition of partisan journalism. It isn't as entertaining as *The American Way of Death* because Miss Mitford admires the defendants, but she sinks her teeth nicely into the government and all its stumbling spokesmen. And, of course, what she is saying about this part of how we live is far more important than her dissection of our funerary practices. Toward the end, she comes out strongly for the ancient British prerogative by which juries may ignore the judge's charge, vote according to their conscience, and by their verdict nullify unjust laws and repudiate unjust government policy. There is precedent in America for such courageous action, and we need it now. The Spock trial sounds too much like the police state coming. Listen. You can hear it: Clump, clump, clump.

1969

Seven

. . . . An Eye
for Celebration

She is always there, wherever there's a showing of Picasso, an old woman
in a black dress and shoes with gummy soles. She remembers the day it
all began, a day at the Armory Show when she was just a slip of a girl
with a keen eye for a canvas. As she stared in disbelief at the *"Les
Demoiselles d'Avignon,"* she felt a stir within her. *"I* can draw better
than that!" she shouted. She hasn't missed a Picasso hanging since, and
here she is now, mumbling over Picasso's *"347"* sequence of engravings
before she turns upon the guard. "I can draw better than *that!"* she
bellows. "I *know* I can!" The guard's face crumples, but the woman
pushes past him. "I may be old-fashioned," she says, "but for me,
beautiful is Vermeer."

The series lacks a formal name. It contains 347 engravings—
drypoints, etchings, aquatints, and mixed-media impressions—which
Picasso produced, sometimes at the rate of half a dozen a day, from
March 16 to October 5, 1968. Because there is so much of it (posing a
problem for museums), because it takes so long to look at, and because it
is meant to be seen sequentially, not bunched together on a museum's
walls, it seems a work of art uniquely suited to presentation in book
form. Random House and Maecenas Press have assembled the series
under the title *Picasso 347* (two volumes boxed, $150). The result is
astonishingly faithful to the original impressions and is, perhaps, the
most satisfactory art book ever made by techniques of mass production.
It is certainly the heaviest: I have to ease it up on my knee, mindful to
keep my back straight while slowly standing up.

I believe this series is one of the great works of art of our century. It is something worth living with: the symbolism, for instance, is elusive and complex, and the references to other paintings, an old trick of Picasso's, are sometimes more than I can cope with. But the greatness is clear even after a brief examination. The sheer size of the thing is part of it, the imaginative stamina that produced so many variations on a handful of themes without fumbling, banality, or repetition. The speed of the thing is part of it, too: so much done in so little time because Picasso has, in nearly ninety years, learned everything. You can see in his line both the speed and the perfection. A lamb hangs over a woman's arm. It may seem like little more than a mass of curls, but it is the quintessential lamb, and the woman holding it—you can tell from the line of her neck—is used to holding lambs. The speed, too, shows in Picasso's mastery and mixture of techniques. In the 281st engraving, a man pursues a woman—they are sketched in drypoint—but all the violence of this remarkable picture is in the tree toward which they race, an aquatint tree that cannot be forgotten.

The series proclaims no theme, but it is not hard to discover the link that holds these pictures together. The first shows an adolescent boy dreaming. Various figures keep watch, as they do in so many of Picasso's engravings. A noble horse writhes as a beautiful woman, her breasts falling from her dress, sits on its back. A kindly giant offers the boy something—what? Perhaps his masculinity. In the last, and most beautifully serene picture, a man plays a guitar in a wood by water while a naked woman strokes her shoulders. We have begun somewhere, and it seems, come out somewhere: In between there are 345 pictures illustrating men's admiration for and obsession with women. There are variations on the Nativity (in the most beautiful, Mary has given birth to a dove), variations on an abduction, and on familiar Picasso themes: the artist with his model, warriors in chariots, satyrs, circus folk, and a climactic sequence of twenty-four pictures of copulation. Picasso leads us gently there, first drawing men and women with their genitals exposed, even men staring between women's legs. The scenes are not pornographic; they are erotic. That is, Picasso expresses sexuality with dignity and joy. He exults in sexuality, finding it in the demonic energy with which an artist paints a woman, and in the liquid line of a woman pulling back her hair. The ecstatic sensuality of sight and touch—this is what Picasso celebrates in these engravings. Leafing through them is like listening to the Mass in B Minor or *The Marriage of Figaro*: One cannot finish without feeling that there is now, as always, hope for man and joy in his condition.

1970

. . . . In Search of "The Sum of Human Knowledge"

Have you discovered what fun it is to read an old encyclopedia? After a decade or a generation, of course, you must distrust much of its information, but it still reflects with accuracy the concerns and beliefs of the society that created it. You can study an age by examining the way it records information it thinks worth preserving. You can trace man's progress (if that's the word I want) by noticing not only what he includes but what he drops from his compendium of "the sum of human knowledge."

In an article on logic in the first edition of the *Encyclopaedia Britannica,* the following syllogism appears:

Every creature possessed of reason and liberty is accountable for his actions. Man is a creature possessed of reason and liberty. Therefore man is accountable for his actions.

We may have lost some of our faith in man's reason and liberty, and therefore in his accountability, but this kind of humanism was the faith that created encyclopedias. All man's knowledge could be brought together in one place. A man could comprehend all knowledge. We don't believe this anymore, but we still make encyclopedias as if we did believe it.

The first *Britannica*—three volumes, 3,000,000 words, 2,689 illustrations—appeared in 1768. To honor the encyclopedia's two-hundredth birthday, Praeger, a publishing firm owned by Britannica, has put forth a nifty facsimile of this first edition, complete with long *s*'s, leather bindings, and facsimile stains and watermarks. Priced at $79.50, it won't sell very well, which is a pity, because it is an invaluable guide to understanding eighteenth-century England. With its gatefold charts on grammar, trade winds, and chemistry, its elegant architectural engravings, and its map of western Canada labeled "Parts Undiscovered," it is—like its most recent successor—very much a child of its time.

In an age when specialized help was often far away, country squires must have found it indispensable. If your horse had glanders, your wife, a baby, or your groom, a swollen gall bladder, you reached for that ultimate how-to-do-it manual, the *Britannica.* There are, for instance, twenty-two pages on gardening ("You may now give your melons air in the middle of the day"), and one hundred and twelve pages on medicine—an attempt at summarizing what was known by an age teetering between art and science in its approach to the cure of human ills. A long, detailed article on surgery is obviously directed at the man who may have to try his own hand someday ("Having laid your patient on a table . . ."). The same applies to the article on midwifery, which contains illustrations that caused a scandal in their time. The thirty-nine pages devoted to farriery, "the art of curing the diseases of horses," have shrunk, in the 1968 edition, to two short paragraphs, and farriery itself has become "the shoeing of horses and other ungulates."

Some people still prize the eleventh *Britannica*—twenty-nine volumes appearing in 1910 and 1911—which today can be bought secondhand for a price between $50 and $100. Like the age that produced it, the eleventh is both literate and self-assured. Its essays, by towering and sometimes cranky scholars, tend to be lengthy and tolerant of entertaining digressions. When the eleventh errs—either in fact or opinion—the earth seems to shudder: "Mentally," the eleventh proclaims, "the negro is inferior to the white." "The influence of Donne upon the literature of England was . . . almost wholly malign." There is no mention of Marx in the article on Communism. The editor of the whole encyclopedia insists that George Meredith was "among the few creators in English literature," ranking in "the highest class of all, by Shakespeare."

Such ham-handed errors are, however, part of the sinew of the eleventh; when later editors ripped them out by their roots, a great deal of rich soil fell away, too. The great, long crotchety essays were disemboweled: Instead of the eleventh's stylish essay on the history and literature of fencing, for example, the 1968 edition tries to teach its owner *how* to fence by following diagrams. Instead of the eleventh's teeth-rattling tale of the execution of Guy Fawkes, the 1968 edition offers only a bloodless affair. Of course, Britannica, still trying to represent "the sum of human knowledge," needed the space to make room for all the new goodies man has come up with since the First World War. Thus, the editors have shaved the biographies of Gabriello Fallopius (he of the tubes) and Frederic Falloux (agent to the Bourbons) so that an article on fallout might be squeezed between. Each age gets the encyclopedia it deserves.

The 1968 *Britannica* is not a new edition in the sense that the eleventh was. For years, Britannica has pursued a policy of planned obsolescence called "continuous revision," which means that minor changes are made *every* year, with the result that—depending on how you look at it—the encyclopedia you buy today (and it will cost you $459) is as up-to-date as it can be, but it will be out of date within the year. Even so, it is an impressive hulk of a thing to have around the house: 24 red royal volumes, 28,264 pages, 36,428,800 words, 29,916 articles signed by 10,179 contributors, and 22,492 illustrations. Whether it will do for you what you want it to do depends on whether you buy it for the right reasons and know what to expect from it.

Rule #1: Don't look up anything you know much about (though, of course, everybody does precisely that) because what you find will usually prove disappointing.

Rule #2: When looking up something you don't know about, treat what you learn as provisional information—good until you get a more up-to-date and authoritative book.

Rule #3: Remember that some information, to be properly presented, requires more emotion, more of a point of view, than an encyclopedia will provide. Try reading about Bach's music in the *Britannica*: the unbelievably marvelous made unbearably dull.

Rule #4: Don't buy an encyclopedia for its science or technology. The science in the *Britannica* is like a leg of lamb in your freezer: It will last for about a year, but it's decaying a little bit every day. Instead, buy cheaper books on science that you can replace often.

Rule #5: Remember all reference books are fundamentally square—cautious about what they dignify by admission to their pages. In fact, the *Britannica* is positively cube. It has a fine article on home pickling and freezing, but nothing on the Beatles. John Cage is not mentioned in any article on modern music; Pete Seeger is omitted from "Folk Song, U.S."; and Dave Brubeck is absent from the article on jazz. But the *Britannica*'s antiradicalism goes further than that: John Reed, the American supporter of Lenin, is not mentioned, though he's been safely dead for years. There's a well-balanced piece on De Sade, but no mention in the bibliography of the excellent, widely available translations of his works. There's an article on Negro leaders, with pictures of W. C. Handy and Ralph Bunche, but no mention of Malcolm X or Stokely Carmichael. No mention is made of Happenings, Pop Art, McLuhan, or miniskirts. There is nothing on the Death of God.

There are three dandy pages on baseball jargon, but the man who wrote the baseball article didn't read them: He talks of players who "traverse the bases." We learn when W. C. Fields moved to Hollywood, but there is not a word about his love of liquor. One of Buckminster Fuller's domes is illustrated, but Fuller's name is not mentioned in the article on domes. The motion pictures article is at least eight years out of date—thus, all important contemporary films are ignored. The article on textiles emphasizes history and aesthetics; the textile technology is unsophisticated, its economic significance is ignored. There is jingoism, too: Nobel Prize winners who have contributed to *Britannica* have stars beside their names, and there are long articles on both Britannica and Robert Hutchins, its chief officer.

And yet—most of it seems very good. The best people have been hired to write about Donne, Danton, Hemingway, and the war in Vietnam. Pictures of the moon taken in 1967 are included. There are new articles of impressive length on information processing, the Cold War, and the history of technology. Whatever the *Britannica* has on any subject is better than having nothing. And nothing is what most American families have concerning almost everything in it.

1968

..................Taking Crime Seriously

Detective stories are to the serious reader what recess is to the schoolboy: a few moments of fun and games scratched from the serious business of living. They may look like real books—the reader must turn the pages to encounter people, places, and plot—but they aren't. Crime fiction is familiar and therefore comfortable. By subjecting characterization to story and story to an absurdly rigid moral construction, crime fiction becomes the antithesis of serious fiction. At its best, it is an intellectual puzzle; at its worst, a ritual game that improves by the frequency with which one plays it. Here, as elsewhere, ripeness is all.

A ritual morality pervades these stories. If they seem alike, it is because they are, they must be. The genre allows only for surprises of detail (poison this time, M. Poirot, not strangulation), but never for a surprise in the basic structure, which *always* concerns the restoration of moral order to a closed society that has been rent first by a murder and then by mutual suspicion. The mystery also requires a passion for order quite alien to much serious fiction: Fear becomes fear confirmed and then, at the end, the fear is removed. Evil is generally the business of only one man in each story and (in the peculiar moral world of detective novelists) an evil act necessarily triggers others so that it becomes imperative that the evil be purged so that all may be left at the end feeling cleaner and more decent than before.

Crime fiction also relies on mini-characters who amount to no more than facts with which the reader must cope, pieces in the jigsaw puzzle that he is trying to solve. The function of character in the crime story is to keep the reader involved, to allow him room to speculate on motivation. The more complex the character, the less useful he is in solving the puzzle: Dmitri Karamazov, for instance, is capable of anything because he is a whole person, but Colonel Belcher, who was seen in the conservatory just before the vicar was garroted there, must be innocent because he is so obviously incapable of writing the villanelle that the murderer left behind him.

There is, however, a gray area between crime fiction and serious fiction about a crime. One thinks of Hammett and Chandler. "I'm a novelist," says one of the characters in *The Dain Curse*; "my business is with souls and what goes on in them." I can imagine Hammett thinking that about himself—there is a certain amount of pretentiousness in this kind of writing and rather more among readers and reviewers who testily insist that these novels are as good as most that America has produced—but I have never been convinced that souls have much to do with this fiction. Talk about souls, yes, but it is always the same talk, carefully honed and never varying from novel to novel, or even, in the Hammett-Chandler-Macdonald tradition, varying much from novelist to novelist. I am very fond of this kind of fiction, which is exceedingly difficult to write well, as Ross Macdonald does, and is perhaps even difficult to write badly, as Roderick Thorp did.

Roderick Thorp's novel *The Detective* is five hundred and ninety-eight pages long and a selection of the Literary Guild. A paperback publisher will pay $250,000 for the rights to reprint it and a film company has bought it as well. Not much more can be said in its favor. *The Detective* is a work of surpassing dullness, an ungainly and unconvincing monument to the banality of much of human existence, and a further reminder—if one were needed—that nobody since Dostoyevsky has managed to convert a detective story into plausible serious fiction.

The story starts out well enough, in the classical manner made famous by Hammett and Chandler. Norma MacIver, a pretty, pregnant widow, turns up in the office of Joe Leland, a war hero and quondam cop who, for private reasons the author will reveal at excruciating length, has set himself up as a private eye. Norma's husband is dead; the coroner said suicide, but Norma thinks it's murder. Leland takes the case which turns out to be far messier than he supposed, exposing not only a conspiracy to defraud the public and a homosexual murder, but also a great deal about Leland's own past and messed-up marriage.

Most messed up of all, however, is the novel, in which nothing works right. As if to prove he's writing a "different" kind of detective story, Thorp allows no trace of action or excitement to sully his narrative until page 533. Everything that takes place before and after develops through interminable conversations and interviews in which dismal people most improbably reveal everything they know—particularly about their sex lives—to the patient Leland who, out of fairness, replies with details about *his* sex problems. Even the dead man, speaking on a tape recording, holds forth for pages on his unhappy youth and his sex life. The novel needed only this.

No detail is too trivial to escape Thorp's rapt attention, with the result that some details of importance are likely to escape the reader's. But if this lack of selectivity cripples the action one might expect in such a novel, it is entirely fatal to the author's attempt at style. Hammett and Chandler wrote crisp, tough, occasionally witty stories with a personal point of view that was, in its own terms, completely convincing. But *The Detective* is no more appetizing than a great damp lump of unleavened dough. Traditionally, such a story should be told in the first person, but Thorp can't make Leland interesting enough to carry the load.

Whenever one tries to do "something more" with the detective story he winds up doing something less. We don't admire detective stories like *The Nine Tailors* or *The Maltese Falcon* because they are as good as the best novels, but because, *as detective stories,* they reveal as much skill and afford as much pleasure as most good novels. A good mystery writer knows that characterization serves situation; the serious writer knows the reverse. The good mystery writer, like the serious writer, is concerned with form and style, but he is bound by traditions detrimental to serious fiction and one of these is the avoidance of uncalled-for characterization. Thorp is incapable of creating an interesting character, but he properly feels that a "serious" story requires it. So he simply extends his characterizations horizontally, tacking on tedium by the yard. The result is inhumanly boring.

1968, 1966

I have read only the last two of Ross Macdonald's novels, *The Goodbye Look* and *The Underground Man.* They are both very skillful, but perhaps it is not necessary to promote Macdonald, as some reviewers have suggested, from the ranks of mystery writers to the class of social critics where, I think, he would fare indifferently. In *The Goodbye Look,* a story about a missing heirloom, half a million dollars, three murders in fifteen years, and a boy about to go around the bend, Macdonald runs lightly over the surface of Southern California life, a surface that seems to conceal all the violence, all the corruption of the flesh and spirit that the world has ever known. Private eye Lew Archer is pulled into what appears to be a trivial affair, but one person leads to the next; everybody is close-lipped and each has his shady history and sinister connections that must be pursued. It is a novel about desperate people, people who are rich and on the run. They make wan little jokes, but survival is their main concern, and they'd just as soon not think about the violence they have seen. Sex is of less interest to them than money. "There's nothing people won't do for money," one character says; "I know that," Archer replies.

This kind of toughness, made famous by Hammett, Cain, and Chandler, may reflect less insight into the way people really are than it does the rhythms and expected responses that lead to the ambience of romantic melancholy that this kind of fiction requires: "I have a secret passion for mercy," Archer says toward the end, "but justice is what keeps happening to people." There is some substance to this remark, and rather more style, but yet the substance *and* the style *and* the plot, which depends on the most implausible tangle of identities, are all derivative, very much so.

The Underground Man, I think, is a little better. The tangle of generations, of son to mother and daughter to father, which was the concern of the earlier book, is repeated here, though in the form of a mother searching for her son and a son searching for his father. The aura of loneliness and sadness seems even more pervasive than before. Macdonald does manage to convey an astonishing sense of the uprootedness in American life and the fragility of its society: Fathers disappear and wives walk out in patterns repeated through generations; upward and downward social mobility prove equally awkward and unfulfilling; meanwhile, a consuming forest fire laps at the edges of all.

Lew Archer emerges as a more interesting man than he seemed in *The Goodbye Look*. He has a talent for making people who have bottled-up emotions or just plain secrets tell far more about their lives than they ever intended. He has a sense of irony, too, which is rare in detective heroes. More important, he has a definite moral character—a moral character, I should add, that is about as sophisticated, if rather more articulately expressed, as that of Paladin in the television series *Have Gun, Will Travel,* but a moral character nonetheless. Archer stays aloof from involvement with people, perhaps because he has been hurt himself by his wife, perhaps because he sees only how human involvement results in injury; he refuses even to sleep with a woman who offers her services— not, I suspect, because he doesn't want her, but because to take her would be to change the subtle nature of his services to her. This concept of service is important to a morality that seems otherwise based on exhaustion and pessimism. If Archer realizes that he "sometimes served as a catalyst for trouble, not unwillingly," trouble, in time, depresses him. "The hot breath of vengeance was growing colder in my nostrils as I grew older," he says. "I had more concern for a kind of economy in life that would help to preserve the things that were worth preserving."

1969, 1971

It is a truth universally acknowledged that a popular writer who cannot maintain suspense must take refuge in romance. I don't know why Helen MacInnes has a following for her glutinous fiction that exceeds that of any able writer of suspense stories, but there must be something of the fat woman who can't stay out of the candy store to it all: Her readers, stout consumers of vapid romance and tinted travelogues, surely do not *want* plausible novels of international intrigue, or even highly styled implausible novels, and couldn't stick with one if they began it.

In *The Venetian Affair,* Miss MacInnes serves up again the comfortably preheated formula from which her customers have no apparent desire to be weaned: a minimum of suspenseful action folded into a maximum of muddle, the whole mixture larded with excess verbiage. Bill Fenner, an unlikely drama critic, is, upon his arrival in Paris, recruited into the even more unlikely role of intelligence agent. In the first half of the book he stalks around Paris, keeping his eye on the easily identifiable enemy agents, and meets The Girl; in the second half he scampers around Venice, still dodging the easily identifiable enemy agents, and saves The Girl.

This may seem like slim pickings for even the most modest spy novel, but there is nothing Scotch about Miss MacInnes, who cheerfully spins her yarn to more than four hundred pages. By the time the professionals in this kind of fiction are winding up their stories, Miss MacInnes is just lumbering under way. Her banal world includes a host of well-scrubbed good guys and antiseptic bad guys. We may get confused by the quantity of characters, but the author, by making us privy to all their thoughts, takes care we shall never be surprised. What's more, drama critic, professional spy, and Communist thug all talk exactly alike; without all the "Bill said's," the reader would be thoroughly lost.

Nor does Miss MacInnes believe in cheating her reader by scrimping on the scenery, by setting her action in, say, the men's room at some dingy bar. She knows what her fans want and, well, it's a little hard to think of international affairs as an indoors kind of thing, so what little action there is unfolds at Orly, the Crillon, the Tuileries, the campanile in the Piazza San Marco, on and above the Grand Canal and any other place where a tourist might feel at home. Finally, Miss MacInnes does not believe she should strain her readers' faculties by making them guess what has just happened or the reason therefore: We always know all about it long before the characters do, and when, after many pages, they are let in on the secret, too, we get a windy sermon on the subject. After reading this one, I felt kind of fat for days.

1963

......................How to Write a Spy Novel

Since spy novels are selling better than dirty novels this year, here are a few pointers on how to write them:

A. The High-brow Spy Novel. References: *The Spy Who Came In from the Cold; Funeral in Berlin.*

1. Remember that there are only two kinds of spy novels: the story in which the spy is a professional and the reader's interest lies in sharing the author's expert knowledge of the actual machinations of contemporary intelligence; and the story in which the spy is an ordinary man, forced by powers beyond his control to participate in an operation he may never fully understand. Here the reader's interest is to see how he survives at all; we delight in the author's implication that a similar muddle might engulf any of us. The former, the high-brow spy novel, is of course the harder to write. The best of them, like *The Spy Who Came In from the Cold,* will be endowed with the trappings of a detective story, not quite a whodunit, but a challenge to the reader to unravel what is *really* going on before all is revealed. The clues must be there. The plot must be involved, but it need not be clear. Characters, action, and dialogue, as well as individual scenes, should be expertly fashioned and written with just the right amount of ironic detachment.

2. Remember that the best high-brow spy novels are actually comedies of manners peculiarly suited to the perplexities of modern times. In the Cold War, fallible and anonymous men, struggling in gray and private arenas euphemistically called "intelligence and operations" may succumb to the conflict of idealism and pragmatism. It helps if this failing can be made funny.

3. Choose a credible and all too realistic hero. If you want to kill him off, write your story in the third person. Otherwise, use the first person (more chance for jokes, queer perspectives, there). Keep the focus on the hero: Don't waffle off to tell us what the commissar is thinking. Develop the hero's character through idiosyncrasies.

4. Pretend to be realistic. Information about the Cold War can be obtained from numerous sources and can be thrown, undigested, into your book. In Len Deighton's world of espionage, coffee cups and expense accounts are as vital as pistols and secret dossiers.

5. If you can, write well. Spoon in the *Weltschmerz*. Irony and wit are always useful. If a man is about to be killed in the most horrendous manner, talk about cats prowling around in an apartment; spend more time, or at least more clarity, on the cat clawing at the sofa than on the man clawing at the noose around his neck. This is very sophisticated. Overall tone should be Ignorant-Armies-Clash-By-Night.

6. Be confusing. Espionage confuses our government, the public, the spies themselves, and maybe even the Russians. You will be unrealistic (see #4) if you do not confuse the reader, too. The best way to do this is not to tell *what* happened until after it happened, and save *why* it happened for the end of your book. *Example*: If somebody is to take a shot at your hero, write it this way: "The bullet from a small 8 mm. short-trigger Pelmann and Rosenthal Mark IV spins in the region of 2,000 revolutions per second," etc., carrying on like this for a paragraph or two before allowing your hero to pluck the bullet from his bicep.

B. The Low-brow Spy Novel. References: All the James Bond stories, the Helen MacInnes stories (never to be mentioned again), and Frederick Ayer, Jr.'s *The Man in the Mirror*.

1. Choose an incredible hero. Ayer uses a former Waffen SS colonel who drops his disguise as an Argentine businessman when impressed by the MGB to impersonate an American Special Presidential Assistant for Security Matters. You can't do much worse than that.

2. Be grotesque. This kind of spy novel is really only a comic book in prose. Your situation is so stupid that readers will either ignore your book or be held numbly in thrall to see how you muddle out of the mess you have wrought for yourself. Remember that Ian Fleming never allowed moral or political ambiguity to grace his cretinous extravaganzas—and the reputation of the spy novel is still staggering from the shock of his popularity.

3. Forget about character, style, probability, and plot. The general rule here is: *The more absurd the situation, the less story required.* Ayer's Nazi working for Russia in the American Cabinet is understandably concerned only with attempting to avoid exposure.

4. Pretend to be sophisticated. Your readers are not, but they expect you to be. In Low-brow spy fiction there is an inexplicable but inescapable link between high living and the dirtiest of professions. You can safely choose the wrong clothes, the wrong engine ratios in jazzy cars, the wrong years for wine, the wrong prose style when quoting from

Time, because none of your readers will know the difference; it is the seemingly knowledgeable chatter that they care for.

C. The Middle-brow Spy Novel. Between these two extremes, you would expect a compromise. Reference: Adam Hall's *The Quiller Memorandum.* It combines many of the best qualities of the high-brow stuff with a preposterous James-Bond-style internal situation. Quiller is an Englishman, working for British intelligence in Berlin. He is tapped to catch the head of Phoenix, an undercover Nazi military organization about to restore Nazi domination in Europe. (Just the kind of thing we're all worried about; more so than Alec Leamas dying against the Berlin Wall.) Like most fictional operatives, Quiller is a master of many trades, and a bit of a pedant to boot. He provides us with short lectures on how to shadow a man and throw off a shadow; the psychology of defecting spies; varieties of plagues and anesthetic drugs; principles of cryptology; how to stage a faint or prepare the body invisibly for action. "We are not gentlemen," Quiller says from time to time, "and we have our little ways."

Quiller's little ways, abetted by the Opposition's traditional reluctance to kill off the Good Guys before he brings them to ruin, see him through an impressive number of horrible encounters, including a fine interrogation scene (conducted by a psychoanalyst using narcotics). Plenty of action, plenty of menace, plenty of "inside" information about the techniques of espionage, and several reverse twists at the end. Who cares if it's a bit hard to follow, or remember?

1965

. . . . A Handful of Air

No one can convince me ghosts don't exist. In our house they not only flourish, they also come to collect their own. In the last four months (the date is exact because that is when we hired a new baby-sitter) the following volumes have mysteriously vanished from my library shelves: Algernon Blackwood's *Tales of Terror and the Unknown*; M. R. James' *Ghost Stories of an Antiquary* and *More Ghost Stories of an Antiquary*; Shirley Jackson's *The Haunting of Hill House*; and Truman Capote's *Other Voices, Other Rooms,* which, though it had not occurred to me, might strike a novice apparition as having a spooky sound to it. Those who don't have much experience with baby-sitters might suggest an alternative solution to our household mystery, but we *do* know baby-sitters—once she brought her teen-age son and that evening a book of photographs called *The Nude* vanished—and we prefer to take our chances with the ghosts.

There are three kinds of ghost stories. The oldest variety—of which M. R. James was the last and greatest practitioner—offered the reader real ghosts and the *frisson* of seeing nature running amok. Next came the genre which starts out like a ghost story, but is later explained in terms of human machinations. A disappointing business, of course, but it allowed G. K. Chesterton in "The Blast of the Book" and John Dickson Carr in *The Burning Court* a different way to exercise their considerable talents. Then, with Algernon Blackwood and Henry James, came the modern synthesis: A complex narrative concerned with unnatural death, but leaving some doubt as to whether this disorder is the result of super-natural intervention or the madness of the principal character.

The difference between M. R. James and Henry James is the difference between the nineteenth and twentieth centuries. M. R. James wrote in the time of La Belle Époque, a time when the world was secure, when communication was poor, when the conflict of rich stability and the primitive unknown was more marked than it is today. To believe in real ghosts one had to believe in oneself and one's position in the world. By Henry James' time the world had changed: Men had learned of the greater horrors of the human psyche and the social establishment. All confidence collapsed. As Dorothy Sayers said, "We are afraid where no fear is."

In the new ghost story the supernatural is a question mark, reflected in human dissonance which is in turn revealed by a situation of illness and sexual disorder. The best example of this kind of story we have had since Henry James is Shirley Jackson's *The Haunting of Hill House*. But hardly anyone writes such stories anymore and so, when a novel like George Lanning's *The Pedestal* appears, we grasp at its insubstantial charms and find we have caught no more than a handful of air.

Lanning adheres closely to the formula. His narrator is a rich man in his thirties who, while recovering from a mental breakdown, moves his wife to his family's house in the country. At an auction they buy a pedestal made of wood, a grotesque object with clawed feet. The pedestal, once they have moved it into their gigantic house, assumes a will of its own; on several occasions John catches it moving around the place. More mundane problems, however, take over the story—a woman is murdered, the local priest is implicated, and John's marriage breaks up—with the result that the perambulating pedestal can hardly obtain the audience it deserves.

And this is the trouble with Lanning's novel. The pedestal, the supernatural element of the story, is pushed so firmly into the background that it seems irrelevant. What we have is an expert domestic tangle, graphically realized in everyday terms. Ghost stories, however, cannot tolerate the sticky intimacy of ordinary life, so the pedestal, when it heaves into view, is almost ludicrous. It is, I suppose, a symbol of John's problems with impotence, but the story is most unsatisfactorily resolved, to quote Miss Sayers again, in a "platitudinous emphasis on the horrible."

1966

.... You're Putting Me On, I Hope

When I was eleven and pushing into puberty, I discovered the first great passion of my adolescence. It was certainly not for girls—those braying and lumpish creatures that I chased and bumped at recess. Girls would come into fashion the following season, but that year, the year after Hiroshima, my passion was for science fiction.

Seven years and about two thousand stories later, as my more literate relatives began to think that special schooling or perhaps an *auto-da-fé* of my entire library would set me right again, I kicked the habit. I rarely look back, though I regret none of the hours I spent with moldy magazines and tacky hard-cover collections. Most of the stuff I read, of course, was written by and for adults with the minds of children, which was dandy for me because I met it coming from the other direction: a child who was beginning to appreciate adult books. What turned me off science fiction, however, was that something went wrong with it. It could not keep up with the excitement of real science in the postatomic age. It changed, but it failed to change imaginatively or improve significantly after the late 1940's, when Groff Conklin and August Derleth built their anthologies by burrowing through back issues of *Astounding Stories*. This spring, we suddenly have two excellent science-fiction novels; if the trend continues, there may yet be hope for the entire genre.

Michael Crichton's *The Andromeda Strain* lacks the literary tone of the best novels of Jules Verne and H. G. Wells, but it is surely the best science-fiction story of the last few decades. Its success is due to Crichton's use of modern biological discoveries and theories (our knowledge of biology, it seems, doubles every ten years), and to the skill with which he extrapolates from what is sure to what is possible, leaving readers as ignorant as I to wonder where fantasy cuts loose from fact.

The title refers to the code name given to extraterrestrial bacteria brought back from space to earth by a damaged American satellite. The satellite was supposed to collect space bacteria for use in biological warfare, but it was not supposed to fall near a tiny Arizona town. Within hours the bacteria had killed the townspeople: Some died of instant blood coagulation; others, driven insane, committed suicide. Two people survived: a sixty-nine-year-old man who drank Sterno to calm his ulcer, and a two-month-old baby.

The satellite, the survivors, and a team of scientists are hustled off in darkest secrecy to a classified government installation in Nevada. There, deep underground and perched on top of an atomic bomb (to be used if needed), the scientists work in a totally isolated and sterilized laboratory, racing to discover what breed of life this is, how malevolent, and how best it may be controlled before it kills off the better part of the country. Naturally, everything goes wrong: The bomb starts ticking, the bacteria start spreading, and the scientists make disastrous mistakes.

A typical science-fiction story? Hardly. *Andromeda* acquires a spurious air of legitimacy because Crichton seems to know a lot about government security procedures: Just for fun, he hides some of his story's most dreadful revelations in the officialese of government reports. The story also acquires a decorative air of legitimacy because Crichton has decked it out with a phony bibliography and computer charts and print-outs; much of the book is printed in the curious characters computers use. But this is just window dressing. Crichton's apparently genuine knowledge of microbiology, with all its attendant chatter about epidemiology, metabolic disease, parasites, and pathogens, makes the reader feel he is soaking up an education as well as an entertainment. It is a dangerous assumption; much of the information is obviously sound, but just as much is not, and Crichton cleverly conceals his borders.

The story of the Andromeda Strain is frighteningly relevant. Long ago, H. G. Wells speculated that Martians invading earth might succumb to the germs they found here, but only recently have we worried about infection brought to earth from our probes in space; our lunar astronauts, in fact, will be thoroughly decontaminated on their return. Crichton's description of "how to disinfect the human body—one of the dirtiest things in the universe—without killing the person at the same time" is, like most of the book's details, entirely plausible and quite ghastly. Still, this is the kind of fare that any skillful journalist or researcher might provide. What sets *The Andromeda Strain* apart from most science fiction is the consistently varied playfulness of the theories and questions Crichton introduces: What actually is life, and are we sure we can recognize it? Must complex forms of life from all parts of the universe grow larger in size, as they do on earth? To what extent do we adapt to viruses and bacteria and come to depend on them? What is the most economical way for a planet to tell others it exists? Lots of stuff like that, and it's all great fun.

Robert Merle's *The Day of the Dolphin* is a French novel that uses a science-fiction gimmick to support a heavy load of satire and social criticism, but, like Crichton's story, it has an uncanny aura of immediacy about it. Secretary of Defense Melvin Laird said recently that Polaris submarines will soon become vulnerable—but he didn't say why. Merle tells us: because dolphins will be trained for warfare. Patrols of dolphins using their natural radar will detect nuclear submarines and then destroy them by sowing mines in their paths or by planting bombs against their hulls.

The great virtue of Merle's story is that he explores this possibility as if it were a monstrous betrayal of trust and friendship, a gross unbalancing of nature, and the loss of man's last, best hope to come to terms with the world in which he lives—and of which he knows so little.

Dolphins are intelligent, have brains as large as ours, and have a language of their own. "Dolphins like people," one of the characters in this book says. "God knows why." Merle takes dolphins a crucial step further. His hero, a scientist named Sevilla, studies communication with dolphins under a grant from the American government. He has taught one dolphin, Ivan, how to whistle forty monosyllabic English words with his spiracle, the hole through which he breathes. Immediately, rival American intelligence agencies close in and give Sevilla's naïve ideals a battering. "We live in glass cages," Sevilla says, "observed, analyzed, dissected down to the last detail." The parallel is heavy-handed but nonetheless effective. Eventually, Sevilla teaches Ivan—and Bessie, Ivan's wife—how to talk fluently in English. The dolphins prove bright and affectionate. They hold a press conference to explain that they are not fish but cetaceans and that man, for them, is like God: "He is good, he is smooth, and he has hands." Soon men who are not so good take over: The government abducts the dolphins to train them for their deadly missions. Sevilla despairs; the world approaches nuclear disaster; the dolphins lose their faith in man.

The Day of the Dolphin is melodramatic and overlong, but it is also provocative and uncommonly entertaining. Like many Frenchmen, Merle loses his cool, succumbing to misinformation and cynicism when he talks about the paranoid qualities of life in the United States, but we say worse things about ourselves, resenting them only when they come from foreign sources. I found the book often funny, sometimes coarse and sometimes poignant, a thoroughly enjoyable story.

1969

A quick cram course in what has happened to science fiction since you were a kid and used to read it:

• It is no longer as exciting as books about real science. In 1950, *Astounding Science Fiction* presented Ron Hubbard's crackpot theory of Dianetics as if it were a matter to be taken seriously by insisting that medical journals took too long to get the important news to the public. Since then, Ron Hubbard has founded a religion, Scientology, and the rest of us have landed on the moon, discovered DNA, and made blueprints of the coming ecological catastrophe.

• Science fiction has turned to sex, sentimental religion, and inept experiments with style. For sex and style, it is hard to beat George Macbeth's "The Silver Needle":

> *. . . through four orgasms*
> *in the new Janssen feelie, flicked*
> *the in-switch for a re-fill . . .*
> *of Semen Number 5 (those*
> *thigh-borne odours!)*

And for sentimental religion, pleasingly expressed through sex, no one can surpass Robert Heinlein's *Stranger in a Strange Land*: "As they merged, grokking together, Mike said softly and triumphantly: 'Thou art God . . . We grok God.' " You may say you can't read this stuff without laughing, but hundreds of thousands of teen-agers can, as well as many adult illiterates who defend, with a kind of locker-room machismo, what Harlan Ellison pretends is a "revolution" in science fiction today.

• Science fiction writers, unlike detective story writers, continue to lust after respectability, attempting to drag anyone who writes with imagination into their camp. In fact, science fiction, like pornography, is rarely respectable in itself but provides for good writers a rhetoric that can be applied to serious fiction. The best we can hope for from routine science fiction is a sequence of ingenious speculations and pleasing images that prod us awake as we doze over the prose and return, perhaps, to prick at our memories after the stories themselves have long been forgotten. And the best is none too easy to find. The rule is to avoid the writers you have heard of (if they have survived, they are simply stuffing a little copulation and village atheism into the same stories they wrote thirty years ago) and avoid as well the writers you haven't heard of because they are doing the same, only writing it worse: "In the flushrush of blood of dawn of I-am-the-erection-and-the-strife," as Philip José Farmer says. The only course is to choose novels that are being pushed by their publishers as real fiction and even then you will lose two times out of three, as I did.

Kate Wilhelm's *Margaret and I* has a cute trick: It is narrated by Margaret's unconscious. Margaret is a distraught woman, abused by her husband and oppressed by a pair of scientists who know that she has in her care the notes of a man who has escaped from time. Margaret's unconscious keeps warning her who the bad guys are, but it doesn't do much good, and Margaret, under hypnosis or in dreamlike trances, slumps into sexual orgies. Very detailed sex it is, too, as if science fiction writers had something to tell us about the way it works that hasn't been told before. Anyway, it kept me awake, most of the time, while Margaret made her way toward another plane of reality, or dimension, or something, where her lover lives. Count this as minimal science fiction: little more than a soap opera about female problems with a fantastic twist.

William Hjortsberg's *Gray Matters,* by contrast, is maximum science fiction, by which I mean that it is a book that begins with machines scuffling around on obscure errands in a world where machines are about all that is left to function efficiently. There is also, of course, the gray matter, the human brains that have been removed from their tiresome bodies and left to swim in safe deposit boxes. The machines service the brains, educating and amusing them by tape-recorded courses and entertainment, including orgasms which seem to be required, for centuries until the brains are enlightened enough to be given new bodies. One day a brain revolts . . . escapes . . . though I'm not quite sure why, when you consider the fantastic sex lives that these disembodied brains can have. Glinting among the gobbledegook are a few beams of wit, and a nice little antitechnology moral, too, to make it all worthwhile.

Ursula K. Le Guin's *The Lathe of Heaven,* however, is really a very neat performance, accomplishing what science fiction is supposed to do. The time is 2002, the hero a passive man who discovers that his dreams are out of control. George's dreams change reality. Whatever George dreams comes true as he dreams it; moreover, his dreams cover their tracks, changing the past and what everybody except George remembers of the past as well. Naturally, people are reluctant to believe George's story— but George is terrified. His "effective" dreams, as he calls them, begin in a small way—a relative killed, a picture changed—but in time he dreams of alternative visions of the world and history. The earth's population is decimated; its wars intensified and then halted; an alien planet attacks . . . and all because George dreamed it. An ambitious psychiatrist discovers that under hypnosis George will dream what he is told to dream and so the psychiatrist can play God, advancing both his own career and history as he wishes—except that, as we know from Freud, dreams like to play tricks.

Mrs. Le Guin is extremely inventive. She shifts her continuum of the world and its past every few pages, playing expertly on alternative suggestions as to what we may expect from violence, war, and over-population. She has a nice sense of irony, too: For all his tremendous power, George remains virtually a prisoner; for all the horror of his dreams, the world seems actually to improve. Science fiction is rarely able to offer a sustained vision of an interesting alternative to the world we know, and Mrs. Le Guin does not attempt to do so; instead, she provides the brief glimpses, the partial speculations that I have suggested are essential to a story of this kind. Even her moral—that we cannot stand outside the world and direct it but must be content to be part of the whole—is gracefully developed and is, after all, what the ecologists are still trying to tell us.

1971

. . . . .Paper Reveries*

What a destiny for Blackhawk! The ironic fates sneer as they weave their pitiless web for the Flying Freedom Fighter and his Funny-talking Foreign Friends! Will Blackhawk's most perfidious foe, GRADUATE STUDENT, *drown out the famous cry of* "HAWKAAA!?" *Listen!* "Wilna polarizes Blackhawk's pattern of violence, suggesting that his

*A review of *Comix: A History of Comic Books in America* by Les Daniels; and *75 Years of the Comics,* Introduction by Maurice Horn.

heroic stance in favor of a certain kind of freedom is simultaneously a sort of repressiveness. This problem is posed beneath the surface despite the obvious Blackhawk position . . ." KA-POW! Right in the kisser, Les Daniels. Don't miss the next episode when Maurice Horn explains that comics artists "have created spatiality out of the multilinearity (horizontal, vertical, diagonal) of the layout by means of expanding or projecting the figures along carefully worked-out vectors." (Blackhawk may be dead, but Horn doesn't suspect that I carry a tear-gas rocket concealed in my cape.)

Most comic strips are pretty dreadful, but their critics have been worse. We have no vocabulary to talk sensibly about trashy art that chafes at the erectile tissue on our brainstems. Instead, we talk about the drawing in the same lame language that the *Art News* boys applied to Rothko's paintings, and among all the Nazi-nabbing and Commie-crushing, we scratch for political polarizations. Churchy La Femme, Okefenokee College's spokesman for the Turtle school of criticism, put it plainly: "A comic strip is like a dream." Daniels and Horn may sputter, but there is not much more to be said. "A tissue of paper reveries," La Femme continues. "It gloms an' glimmers its way thru unreality, fancy an' fantasy." Even Charles Schulz, our most popular theologian, insists that "things come to me and I draw them, that's all. . . . No hidden motives or meanings. Whatever people get out of them, that's what's in them."

Schulz's passive approach to interpretation is the only way to "understand" comics: Their success lies less in what is represented than in what we infer. We all (men, anyway) dream of flying, of smashing the small-time punks who heave across our prows. It doesn't matter which super-hero comic we are reading—Trashman acquires super powers by smoking a joint; the aim is satirical, but not entirely—because the release is the same. Even years later, as captains of industry who don't really need capes and ropes anymore, we are not wholly immune. We do not grow out of Batman as much as he lets us down—by sending Robin to college, as he did recently, where Robin smashed the SDS.

Realism is bad news for comics—a point that eludes the comics critics. The closer comics come to realism and conventional irony—as they did in their decadence, in the fifties and sixties—the worse they become because other art forms can handle realism and irony better. *Mad* magazine seems like good satire only to those so numb of intellect that they have no access to the inspired satire that sprouts like toadstools from the dirt at every hand.

Comics critics forget just how bad the drawing and writing of most comics are; because there is something in bad comics that we like, we start to praise all the wrong things. "Tarzan" and "Prince Valiant" were never well drawn, in spite of what the comics critics say; they were slickly drawn. And we must bear in mind that in bad comics like "Superman" the inventiveness is all in the conception—in the kind of heroes and the circumstances of the stories built around these heroes—and not in the stories themselves. In good comics, the opposite is true. In "Krazy Kat," "Barnaby," "Pogo," "Peanuts," and "Donald Duck," the conventions are soon forgotten: The point has nothing to do with talking ducks or alligators, but with the wit and inspiration of the continuing stories. Of the great comic strips that can claim to be a significant part of our popular culture, only "Donald Duck" has not found immortality in book form—perhaps because publishers are unaware just how good Donald was, from the mid-forties until 1952, when Carl Barks was creating most of the episodes for Disney. Few stories in comics were ever wittier or more inventive.

Both the collections reviewed here are disappointing, but of the two Daniels' is by far the better. His tedious text does yield the necessary information, and the selections he has made from the entire history of comic books are complete and well chosen, except for an indiscriminate affection for the really bad stuff in the fifties and sixties. He is good, however, on the contemporary "underground" strip, and his book is worth buying for the selections alone. Horn's book, based on the current exhibition of comic-strip art at the New York Cultural Center, has a nearly useless text; and the selection of strips, many of which are blurred in reproduction, are incredibly badly chosen: "Terry and the Pirates," for instance, without Dragon Lady; "Tin-tin" without Captain Haddock, Milou, or Tournesol; "Steve Canyon" represented only by a gasping Poteet!

1971

. . . . Family Reading: Books Rated "AA" (Acceptable to Adults)

Happy families are all alike; every family that reads books together has its own problems. Consider this scene, which couldn't happen in *your* house. The father reads a book in the room where the kids aren't supposed to come because it is the room where Father works. As usual, the father has a deadline leaning on him and, as usual, there is a kid in the room. She is seven, an articulate critic of literature and life, and her father loves her for her yellow hair.

"Go away!" the father suggests.

"Read me a story," the kid replies. In the ensuing scuffle of wills, the kid sees the book her father is reading. "Daddy!" she wails. "You're supposed to be reading that book to *me!*" She's right. It's her book. For the past two weeks, I've been reading kiddies' books on the sly. "Daddy," my daughter asks, "am I *lucky* to have a father who loves books?"

I couldn't say. At that moment, I was engaged in what Secretary Laird and I call a "protective/reactive intelligence probe": I was looking for books an adult could enjoy reading to children. Sixteen times through *The Cat in the Hat* will do that to a man; so will assorted stories of pigs and chickens who remorselessly repeat the same nouns and verbs. This season, kiddy biographies of Nat Turner and Cesar Chavez are much in demand, but I wanted something better. I wanted books an adult could read without condescension even if children were not available, books with imagination and a sense of the marvelous. Most of the books below are like that, and are aimed at the four-to-eight-year-old market. That's my level, and I hope it's yours, too.

1. Mainly for the Pictures

Many children's books are set in the framework of a dream, but Maurice Sendak's *In the Night Kitchen* more closely resembles a real dream than any such book I know. It is not so much like the story of a dream as it is a dreamlike experience itself: partly fun, partly heroic, partly ominous. A small boy falls through the dark and out of his clothes into the batter of a cake being made by three cooks who all look like Oliver Hardy. Like a real dream, the story does not move forward but slips from here to there, while in the background a night city of corkscrews, eggbeaters, and coffeepots slides by. Sendak's colored drawings are gay and just a bit disturbing.

Of *The Angry Moon*, my daughter says, "This is a beautiful book. You can hardly tell what's happening." She means Blair Lent's illustrations ("The pictures have a lot of light," she says), which she has studied because she likes to screen books before I read them to her. William Sleator's text follows a Tlingit Indian legend of a girl who mocks the moon, is captured by it, and is later rescued by a boy who shoots a ladder of arrows to the sky. Ethnic folktales are in vogue with children's writers now because the magic is much the same, whether it comes from an Estonian or Ethiopian source. This story is much like many others, but it is made memorable by Lent's dramatic paintings, particularly those of a malevolent moon with fearsome eyes and a mouthful of stubby teeth.

2. Balancing Pictures and Story

Most of the writers who attempt old-fashioned fairy tales today—complete with orphans, witches, and wicked woods—botch the job. They don't know how to handle in print what is essentially an oral form of storytelling, and they are unwilling to admit how much violence and cruelty such stories require. My children reject the laundered version of the Gingerbread Boy in which the cookie escapes unchewed; they know he *must* be eaten at the end.

Harve Zemach's *Awake and Dreaming* has too easy a happy ending; in fact, you can see where the hero should have become greedy and suffered for his sins. Still, it is an intriguing and roughly traditional fairy tale in which a young man, aided by a witch, conquers the nightmares sent by the King of Dreams and finds in his sleep the maiden he will marry. Margo Zemach's drawings are equally important: They have grace, color, and disarming style.

I like even better Isaac Bashevis Singer's *Joseph and Koza,* the story of a Jew who comes to save the daughter of a Polish king from being sacrificed to appease the gods of the Vistula—and at the same time gives the Poles a heady dose of monotheism. Singer is a surehanded storyteller. Poland 2,500 years ago, with its harvest dances, its king whose crown is a gourd with candles, and its mad witch Zla who calls on Baba Yaga and the demon of the Vistula to bring plagues upon the land, is irresistible. Symeon Shimin's drawings are both beautiful and as forceful as a poke in the eye.

3. Mainly for the Story

Halfway through Roald Dahl's *Fantastic Mister Fox,* my daughter interrupted to cheer on the little foxes who, with their father, were digging a fantastic tunnel to escape the earth-moving machines of three evil farmers. Little foxes, my daughter said, making her shoulders small, "are more diggable." *What?* "Like when I race you upstairs," my daughter says. "Who wins?" I shouldn't have asked. "I *always* win. You go: *Bur-um, bur-um, bur-um.* I go: *Phweeeeeekapom!* Maybe," my daughter gently adds, "it's because you're so full of wine." Reading to children is a delight. Anyway, Dahl's fox story, written for younger children than his immortal *Charlie and the Chocolate Factory,* involves less of the imagination but more of the guts: It is that rare thing, a genuinely suspenseful children's story. At the end there is a good touch: The fox loses his tail. My daughter knows that the good stories are the sad ones: "Like *Born Free,*" she says. "It was sad because it was true."

E. B. White's *The Trumpet of the Swan,* the most considerable of all these books, is not at all sad, though there are places where it might have become so. *Trumpet,* in fact, often comes close to farce. I have the feeling that no one but White could get away with this: the unexplained transitions, the little flights of fancy escalating the unreality, the sidelong concessions to what an adult thinks is funny. But then White, I have long believed, is one of the best writers we have now in America: He combines wit with seeming simplicity. We haven't had much of that recently, not since Mark Twain.

Louis, a trumpeter swan, is born mute. He is "a swan with a speech problem," which is bad for swans because Louis cannot cry "Ko-hoh, Ko-hoh!" as he flies, nor can he tell the beautiful Serena that he loves her. Louis, however, has a friend, a boy who found him while camping in Canada and who takes him to school to learn to read and write. Louis then travels with a slate and chalk around his neck, but as few swans can read, this does him little good. Meanwhile, Louis' father steals a trumpet for his son. Toward the beginning, Louis' father nearly steals the book as well: "Here I glide swanlike," he is fond of saying, "while earth is bathed in wonder and beauty. . . . All swans are vain. It is right for swans to feel proud, graceful—that's what swans are for."

Louis, of course, learns to play the trumpet. He plays bugle calls at camp, songs for the swan boats in Boston (he stays at the Ritz, where he sleeps in the tub and eats watercress sandwiches), and jazz for a nightclub in Philadelphia. White knows that the trick of a good children's book is to catch a good idea and play variations on it. And it *is* a good book, one that should be with us for some time.

1971

If you want to understand an age, look at the literature it produces for its children. Children's books are invariably moral. Most attempt to convey a moral point of view to the child; most reveal the morality of the society in which the children are raised. Children's books may not show society as it is, but they tend to show it as we would like it to be. As much cannot, should not, be said for the adult literature of ages past; because of this little more than what has been admired by the most intelligent of men has survived. Children's literature, being more easily forgotten, remains a more accurate mirror of a time.

When we read eighteenth-century English literature—the novels of Fielding and Sterne, the poetry of Pope and the criticism of Johnson, the plays of Goldsmith and Sheridan—we are reading what the gentry thought life in England was all about. Children's literature, however, reveals what the middle classes like, and what they liked in the eighteenth century was the pietistic moralizing, the intellectual softness, and incredible cruelty that we associate with Victorian England, nearly a century later. Thus do moral standards filter upward from below.

Leonard de Vries' *Flowers of Delight: An Agreeable Garland of Prose and Poetry, 1765-1830* is an eye-opening book of inestimable value to scholars and such laity as love Olde England. It is a collection of children's books from the Osborne Collection in Toronto. It is no longer, I fear, a book for children. There is, for instance, "A Pleasing and Instructive Story" in which a girl who did not obey her mamma is kidnapped by a woman who sells her into white slavery. She "never saw her kind mamma, or her nice home, any more." And who remembers that Mother Hubbard's dog was addicted to smoking and drinking? You won't find *that* in kiddies' books today.

The collection contains hundreds of such stories and verses and seven hundred pictures as well. Many of your old favorites are here in their unbowdlerized form. A book as gruesome as it is entertaining.

1966

No parent will be surprised to hear that much of our most heady modern literature is written for children. A case in point is *Rabbit Country* by Denise and Alain Trez, which Viking has let loose among our young. "0205," the cabalistic symbol on the jacket flap, says, indicating to the cognoscenti that the book's appeal will be to those from two to five years old. My eye. Viking, I have heard, is currently suffering a bad case of Second Thoughts, and well it should.

Once upon a time, it seems, there was a country of carefree rabbits who played in the fields (as rabbits will) and in the trees (as obviously they won't) and when the winter came, they burrowed underground, like so many Viet Cong, to guard their carrot bin and watch TV. One day the rabbits found a crown in the grass and gave it to him among them who could jump highest, making him the Rabbit King. Unfortunately, he became a corrupt king. As with so many modern rulers, his crown fell over his ears so he could not hear. The king, I'm glad to report, gets his, loses his crown, is king no longer, and all the rabbits are happy again.

End of story. I asked my son, aged six, what it meant. He told me that there are "fifty and a fraction rabbits" on pages 24-25. This may be a clue to the matter, but I suspect he was putting me off. When he had finished the story, he said only, "I like it." No more. Smart man.

But consider. Those more accustomed to the cozening tergiversations of deceitfully simple literature will recognize here a metamorphosis into animal culture of certain dubious political ideas advanced in the eighteenth century: the noble savage, the joys of democracy, and the corresponding uselessness of kings. A most subversive tale, Instigating the Young to Riot, etc.

There's a logical flaw in the story that I'm sure the former rabbit king has noticed. The authors tell us that without the crown nobody knew which rabbit was king. But how did the king get the crown in the first place? Because he could jump higher than any other rabbit, that's how. Ha! He will jump again. If these bunnies have any brains, they'll stage a jumping contest and murder the winner. After the Revolution comes the Terror. Then everybody's happy. A sequel, if not a revised version of this incipient classic, seems in order.

1966

. . . . Another Book to Save Us from Ourselves

Did you know that before your guests arrive you should dust your light bulbs? Remove the detective stories and movie magazines from your coffee table and put copies of *The Atlantic Monthly* and books by Teilhard de Chardin in their place? Do you know the wrong place to put a vase of gladioli on your yacht? Did it ever occur to you that "it is practically impossible to serve a meal correctly when the guests' eyes are all riveted on a television screen"? That "the only really refined way to eat soft-boiled eggs is with an ivory teaspoon"? That if favors in birthday cakes "are wrapped in squares of waxed paper or aluminum foil, there is really very little chance of their being inadvertently swallowed"? One more time, team: Did you know that "It's U to live in a historic private house in Paris"?

Merde, alors. I can't imagine how we social boobs ever got along before Genevieve Antoine Dariaux took mercy on us and wrote *Entertaining with Elegance.* Here, assembled in alphabetical order by topics of presumably general social concern (White Lies, Wine, Xmas), is the fruit of many seasons' study of the craft of social flummery. I admire the sheer brass of the book. For Jane Austen, elegance was an attitude of mind, a generous broadening of the spirit. Jane Austen would have known how to write about Mrs. Dariaux (and did, as I recall, on several occasions). But, as the Army Corps of Engineers cheerfully reminds us, you can't stop progress, and so, a century and a half after Jane Austen, Mrs. Dariaux offers us the New Elegance: great gobs of shellac to cover our natural crudity. Behind the alphabetized areas of social nervousness, the ivory spoon thrust in the soft-boiled egg, lies the unmistakable suggestion that the building blocks of elegance are pretension and deception. *The Atlantic Monthly*, Mrs. Dariaux's idea of an elegant magazine, brought out from wherever she hides it between parties and dusted—just so—and placed on the warm spot on the coffee table where *Real Screen Gems* lay sweating just minutes before.

As I say, it is an admirable book. Mrs. Dariaux may preach deception, but she does not herself deceive. She is straight with her readers, knows their problems, presumably had the same in her own pre-elegance days. She makes no concessions to her readers' intelligence. In fact, there is no discernible trace of intelligence at all in these pages, for which we may be grateful (imagine our problems if there were). The vulgarity comes through as vulgarity should, loud and clear: Elegant entertaining is really an adjunct to advancing your husband's career. Unimportant guests can be insulted if they stay too long; important guests must be flattered always. In case you cannot recognize a bore (which would be unlikely by the time you had worked your way to the *B* listings in Mrs. Dariaux's book), an entire page is devoted to Mrs. Dariaux's definition of one.

Elegance is easy, folks, when you know how. And Mrs. Dariaux is the kind of woman to whom I want to send a gift subscription to *New Left Notes* or maybe even *Screw*—just to think of her, trying to anticipate their delivery (Let's see, this is Thursday, *Screw* reaches Oyster Bay or wherever on Thursday) and trotting out to the mailbox—to get the damn thing before the chauffeur does.

1965

. . . . Thorns from
the Rose

DEAR DR. FRANZBLAU:

For the past few months I've been living with a Dutchman, who like myself is a painter. We often fight because my stuff hangs in exhibitions and he never sells anything. Frankly, he's nuts. Last night he cut off his right ear and sent it to a lady of poor reputation. How can I help him before he does something really crazy? Actually, I don't feel too good myself. My family wants me back in the stockbroking business, but I want a cruise to the islands.

Sincerely,

P. GAUGUIN

Answer: Often those who profess concern for a colleague are simply masking fears of their own inadequacy in the normal competition of the retail painting industry. Your rejection of your family, of which a wife would presumably be a component, and your hostility to the Dutchman's lady friend, suggest that your motives for living with this painter are suspect and should be examined. Your friend's conduct is typical of artists who need therapy before they can conform to normal, acceptable patterns of behavior. His paintings will sell when, after treatment, he realizes that it is the business of psychologists, not painters, to show that reality is not what it looks like. Your fantasy of an island cruise shows that you are trying to escape maturing as an artist. You should adjust to the healthy stimulation of broking stocks.

Like all professionals—doctors, lawyers, soldiers, and the clergy—Rose Franzblau makes her money from other people's miseries. On radio and in newspapers, she has peddled her alarming homilies, her turgid prose, her imperious tone, and her serene faith in Freudian technology. In agony, people ask her help—and she gives them a short right to the jaw. In distress, people cry for reassurance—and she shows them problems they didn't even know they had.* *The Middle Generation,* a collection of some of her daily performances relating to problems encountered by people in middle life, has a certain vulgar fascination and a certain cultural importance.

First, there is the fun of spying on other people's problems: the man who wears women's panties to the office; the mother who takes showers with her teen-age son. Next, there is the fun of watching Dr. Franzblau stiff-arm people who whine about their problems: a mother who complains that her daughter is more interested in art and theater and her girlfriends than in dating is told, indeed, there *is* a problem, but it is the mother's. We who have no formal training in psychology might be tempted to tell the mother to rejoice in her daughter's exuberance and individuality, but joy is not Dr. Franzblau's line of work.

Then there is the fun of watching the Franzblau Gratuitous Transition. A mother writes that her daughter is getting married and is

*Assuming, of course, that the letters are real and not concocted by Dr. Franzblau and her staff. A careful reading of the letters suggests that at best they have been heavily edited.

ignorant of sex. Dr. Franzblau tells her that: (a) the girl has fears about sex; (b) the girl needs "helpful guidance" from professionals; (c) the parent is "the last person" to help the girl because (d) "the parent would tend to spotlight her own fears and failures." The point is, the mother's letter indicates no such complications. Still, a paid psychologist can hardly advise ignoring other paid psychologists or tell the mother to go ahead, make mistakes, and treasure her relation with her daughter.

Finally, the book is unreadable—and yet still important for Dr. Franzblau's transcendent vulgarity: the vulgarity of all who try to paste a determinist Band-Aid on the wounds and weaknesses of the human spirit. She fails to see how her training limits her responses. She won't admit how tentative, even humble, she should be when confronted by the barely articulated grief of people she has never met. She cannot admit that there are many valid, joyous ways to live and to respond, and that, perhaps, the burden of pain and guilt can best be eased by rejoicing in one's differences. "Only connect," E. M. Forster wrote; "only adjust" is Dr. Franzblau's creed. It is a dismal, diminishing approach to life's mystery and openness. The best therapeutic advice is still St. Augustine's: "Love, and do what you will."

1971

................Pornography as
Art and Rhetoric*

> *'Fair and foul are near of kin,*
> *And fair needs foul,' I cried. . . .*
> *'But Love has pitched his mansion in*
> *The place of excrement. . . .'*
> —W. B. Yeats: "Crazy Jane Talks with the Bishop"

Can anything intelligent be said about pornography? Like prayer, it causes an alteration in our brain waves and our blood. In both prayer and pornography, sparks are struck from some part of our cortex that

---

*A review of *The Aesthetics of Pornography* by Peter Michelson; *The Sensuous Man* by "M"; and *The Couple* by "Mr. and Mrs. K."

knows no language; the sparks from prayer fly up, the sparks from pornography fly the other way. We distrust the stuff because we can't control it—the trembling in the loins, the intense curiosity and rapid satiety—and if we can't control it, what's an education for? Down Darwin! Flake off, Freud! Yet here is Peter Michelson proposing an entire poetics of obscenity. Pornophiles will rejoice to see unexpected Brownie points awarded to the most vomitory narratives. Pornophobes will be pleased that Michelson classifies pornography, fitting it firmly into the aesthetic history of Western literature; they will be pleased because what we classify we have begun to understand, and what we understand we have begun to control.

Pornography, says Michelson, is "the imaginative record of man's sexual will," documenting "both man's neurotic and archetypal concerns with sexuality." It is a kind of romance, no more pernicious than the romances of passion that rule the lives of Heathcliff and Emma Bovary. Like Aristotle, Michelson believes that literature is a mode of knowing, one of the ways, ever changing, by which we explore life. And because art needs to find a metaphor through which life can be examined in a narrow compass, a metaphor of love or sexuality will serve as well as any other. In recent years, we have overturned the aesthetic dialectic that "truth is beauty"; in fact, "our literature adopts an aesthetic that aims to reveal the ugly as the true."

Michelson argues that even the ugliest pornography tells us something worth knowing about ourselves. However exploitive, it reminds us of "the rhythm of expectation and frustration which marks our sexual lives." Hard-core pornography like *Fanny Hill* reminds us of our animality, approves it, and suggests what possibilities await it. Soft-core pornography like *The Adventurers* thrusts measured quantities of sex into silly stories designed to satisfy the reader's expectations. Unlike the really dirty stuff, there is here no threat of moral anarchy but rather a celebration of man's lust for wealth and power. On the other hand, artistic or complex pornography like *Lolita* and *Story of O* lays claim to art because it is committed to exploring morality and the full consciousness of love.

This is brave and useful thinking, but it needs refining. Like many a scholar in search of a system, Michelson proves something of a Procrustes, stretching an arm here and whittling a leg there until the body fits the bed. Pornography cannot usefully be defined as the literature of sexuality; if we cannot be more specific, we shall have to include *Anna Karenina, Ethan Frome,* and *The Ambassadors.* Artistic pornography is a term we may usefully apply only to books that cope with sexual material that, in another context, would be outrageous.

As for hard- and soft-core pornography, they remain constant. History intervenes in pornography only when some writer from the mainstream borrows its techniques for his own purposes. The goal of the worst pornography is not art but incantation: repetition in the service of release. What our need for it tells us of ourselves may be true, even important in terms of the myth of culture, but because it is expressed in naturalistic terms, it may be mistaken for fact, thereby causing more grief in an area already overburdened with misery. If Sir Ravenell Rakehell can make ten women happy in one evening, why can't I? Or, worse: If Sir Ravenell's wife likes what he does to her, why doesn't mine?

One man's myth is another man's perversion. A lady I know, asked to comment on a book of erotic paintings, replied: "Once you've seen one Persian penis, you've seen 'em all." Sex, in human affairs, needs such balance, but the dirty books cry: *No balance!* The books lie. The truth about sex is probably closer to what George Steiner calls "imperfect striving and repeated failure" than to what the pornographers acclaim. The essence of pornography is mendacity, a point Michelson overlooks, though he comes close to it, and then veers away, in a passage made difficult by the quest for antecedents to his pronouns:

> *Pornography, the kind represented by the* Story of O, *is a manifestation of the ugly. It does not romanticize sexuality; sex, unlike John's other wife, is not beautiful. It is simply* there, *dominating love, aspiration, happiness, all human experience. Its extravagance is often fearful because it so ruthlessly reflects our own libido.*

The problem of understanding this precisely lies with our growing uncertainty as to which of the "it" and "its" refers to sex and which to pornography like the *Story of O.* Still, the general meaning is clear: Sex in this book is ugly, and sex is always there; it dominates other aspects of our lives; *pornography is not romantic because it accurately reflects this imbalance.*

There is some loose thinking here. *Story of O* does not represent the ugly, except in Michelson's moralizing terms; it reflects sex as a totality of experience and as a justification of a life-style—and that *may* be ugly, if one thinks it is, but the author of *O* has nothing to say on the subject. I think critics have a right to make moral judgments on the art put before them, but they must make it clear that it is *their* moral judgments they are making. Part of the cleverness of the *Story of O* derives from its author's ability to avoid, without our lamenting the lack, any moral comment or frame of reference at all.

On the other hand, I am convinced that *O* does indeed romanticize sexuality, not by making sexuality seem better than it is, but by making it seem more all-pervasive, more all-determining than it is. Michelson claims that *O* is not romantic because he assumes that romanticism stresses beauty—a very poor assumption. Beauty is often a by-product of the romantic imagination, but romanticism is more regularly concerned with obsession. *Wuthering Heights,* for instance, is a romantic novel, but it does not suggest that Catherine and Heathcliff's relationship is beautiful. The metaphysical shudder we get from the book is not prompted by a conviction that this is the way it really is—thousands of girls throughout history yelling "Heathcliff!" over the moors—but from our sense that this is, if matters got out of hand, how it might, just possibly, be. And so it is with *Manon Lescaut, La Belle Dame Sans Merci, The Ancient Mariner, The Lady of Shallot,* and any number of romantic works that attempt to show, through metaphor, what life might be like if obsession took control, and attempt to show it in relatively realistic terms.

To this extent, *Story of O* is romantic—yet it is not a romantic novel. Michelson implies that the book is an accurate reflection of our libido. "Ruthless" is the word he uses. It is nothing of the kind. The novel's romantic hypothesis is that of a dream made plausible by its calm and understated tone, its assumption that such designs and acts are not only possible but probable and acceptable. And yet the author reminds us that it *is* a fiction; like a dream it can start and end in different ways. Surely the author never meant us to take it seriously; no sophisticated reader could be fooled by its convention of straightfaced ingenuousness. All that is part of the fun: The book is not ruthless, it is decadent. By this I mean the author is fully aware that although her metaphor brushes against a partial truth, it is, as she has realized it, antiquated and deceitful; yet she invites us to share her ruse and enjoy it anyway, for the sake of old dreams or more earnest books read long ago.

Michelson is, I think, on stronger ground, when he says that pornographic rhetoric will be more important to the future of literature than pornographic books. But the pornographic rhetoric we have now demeans sex while pretending to extol it, as one can easily see from reading our nonfiction books that pretend to offer advice and consent. "If you can get *at* a woman, you have at least a chance of getting *into* her." That about sums up what *The Sensuous Man* has to offer us. The book is a mirror image of *The Sensuous Woman*—it is impossible not to believe that they were both written by the same androgynous flunky in Lyle Stuart's office. "Every book should have an orgasm," the author coos. And: "May your every orgasm surpass the last!" This is a book to make one think of Gibbon, Spengler, and the general collapse of civilizations.

Even more appalling, because it is less clearly meretricious, is Harold and Joan K's account of their two weeks in St. Louis at the Masters and Johnson clinic in search of Harold's potency. "We really have a desperate situation here," Joan says, and Harold adds: "A woman who needs satisfaction is my nightmare." Well, there is no sense smirking. Their problem was real enough. The $2,500 the cure cost them was real enough, and I suppose the lotion they smeared over each other's bodies was sticky enough. A generation ago, Joan and Harold K would have been bombed out by the blitz and sold their story to the newspapers. Now their ghostwriters, with an eye to titillation, have stretched out the Ks' sex stories. Harold and Joan both tell every episode, not together, which might have told us something, or apart to create different and informative perspectives, but apart to provide a kind of instant replay of the sex. One almost looks for Howard Cosell's commentary.

"As I tell this story," Harold says, "it occurs to me that I haven't even mentioned Joan. Maybe that's part of it. My mind was only on one thing." I cannot imagine sadder, truer words.

1971

Eight

. . . . Food for
Second Thoughts:
The French Attack

The bill came to $116.20 which, we agreed, was about as much as four people should pay for a meal in the middle of a working day. We might have lunched for less at a cafeteria three or four doors down the street, but greasy smoke coiling from countless hamburgers had left a film upon its windows, and, anyway, there is no *challenge* to that kind of eating, nothing you can fairly fault the surly waiters for. We went instead to the Café Chauveron, which ranks as one of the half-dozen Manhattan eateries most admired by critics of French cuisine.

"We ask first for something simple," said Henri Gault, "*a salade de tomates,*" which, at Chauveron, costs $1.25. "It is cheap. We watch the waiter's face when he takes the order. He may not like it, but he must not show displeasure. If his face is not impassive, we will grade him down."

"They bring a cut tomato," Christian Millau explained, making chopping motions with his hands. "It is peeled, the—how you say?—pips are removed, and there is oil and vinegar. It takes a long time to prepare. Few restaurants do it right."

Millau is thirty-nine; he has dark hair and a mobile face that breaks into a grin like Fernandel's; Gault is forty, grayer and more serious.

Few men have had so wide an experience of French cooking. They have built their reputations by the way they reject a platter of *Belles Crevettes Roses à l'Indienne,* by the flurries of French with which they return an offending *Cassoulet Toulousaine* to the kitchen. Their new book, *A Parisian's Guide to Paris,* examines French restaurants more fully, more ruthlessly, and with more *élan* than any other, and now they plan a sequel on restaurants in New York. "We are not so difficult with

New York restaurants," Gault says. "We are too polite," Millau explains. "The French know what good food *is,* but Americans don't, and so the restaurants here, which should know better, lower their standards."

The evening before, at Stonehenge, a famous restaurant in Connecticut, I had ordered *Faisan Printanier* and a bottle of Chambolle-Musigny, which were delivered at eight thirty. When the maître d'hôtel uncorked the wine and announced that Connecticut state law required all glasses to be removed from the table at nine, I felt a hot flush run from my liver to my esophagus. No, I said to myself, one cannot judge a restaurant in anger; let us see how these cool and rational Frenchmen, who really know what food is all about, evaluate a place as great as Chauveron.

"We French are a nervous, excited people," Millau told me. "We don't understand why waiters don't rush. Why do they want me to wait twenty minutes for a cup of coffee?"

"Nor do we understand why you Americans want to set flame to everything," Gault said. "In the Pump Room in Chicago, they set flame to the salad and to the soup, too."

"Most Americans eat with their eyes, not their mouths," Millau said. "You like colors. You like to *see* things. You flame everything but milk."

"At The Forum of the Twelve Caesars," Gault said, "I had a flaming artichoke, a napalm artichoke. It's like Vietnam, everything burns. When you see everything cooked—*pouf!* like that—it is usually hiding the bad taste."

At Chauveron, Gault went to wash his hands—"The men's room is not exciting," he reported—while Millau complained to me about the poisons that we put into our water. They spoke in rapid French to the maître d'hôtel, a sullen man who had no suggestions except what was implied by his manner: Eat what is already cooked and get out so others may come in.

"Very bad, that maître d'," Millau said.

"He's in a hurry," Gault said, "he pushes you. He's nervous, he has two or three minutes for you."

"Zero for the maître d'," said Millau.

"But," said Gault, "we are acting different from other people." We were, indeed. When the maître d' told us there was no tomato salad, Millau persuaded him to look again, and when we ordered fresh scallops as appetizers and were told they came only as a main course, Millau exploded—*absolument absurde!*—and demanded that the dish be divided. Irritated and a bit pale about the jowls, the maître d' agreed. We ordered *Coquilles de Fruits de Mer* and *Terrine de Canard Truffé—*

very difficult foods to prepare properly and a test of any kitchen—and then, for main dishes, still working wide of the standard menu, we asked for *Ris de Veau Périgourdin et Purée de Marrons, Foie de Veau Sauté Bercy, Poulet de Choix Sauté aux Chanterelles* and, for the lady with us, a rare sirloin steak *Grillé au Feu de Bois.*

"Now," said Millau, "he is very mad at us."

"Yes," Gault agreed, "but he should not be. We are spending a lot of money. He should ask us if we want some wine. I will call him back."

There was no wine steward at Chauveron at lunch, no one, in fact, who cared to recommend a wine. We ordered a Chablis Vaudésir 1966 at $8 a bottle to begin with, "*et puis,*" said Gault as the waiter was about to scurry off, a $30 bottle of Château Margaux 1953. "Now they *must* be different," Gault said. "They must pay us some attention. If they don't, they are mad. We have shown we know what we are doing, that we care."

Millau disagreed: "They think we are crazy people. They are not used to serving meals like this. But we will have another test. I will call the maître back, and we will change our order."

"They don't make any effort," Gault said later. "They should take time when they see we care. They want money, that's all. What they want to sell is not exciting. Did you see that cold chicken? Who wants cold chicken?"

We stabbed back and forth with our forks at each other's food. "When we test a restaurant, we eat like pigs in a trough," Millau said. The tomato was unripe; there were seeds in the lemon slices; a cigarette butt was left in an ashtray throughout the meal. The scallops were badly cooked—"You are eating flour and nothing else," Millau said—and when the white wine was served, Gault learned that the bottle for which we paid $8 had cost Chauveron $2. The red wine, our $30 treasure, was forgotten altogether until Gault summoned the maître d', who then tried to pass off an inferior vintage that he wanted to serve in tiny glasses.

"Do you sell many good bottles of wine?" Gault asked him. "Oh, yes," he replied, cracking a smile for the first time. "We sold yesterday a thousand dollars' worth of wine."

"You see how they think?" Millau asked. "He smiled. He is nice now. I am sure he is a nice man, but he is not used to people like us. Now for a final test." Millau smiled to himself. "*Haricots Verts Frais au Beurre.*" The green beans came and Millau took three. I asked to try them, watching Millau's face. "Here, take them all!" he said, nearly flinging the plate at me, "*do not return them! Please.*" He sighed. "They are fresh, yes, which is something, but cooked in advance, not warmed up enough. They are *over*cooked; they have no taste. Americans need to learn simplicity. You have a simple way of life, but you are carried away by food; for you, it is a way to show yourself off to others. Americans don't understand if you just ask for beans—or scallops—and butter. For Americans, that's not *cooking!*"

The crisis came when I realized I would be sick if I ate my sweetbreads with their sticky, candy-sweet sauce. Gault took a taste. *"Incroyable,"* he said. Millau tried them and summoned the waiter: the sweetbreads were on their way back, not with timid suggestions, as we Anglo-Saxons do it, or with humble deference to the chef, but with Millau flapping his arms and crying *"C'est mauvais! Terrible!* UN-EAT-ABLE!" The waiter agreed. "I always said it was no good," he said in French. "I don't know why Americans like it."

"You see," said Millau, "they know better, but they are *weak,* they cave in!" We agreed that it was not just Chauveron's cooking that was bad, but the restaurant's philosophy of cooking: an indecent amount of food floating grossly in a sea of pre-cooked sauce. When my sweetbreads returned, the old lot, scraped of its sauce, was still there, nestling by a new lot, the whole covered in brown sauce with peas. Gault took another taste. "That is the same sauce they put on my chicken," he said.

For dessert, we had *Mousse au Chocolat.* "Excellent!" said Millau as he took a taste, and as he said it, the waiter slammed a gob of cream over the whole. The blood drained from Millau's face. "Why did you do *that*?" "It is too dry, *monsieur,*" said the waiter. "Now," said Millau, "you cannot even taste it. The cream is not good."

As we waited for our bill, Gault pointed to a painting that hung over our table, a sickly sight lacquered in caramel brown that said *"Eglise de St. Pierre"* in the lower left-hand corner and *"Après Utrillo"* in the lower right. "After Utrillo," he said. "It is an imitation, like the meal we have had. You can say of this meal that it is 'after French cooking.' "

1969

The Café Chauveron closed its doors in 1971, an occasion that, for some reason, caused considerable lamentation. I wrote my piece about Chauveron because I had always wanted to see how people who really understand restaurants go about evaluating them, and because I could hook my investigation to the publication of a book. The following piece appeared as a review of Gael Greene's book, Bite: A New York Restaurant Strategy:

Fragment of taped interview with veteran of the Great Restaurant War:

Q. Those scars on your ego, sir, are truly pitiable. Where were you wounded?

A. In all the big campaigns, my boy. My blood flowed first at Lafayette (a nasty skirmish, that one!) when the owner, just introduced to me, asked how long my family had been in America. This laceration came at Pavillon, where a waiter bumped my chair seventeen times at a single lunch and poured water on the tablecloth.

Q. And what honorable defeat produced that scar?

A. Oh, that was dealt me by the onion soup at The Four Seasons. I was our unit's cut-and-stab man, see, so when the soup came with a crust of cheese so thick it bent my spoon, I pierced it with my fork and hauled long strands of goo above my head while hacking at it, about nose-high, with my knife. Even my squad leader was appalled. "War crime!" he shouted, "Atrocity!" But all's fair in *haute cuisine,* my boy; there are no rules at all.

Q. A moving story, sir. Has none of our troops survived the war?

A. Yes. One. Gael Greene.

Q. Gael Greene! Do you know her?

A. No one knows her, son. No one knows where she comes from, or what she looks like without her disguises, or why she devotes her life to the Cause of the Common Man—the man with $30 to spend on a lunch for two and $60 for a dinner—though some say that when she was two, her mother put ketchup on her zwieback. All we know is that when a restaurant goes wrong, you can hear Gael Greene's cab come honking out of the smog, and a few weeks later there will be a scorching review in *New York* magazine. She knows what good food should be, although there is nothing duller than news of yesterday's *céleri rémoulade*—you can skip those parts. But she describes better than anyone the cult of "*haute* snoot" that the snobbiest restaurants perfect, the contempt that is served with the *quenelles*—"Orsini's," as she says, "serves memorable cold shoulder."

Q. But, sir, only masochists would volunteer for that duty.

A. Exactly. What can you expect from people who allow themselves to be classified by headwaiters? Who cares for the conversation of a maître d'? I want him to serve me a perfect meal and stay out of my way.

Q. You're a snob, sir. You must understand that if he charges you $60 for a dinner, he has a right to insist you listen to him, too.

A. I'd rather listen to Gael Greene putting down the food as well as the service: "That is surely antique eggplant in the Automat-style applesauce dish ($1.75), and the string beans are limp with embarrassment." She tells you how to buy a $38 picnic for two from Chauveron, but also where to buy the best ice cream. Some of the restaurants she recommends are even inexpensive. Her book—the memoir of her campaigns—is long without being all-inclusive, but it is the sharpest account we have yet had of the war.

Q. Sir, to return to your own scars. What is this curiously twisted cicatrix?

A. That was my Waterloo, boy. The Battle of the Frog Pond; the Frenchies call it La Grenouille. In those days I was inspecting the battlefields with the Clausewitz of *couture,* a man so feared in gourmet-garment circles that bottles of Dom Perignon popped up unbidden at his table. Once, as we dawdled over our *duxelles,* he turned to an elegantly attired flunky who may have run the place. "I want you to be nice to Mr. Prescott when he comes again," the Clausewitz said. "But of course," the flunky murmured. "Put his name in the book," the Clausewitz said, and lo! a golden book appeared and my name was inscribed therein.

Q. You won the battle, sir!

A. So I thought. The next day I took to lunch the women's-news editor of The New York *Times.* "Call Grenouille," I told my secretary. "Tell 'em to check their golden book and get me a table up front. I want to be earlobe-to-earlobe with Mrs. Onassis. Use your English accent." "My Mick Jagger accent?" she asked. "Try Princess Alexandra," I suggested. (*Silence for three minutes; the tape whirs on.*)

The rest doesn't bear thinking on, boy. I'll say only that when the editor arrived, she found me up against the rear restaurant wall, with the kitchen door banging into our table every twenty-seven seconds. I resigned my commission.

1971

. . . . The Novel Glut

"My second novel," writes Mrs. Florence Bonime, "seems to have fallen into a well. After all the long years of writing, teaching, and working as an editor, to find it so completely ignored has been a terrifying experience."

Mrs. Bonime's novel is *A Thousand Imitations.* Harcourt, Brace & World published it on May 17. A couple of hundred book reviewers across the country received advance copies some time in April; and it seems that all, or nearly all of us, ignored it. Mrs. Bonime wonders why.

"I can't believe it is utterly worthless," she writes. "Maybe the book's very slim beam shines from some disagreeable point of the spectrum running from comedy to tragedy. Perhaps this place in the spectrum made the reviewers too impatient to read the book. Perhaps it is irritating because it is inconclusive. How I wish I knew!

"I can hardly believe it bored them. . . . It was written with the conviction that turning pain into laughter needs doing and is worth doing. . . . It isn't black humor, not as bitter as that, but more the comedy of quiet desperation exploding, at one point, into a sorry and absurd violence. Isn't there room for this kind of comedy? . . . When someone of long experience undertakes this kind of project, can't there be somebody who will look?"

Mrs. Bonime, writing in behalf of her own neglected novel, stresses a part of the peculiar agony of the creative writer in this country today. Actually, the current condition of fiction—the manner in which it is published, distributed, and criticized—verges on anarchy.

To begin with, Mrs. Bonime is luckier than most writers. Her novel has been published. Nobody knows how many novels are written in America each year, but one major publisher considers about a thousand novels annually and publishes about thirty-seven of them. This is not as good as it sounds because twelve of those novels will be mysteries, eighteen will be novels by authors who have published before, and perhaps two or three more will be new novels by foreign writers. The management of this publishing firm, like most management, is conservative and would prefer to cut back on the number of novels it publishes.

Why is the record so grim? Publishers know that fiction is in trouble. Experiments with the form of the novel since the war have proved sterile; most new fiction is familiar simply because, one way or another, it has been written before. Television and a vigorous rejuvenation of general books have drawn away much of the talent that once wrote fiction; moreover, they both offer what readers once looked only to fiction to provide: Character, narrative, a sense of place and drama.

Publishers know, too, that only a couple of score hard-cover best sellers sell well in any given year. Most fiction sells only to libraries; sales of three thousand copies for a novel are common; if a novel sells five thousand copies, its author will be urged to write another. Yet no publisher makes money by selling five thousand copies of a book. Fiction sells well only in mass-market paper editions. Hard-cover publishers hope to make money on fiction by selling rights to their novels to such paperback houses.

If we don't know how many novels are written, we do know how many are published. Of 21,819 new books published in America last year,* only 1,699 were classified as fiction. This pitifully small percentage of the whole obtains far more than its fair share of space in review media around the nation. Still, the space that it gets is insufficient to do justice to the books themselves. Reviewers tend to give less space to a novel than to a general book; often an ill-chosen assortment of novels is lumped

*The figure is now about 30,000.

together in a single review. Writers like Mrs. Bonime, who spend years creating the best work of art they can, complain. They should.

Their problem is the dark side of the most spectacular flowering of literature the world has ever known. More books are, of course, being published today than ever before in history—and books are only part of the general communications explosion—but what is important is that although our century may have seen only its fair share of great books, more reasonably good books have been published in our time than in all previous times together. This is what is so exciting—and so baffling—about trying to sort them out: Which books shall be discussed; which books have we time to read? With so many good books available, too many are shunted aside, ignored. Probably the abundance is worth what is lost. What is happening to the novel today is what happened in Renaissance Europe, which produced 300,000 sonnets. The novel has been going for two hundred and fifty years; now, as it once was with the sonnet, it may be time to try something else.

Even if this is so, one would think that the proliferation of reasonably good books would force bad books into oblivion. But no, Gresham's Law seems to prevail with books as well as with money: Bad books drive out the good. Our age provides more and better books to choose from, and it produces more people of educated taste, but it has not yet provided a better average of general taste. Moreover, the time and space that a critic has to devote to books is as limited as ever it was.

Finally, our time has seen the development of the cult of the celebrity, a pernicious condition to which critics are not immune. Newspapers and magazines serve authors and publishers only indirectly; basically, their responsibility is to report the news, and book news today is made by writers in the public eye. Norman Mailer, James Jones, Philip Roth, John Updike, and William Styron have all, after early successes, gone on to write many bad novels, all of which have been reviewed at great length while better novels by unknown writers have gone ignored. Yet critics feel they have done their job if they review Jones' *Go to the Widow-Maker,* one of the worst novels ever written, because no one will notice if they ignore all those little novels by unknown writers that might have been good.

Such are the failings of those who write the news. Most good critics review a number of good, unknown novels, but not enough. If Mrs. Bonime's novel is good but unnoticed, have not we, as readers of books, all lost something important?

1967

.... The Treasure
of Your Company

"It's a peacock feather, don't you see? They're perfectly awful things, and what they say about them is all too true."

"What's that?" I asked. I was standing in a cold rain, peering into the window of Serendipity 3, a window festooned in the weak-jointed artifacts of Art Nouveau. Spring in New York is a fantasy conceived by the Chamber of Commerce and that peacock feather, draped over the orange and purple cover of a little book called *Beardsley Beasties,* suggested that even the best inventions of Mr. Burberry are insufficient protection from the cold and wet of the world.

"Peacock feathers bring bad luck," I was told as I dripped on the floor inside. "As soon as I put it in the window, it began to rain." A tiny glass which frothed at the rim was pressed into my palm. Gin-and-egg-white-and-Dole-pineapple miscegenously married in Waring's blender. The party at which "the treasure of my company" had been requested had begun.

When I was a tad, working for my college literary magazine, I knew what literary cocktail parties were all about. When John Crowe Ransom came to town, Archibald MacLeish lined us all up in a semicircle, put Ransom off to one side under a bridge lamp, placed himself in the center, and told us the discussion would progress as we raised our hands to speak.

When T. S. Eliot came to read, *Life* magazine came with him. We literary types, accustomed to serving martinis that would stun a rhinoceros, were embarrassed to find that none of us knew how to make the kind of tea that comes undisciplined by bags. Nevertheless, we borrowed a silver service that had once been displayed at the Crystal Palace, and a toaster to make scones—scones which turned out to be, upon examination, Hayes Bickford's English muffins. Mr. Eliot presided. We crowded on his left hand and his right hand, anywhere within the rangefinder's field of vision as *Life*'s photographer snapped 674 pictures which were never published. Mr. Eliot purred. The temperature was 101 degrees, and butter from the scones dripped down our French cuffs.

When Dame Edith Sitwell came, graciously accepting our invitation while changing the time, date, and place, we swept out our quarters for the first time since Archduke Ferdinand was shot. We dumped out the furniture that had no legs or was broken in the middle; we even bought glasses, guessing that Dame Edith might not be accustomed to martinis served in paper cups. Dame Edith, splendid in Egyptian headdress and emerald rings piled up to obscure the backs of her hands, answered our questions. Was Pound mad? "Oh, well, you know, I know Ezra very well." "The people in front," said an epicene man, "shouldn't smoke. It makes Dame Edith's eyes smart."

When I grew up, I went to grownup literary parties. Sometimes I couldn't find the author. Sometimes I didn't know who the author was or what he had written. But, if I was lucky, I caught a glimpse of a Kennedy or even two, and once William Paley asked if he might borrow my pen.

At Serendipity 3, of course, things are different. Serendipity 3 is described by its owners as "A General Store," which invites images of nail kegs, hard tack, and folksy conversation around a glowing stove. But no: There are some things that even Serendipity's owners won't touch. Serendipity 3 sells snacks and Pop Art neckties, paper begonias, and portraits from the Hudson River school.

In fact, it is hard to tell just what is for sale and what is priceless decoration. Those round white tables—do you buy them or eat at them? What about that surgical lamp hanging from a ceiling where once (it is said) a surgical table hung as well? Or that clock which weighs maybe a ton, salvaged from a meat market on Third Avenue where it hung out, a definite health hazard, over the heads of pedestrians? Or the pair of portraits of nude and scruffy Victorian men, heavy-lidded in their loincloths? And those thirty-seven Tiffany lamps, blazing from the low ceiling! They were bought, I was told, for $2.50 apiece and now sell for $250.

The party, in honor of the book *Beardsley Beasties,* began. It began and began, but it didn't develop. An Aquarian, discovering that I was a Cancer, read my character from a paper-covered kaleidoscope. Four girls in black-and-white minidresses of Art Nouveau design—dresses produced in the upstairs gallery now discreetly quarantined by a tiny chain—paraded back and forth. One had a Beardsley hat, all balls and black wig, Salome style, and eye makeup straight from "The Firebird." Men were present, too, with tinted glasses and five-and-a-half-inch floral cravats; they cocked their hips beneath double-breasted, double-vented blazers of Harris tweed and jangled the chains on their loafers.

And we had fun, yes. "Such a mild drink," said somebody, "so mild until you find yourself climbing the walls." "I can't taste the gin," said somebody else. "You're not supposed to *taste* it, you're supposed to *feel* it. Stand on this mat. You'll feel better when you fall."

"I commute every day from Stamford," said a lovely girl. "All those men on the train, just picking their noses. I hate it." "Well," said her boyfriend, "men have *problems* in the morning with their noses, and they only have an hour to pick them before they get to the office."

"I can understand Twiggy's appeal," said another. "It's the *Story of O* complex. That *vulnerable* face. She's not innocent; she's been cruelly used. Men are excited by her *possibilities.*"

Not all the conversation was so literary. At those little white tables solitary individuals gazed at *Beardsley Beasties* or at the middle distance. At other little white tables groups of people sat motionless, caught in a frieze, staring at right angles to each other.

Eventually, of course, we come around to the book which all of this was in aid of. *Beardsley Beasties* combines Beardsley prints with funny captions written by Messrs. Caradine, Holt & Bruce, proprietors of Serendipity 3. It's a sniggering production, mixing homosexual innuendo with banal vulgarity; the authors stress the laughs the reader cannot muster. It's tough to make Beardsley seem chaste, but the contributions of Serendipity 3 make one jump to his defense.

"I keep looking for the usual crowd," said somebody as I left, "but I don't see them." No, they are smarter than I am.

1967

· ·The Book
People's Thing

It was half an hour late getting started, but we didn't mind. We had waited a year for it. This was *our* party, a party for book people, and all we book people had assembled a thousand strong at Philharmonic Hall in Lincoln Center. There would be a Vice President, prizes, speeches, and drinks in something like that order; the drinks, anyway, would come last. Nothing is ever really free.

The tickets to the eighteenth annual National Book Awards cost $15, or so the tickets said, but it seems unlikely that more than a score of book people paid $15. Book people can't afford $15; the score or so who actually *paid* $15 had to be people who wanted to be book people. Book critics got in free, the National Book Committee paying their way, a kind of thank-you present for writing about books when book publishers don't advertise in many papers. Book editors got in free because book publishers, especially those who haven't had a book up for an award in years, feel obliged to send a contingent. Authors get in free as guests of publishers. Presumably the Vice President got in free.

So here we were, clutching our coats and satchels because you couldn't get near the cloakroom and nobody wanted to be late. Except the Vice President: He was late, which gave the Literary Activists a chance to distribute a broadside:

To the Chairman of the National Book Committee—

A number of those present will leave this room during the address of the Vice President. They do not deem it suitable to listen to one of the highest officials of the United States Government discuss the arts while this Government is responsible for the ever-increasing death and destruction in the Vietnamese war.

Hardly a literary proclamation, but it was signed by Jules Feiffer, Dwight MacDonald, three editors, and a writer. "JOIN US—JOIN US—JOIN US" the manifesto pleaded, and forty people *did* join them, forty of the thousand or so, when the Vice President began to speak. One long-haired man stormed out, his eyes snapping. Snap. "Have *you* seen burned children?" Snap. "Have you seen *burned* children?" Snap.

Nine hundred and fifty-six people remained, thinking it unlikely the Vice President would talk much of books or burned children. They were right. Mr. Humphrey nominated Thomas Paine's *Common Sense* for the 1776 Book Award, and then talked about the books *he* had read, books by Franklin, Jefferson, "Alex" de Tocqueville (a certain familiarity there, either with Alex or his book), Wilson, and Theodore Roosevelt—"he was sort of on our side." Not many royalties paid to those authors these days.

Then Bill Nichols, chairman of the National Book Committee, bemoaned the fact that the *Times* had blown the prizes a couple of days before: "It's chic to break our release date, just like the Paris openings," and nobody knew *what* he was talking about. Then the Literary Activists, who had discovered that the bar was not officially open and that they would have to pay for their own drinks, returned.

And then came the prizes, good prizes for the most part. The NBA has too often shown an affinity for out-of-print books, unheard-of books, books already published in paperback, unreadable books published by university presses, and books by authors who died the year before. None of that this time. Justin Kaplan won it for his biography of Mark Twain, but he didn't win the *biography* prize, he won the Arts & Letters prize. The biography prize went to Peter Gay for his history of the Enlightenment. Only the *Times* can second-guess the NBA.

James Merrill, who won the poetry prize, gave the best speech. (I had

The 1966 model of a Book Editor, with Editorial Haircut

The same editor, with the 1967 refinement: Rimless Glasses for the new French Mathematician look.

—Exclusive fashion sketches for *WWD* by Peter S. Prescott

thought Sylvia Plath, being dead, would win it.) Merrill shocked the book people because he doesn't *look* like a poet: Handsome, clean-shaven, and with a *vest,* he spoke with grace and wit, with a formal, almost sepulchral diction. Two translators then exhausted the book people's patience with their speeches (one recommended his two forth-coming books).

Finally Bernard Malamud, who won the fiction prize for *The Fixer,* spoke. Malamud's novel *was* the best of the year. Malamud has won the prize before; he writes excellent and readable books, but, like so many writers who win important prizes, he choked up when he was forced to abandon the role of writer and become an actor. You can't blame the fiasco entirely on Malamud. The fiction prize is supposed to be the most important and is saved for the end, but an hour and a half *had* passed, and the book people were thirsty. Malamud chose to make a Major Statement about fiction, but he talked about the kind of unreadable fiction we are lucky he doesn't write. Late in his lengthy speech he said

"Time is running short; there are only a few more points I must make," and a great groan arose from the audience.

When he was through, the book people fought for the exits. Had there been a table to the right containing new books and a table to the left containing booze, there would have been an embarrassing scene; fortunately, there was only one table of booze. The book people came into their element, then, glass in hand, because this is what the NBA is *for.* Never mind the authors, prizes, speeches, or the Vice President (who, after that speech, should have paid his $15), book people must go to work.

We had waited a year. Last year they foisted a sit-down dinner on us (what we had thought was hors d'oeuvres proved to be the main course) and I sat between a librarian from Eau Claire and a critic from Virginia City. No mobility. This year they threatened black tie (book people don't own black ties), but this year we moved. Authors flirted with editors. Editors flirted with agents they wouldn't take to lunch. Critics flirted with publishers who don't send them books. Everybody was saying: I didn't pay my $15, but I'm here. I've made it.

1967

.................Being Frightened
in the Theater

One A.M. on a Saturday morning, the last mild weather of the year. The chairman of Yale's political science department and I stood with our wives on York Street, munching hot dogs and sipping warm root beer. Two hundred Yalies were there, waiting with us for the play to end, for the actors to march naked from the theater, and for New Haven's finest fuzz to lay their clubs along the length and breadth of the actors' skulls. All this had been promised us, but that night, the cast was cautious and the cops were cool; only the hot-dog vendor went to bed content.

The previous evening, Julian Beck and Judith Malina, proprietors of the Living Theater group, had strolled with an assortment of actors and audience down the street from the theater where their play, *Paradise Now,* had just finished its first American performance. Some wore bras and some wore jockey briefs, some wore nothing but a string around their hips from which a patch of cloth hung down in front. Just a glance at those sagging stomachs and drooping buttocks would give any man a case of the metaphysical shudders, policemen not excepted. Near dawn, however, someone ponied up the necessary bail, and the strolling players were released from jail.

This was Living Theater all right, much as it must have been in ancient Rome just before Alaric entered with his bulldozers. What the police failed to realize was that this spillover from stage to street is part of the Living Theater's mission. "We're breaking down the barriers that exist between art and life," Beck told the press, "barriers that keep most men outside the gates of paradise."

My barriers began breaking the following evening, when I walked into a theater that, in the best cliché of socially significant drama, offered no curtain, no scenery, no music. I was given a piece of paper, big enough to hide behind, on which two nude men, decorated with mandala wheels and Hebrew lettering, flanked a psychedelic beanstalk on which the scenes were described, crawling crabwise and upward from the Revolution of Cultures through the Vision of the Magic Love Zap and the Vision of Landing on Mars to Permanent Revolution where, I presume, Anarchism overthrows the System and Paradise is now.

Every seat was full, and a crowd of students had been recruited to squat upon the stage. It was clear that it would be difficult to tell actors from audience, particularly as the audience was soon encouraged to shed its clothes and, like witnesses at a tent revival, become part of the action by heeding the call to be saved. It was clear, too, that those with aisle seats would get more for their money than we who sat in the middle. The play began with the cast, in various attitudes of desperation, whispering into those ears that were adjacent to the aisle. *"What are they saying?"* the rest of us demanded, curious and a bit annoyed, already hooked— without realizing it—into the kind of participation and reaction the Living Theater requires.

The choric mumblings swelled into cries of pain: "I am not allowed to take off my clothes!" But they did, of course; once the fundamental themes were out of the way, the clothes came off, at least down to the cop-out point of bikinis and loincloths.

The rest of the performance alternated among three forms of activity: actors running and shouting in the aisles; dancing and squeezing each other on the stage; and harassing the audience, collectively and individually.

The first, anyone can do, but, inexplicably, the Living Theater cannot do it well. Some actors blocked the view of the audience; others, who spoke in favor of burning money and lining cops, deans, and bankers up against the wall, spoke inaudibly. Only a few, apparently, had been trained to project their voices in a theater. But then the actors didn't

seem to have many words at their command; certainly, in their im-
provised harangues, they didn't *use* many: Down with the System, they
mumbled, Up with Love. Whereupon a sweaty couple clutched at itself
in the aisle, four hands rooting for purchase in the flesh. Above all they
insisted, Be Free. Do Your Thing. The audience wasn't fooled. Veteran
foreign-film fans all, they could read the subtitles: "I hate you,
motherfucker! You're not free unless you do *my* thing!"

The dancing and squeezing were more fun. The cast couldn't dance,
but it could hop up and down in a tireless way, looking rather like
Apprentice Sachems of the Order of the Aborigine Lodge. The actors
built themselves into totem poles and living letters spelling Anarchism
and Paradise, then they flopped down into a great caressing pile,
humming the Tantric intonation "OM."

What the Living Theater excels at, however, is harassing an audience.
It not only harangued the audience as a whole, it picked out individuals
who looked vulnerable and heaped abuse upon them, a technique intended to break the final barrier between actor and spectator. No one
who buys a theater ticket is immune to the total experience of what
happens in an auditorium, but that evening I wanted to remain part of
the mass, safe from personal ridicule I had not invited and which, it
seemed, I might not be able to avoid.

The naked actors roved the aisles, ducking in among the seats, looking
for victims. The hatred and vituperation, the obscenities and rusty
rhetoric that poured from these professed lovers of their fellowmen,
made a wondrous and frightening experience. "If they come to me," I
said to myself, "I'll tell them I'm a running dog of the Wall Street im-
perialists. That will be very funny." But I couldn't imagine who,
precisely, would laugh. "Better to tell them I don't speak English," was
my second thought. It seemed no more effective than the first. They
didn't want me. They found a famous theater critic and his equally
famous wife and favored them with five minutes of personal vilification:
"Look at me, damn you! I can't see your eyes!" The critic slumped in his
seat, eyes resolutely forward, but his wife bit back, delighting her tor-
mentor. Frustrated, she broke the theater's cardinal rule by lighting a
cigarette Another man was pulled from his seat by an actor and held in
a damp embrace. A nearly naked actress sat silently in a man's lap,
ignoring both him and his wife. Another actor argued quietly with a
spectator for nearly half an hour. Everywhere, people were nervous: How
can you *talk* back to an actor who may or may not believe what he is
saying?

("I'll tell you what to do," an actor told me a few days later, when I
told him what his naked brethren had been doing in New Haven. "It's
really very easy. You look into the actor's eye and tell him, 'Buddy,

you're not coming across. It's not real. I don't think you believe it. You're not living the role; it's only skin-deep for you.' Then, while he's recoiling from that—because every actor wants to be believed—you hit him with the clincher: 'Tell me, buddy,' you say, 'are you substituting for some actor who got sick?' " At that point, Exit Spectator, triumphantly.)

But that evening, the audience responded in impromptu fashion. Not surprisingly, because it happened at Yale, it proved itself wittier than the performers:

Actor (*moans from the stage*): How can we reverse history?

Audience: Vote for Wallace!

Actor (*planted in audience*): Stop the show!

Audience: No, *start* the show!

Actor: Let the poor people come to the theater!

Audience: At $4.75, they can't!

The play dragged on. During the Rite of Universal Intercourse, in which the actors squirm over each other on the stage for 20 minutes, a woman called from the back, "Why, it's taking longer than the real thing!" Two or three hours into the play, the audience began to move around, to chat with each other and to yawn. Some drifted toward the stage for an unobstructed view; more drifted toward the exits. Few remained until the end. At its worst, *Paradise Now* is a play that, as one woman said, "takes everything that's good and makes it sound so awful"; at its best, it is a play to read a book by.

After three and a half hours, I realized that the evening had become something of a mill-in. There was no possible way—short of walking naked into the street—that the cast could indicate to the audience that the performance was over. I went outside, where the action was, where the kids were waiting for the head-beating to begin.

"They told me I was in uniform," a boy in a three-piece suit announced. "I said I was the only guy with a vest. They were naked: They were in uniform!" In this way, the Living Theater launched a six months' tour of 30 cities in America. At this rate, any town they play in may prove their last.

1968

Index